Sunset BARBECUE COOK BOOK

Sunset

BARBECUE

ILLUSTRATIONS BY CAROL JOHNSTON

COOK BOOK

BY THE EDITORS OF SUNSET MAGAZINE
AND SUNSET BOOKS

Lane Books · Menlo Park, California

First Printing October 1967
All rights reserved throughout the world. Fourth Edition. Copyright © 1967 by Lane
Magazine & Book Company, Menlo Park, California. Library of Congress Catalog Card
Number: 67-24386. Title Number 207. Lithographed in the United States of America.

CONTENTS

BARBECUE TECHNIQUES

THE RIGHT EQUIPMENT 7

Portable Barbecues • Braziers • Covered Barbecues • Gas and Electric Units

BEGIN WITH THE FIRE 14

Lining the Firebed • Barbecue Fuels • How to Light a Fire • General Firemanship

GRILL COOKING 18

General Grilling Techniques • Skewer Cooking • Shish Kebab Combinations

SPIT ROASTING 25

Meats for Spit Roasting • Accessories • Special Techniques

SMOKE COOKING 31

Advantages of Smoke Cooking • Woods for Flavor • Placement of Coals

FIREPIT COOKING 35

Preparing the Pit • Kind of Wood • Timing the Fire • Preparing the Meat

MEATS FOR BARBECUING 39

Buying Guide for Beef Steaks and Roasts, Lamb and Pork Cuts • Photo Guide to Meats

BARBECUE RECIPES

STEAKS, CHOPS, ROASTS 47

Beef • Pork • Lamb • Game • Shortribs • Spareribs • Ground Beef • Variety Cuts

CHICKEN, TURKEY, DUCK 108

Cornish Game Hens • Wild Duck • Goose • Pheasant • Squab

FISH AND SHELLFISH 126

Striped Bass • Trout • Mackerel • Halibut • Rockfish • Salmon • Swordfish • Shrimp

FRUITS AND VEGETABLES 137

Pineapple • Apples • Eggplant • Zucchini • Mushrooms • Onions • Tomatoes

SAUCES AND MARINADES 145

All Purpose Sauces • Marinades for Beef, Pork, Lamb • Fish Sauces • Tomato Sauces

SPECIAL FEATURES

An Inexpensive Portable Grill 13
Grilling Time and Temperature Chart 22
Salmon Broiled in Foil 24
Spit Roasting Time and Temperature Chart 28
An Argentine Barbecue 30
An Indian-Style Salmon Bake 34
Cooking Underground 46
For the Outdoorsman 51
Steak on the Coals 52
Skewered Beef-Oyster Appetizers 56
Making Beef Jerky on the Barbecue 59
Three Snacks over the Coals 62
Hawaiian Bamboo-Beef Appetizers 69
Grilled Cheese Appetizer 75
How to Barbecue Sausages 77
How to Spit-Roast Suckling Pig 85
Grilled Chinese Pork Appetizers 91
Enough Lamb for a Crowd 94
How to Grill Capretto 96
Basic Lamb Sauce .100
The Classic Barbecue Accompaniments 104
How to Grill Chicken 110
How to Spit Roast Chicken 113
Basic Chicken Bastes 115
How to Barbecue Cornish Game Hens 117
How to Spit Roast Turkey 118
How to Smoke Roast Turkey 120
How to Barbecue Wild Duck 123
Tips on Barbecuing Fish 128
Three Grilled Shrimp Appetizers 133
How to Barbecue Lobster 134
Ideas for Grilling Fruits and Vegetables 138
How to Spit Roast Fruits and Vegetables 141
Grilling Foil-Wrapped Fruits and Vegetables 142
How to Cook Fruits and Vegetables in Coals 144
Ideas for Flavored Butters 147
Special Mexican Sauces for Beef 148
Basic Fish Sauces .152

DIFFERENT WAYS, DIFFERENT RECIPES

Where and why the idea of cooking over coals got its start is a moot point. It makes little difference whether the first meat barbecued was pork or beef, whether the first man to subject it to the process of an open fire was a Chinese or a Neanderthal.

One thing is certain. The man who has been captivated by the mouth watering aroma of food cooked over glowing coals seldom forgets the smell . . . or the taste. He may simply stoke a fire and fix a steak a couple of times a year, or he may grill chops or fish every night of the week. He may spend a few pleasant moments turning hamburgers on top of a hibachi in the fireplace, or he may while away an entire afternoon fussing with a roast in an outdoor smoke oven.

In other words, barbecuing is seldom a one-time affair—you try it once, and you go on trying it, looking for different ways, different recipes that will be enhanced by its tantalizing smoky flavor.

Roughly one-fourth of this book is a thorough coverage of the How of barbecuing—the techniques, the equipment. Early in the book you'll find the basics of grill cooking, spit roasting, smoke cooking, firepit cooking. An entire chapter is aimed at helping you choose and use meats that are especially good cooked by these methods.

As for the What of barbecuing, the greater part of the book consists of recipes ranging over steaks, chops, roasts; chicken, turkey, duck; fish and shellfish; fruits and vegetables; sauces and marinades. All the recipes have been tested in the kitchens of Sunset Magazine. All are sure evidence that there is infinitely more than one way to cook a sirloin—or a game hen, or a salmon.

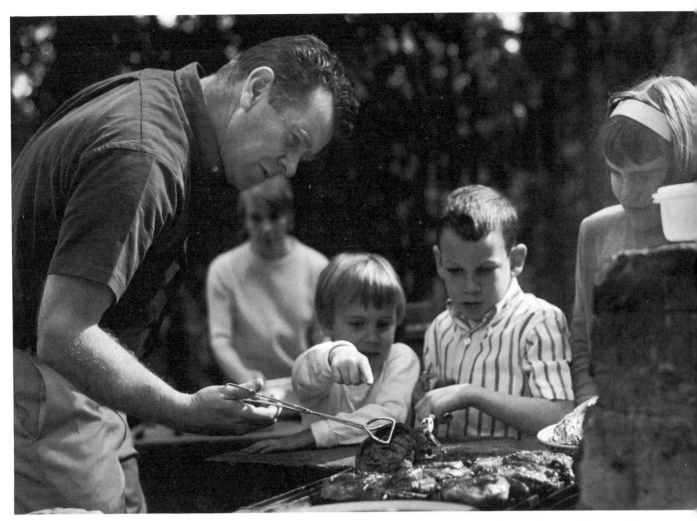

THE WHOLE FAMILY gets in on the act when Dad cooks outdoors. Marinated skirt steaks are the treat here, and everyone has his own picked out. Grill cooking is one of the basic barbecue techniques.

BARBECUE TECHNIQUES

THE RIGHT EQUIPMENT

You don't need complicated equipment for good barbecue cooking. All over the world, hungry people have devised methods to cook their meat or fish on a wood fire with whatever implements they had on hand.

Probably the oldest of these simple techniques is to skewer meat on a stick, the principle of the hot dog roast or the Arab shish kebab. When the food is too heavy to hold or suspend, an alternate to skewers is to bury everything in a heated pit.

Here and there through the first section of this book, you'll find the best of many do-with-what-you-have methods described separately with complete instructions on how to set up and what to cook. On page 30 you'll find the Argentine asador, a gaucho barbecue where meat is suspended over glowing coals on special metal racks. If you want to barbecue a whole salmon, try grilling it under a barbecue hood or under a foil blanket as described on page 24. Whole salmon on the beach? Do it as the Northwest Indians do. The method is described on page 34. There's a thorough-going guide to firepit cookery, or cooking underground, on page 46, and a special homemade portable grill large enough to cook for a crowd, which is described on page 13.

PORTABLE BARBECUES. *Left to right starting at top: electric grill with drip pan, adjustable grill with skewer holders, hibachis, grill with four-position grid, two Mexican braseros.*

Small Portable Barbecues

Most of the foregoing barbecue methods are meant for a crowd of guests. They produce salmon for a village or beef for a trail gang. At the other end of the scale, a great many of the small portable barbecues available these days can go right up on the patio table or into an indoor fireplace. The very smallest, some of the Japanese hibachis for example, can be used inside on the dining table to grill small skewered appetizers.

If you like a traditional approach, you may prefer the heavy metal hibachis or the ceramic Mexican braseros. With just a few coals you can grill skewered meats and seafood for a small family or turn out enough appetizers for a few friends. When you have too many people to do the cooking directly on the grill, the hibachis or braseros can be used as an attractive heat source for warming appetizers and skewers cooked elsewhere.

The Mexican braseros come in terra cotta or in hard-fired black Oaxacan pottery. Too hot a fire can crack or break either kind. It's best to build a fire of no more than ten briquets to begin with, then slowly add more when the pottery is hot. The fire goes into the upper bowl, while the large, lower, decorated bowl is a draft chamber. Frequently, braseros are not sold with grills, so you have to buy one separately to fit the firebowl.

More modern versions of the table-top barbecue have such features as adjustable grills, wind screens, shish-kebab holders, and even rotisseries. Many of them are just scaled-down versions of standard barbecues, while others resemble suitcases, frying pans, or buckets. There are even electric models that use no charcoal at all.

A few of these tiny barbecues are quite specialized. On one your only fuel is newspaper; on another you can smoke cook; still others are specifically designed for hamburgers or hot dogs for picnic outings.

The Versatile Brazier

The next step up in size and complexity is the bowl-shaped brazier barbecue with three or four legs and two wheels for easy transport. At their simplest, braziers are just shallow metal bowls with a grid on top. They are adequate for barbecuing hamburgers, steaks, pieces of poultry, or fish. For more control over your cooking, or for larger pieces of food, you can equip braziers with adjustable grills, wind screens, half hoods, and rotisseries. To do roasts on the grill, or for smoke cooking, you can make a foil dome to fit the entire brazier bowl (instructions given in chapter on smoke cooking), or enclose a half-hood with foil.

Most such braziers come apart for winter storage or for carrying to a picnic site or campground.

Covered Barbecues

A covered barbecue with dampers to control fire temperature makes cooking large pieces of food much easier and more economical. Since you have such efficient control over the heat, even on windy or wet days, the covered barbecue is like a kitchen outdoors combining a broiler, oven, smoker, and grill.

The simplest covered barbecue is the kettle-shaped model. The deep fire bowl has a bottom damper, and the dome lid has a second damper. When you put a roast on the grill and cover it, the reflected heat in the dome browns the top as oven heat would do. If it cooks too fast, just close the dampers a bit to lower the heat. If there's still good charcoal left when your food is done, close both bottom and top dampers to snuff it out and you can relight it the next time.

Another variation on the covered barbecue is the cylinder or rectangular box mounted on a wagon. Some can be purchased without the wagon for permanent installation.

Both the cylinder and box often include an air temperature thermometer in the lid, so there's no guesswork involved in adjusting heat. You can also adjust the distance between food and coals by either raising the grill or lowering the fire grate. Some models have a fire door which allows you to add or rearrange coals without opening the top and letting the heat escape. There are usually dampers bottom and top for further heat control.

If you buy one of these large and expensive wagon barbecues, look for one made of heavy metal with a finish that won't be damaged by heat. Some include grill racks that slope toward a drip trough so that fat doesn't go into the fire. A few of them have a built-in electric coil to start the charcoal.

Many accessories are available for the wagon barbecues. Depending on the model, you can buy rotisseries, smoking equipment, special Dutch ovens, extra grills, and shish-kebab cookers.

The barrel or egg-shaped covered barbecue is influenced by a Japanese smoke oven called the kamado. It is the most specialized and least adapted to ordinary grilling, although you can grill if you wish. It is probably the most economical for long cooking, since a small amount of charcoal can be damped to burn slowly for hours.

The kamado has a damper near ground level and a chimney with lid or sliding door at the top. Inside, a ceramic bowl holds charcoal, and a cylindrical sleeve holds the grill well above it. The bowl is intended to hold only 20 or 30 briquets or the equivalent amount of plain charcoal, and heat is controlled exclusively by the dampers. You light the charcoal with both dampers wide open, then shut them almost entirely for long cooking or for smoking. Since it is difficult to add more fuel (the charcoal is entirely enclosed when the grill is in place) you should start with the fire bowl filled to capacity. If coals are left at the end of the cooking time they snuff themselves out when the dampers are closed.

A side feature of the kamado is that its shape permits guests to circle around it on chilly evenings and use it as a garden heater while the roast is cooking.

Kamados are heavy and difficult to transport, so don't expect to trundle one around much once you've found a good place for it.

Gas and Electric Units

Traditionalists may stop reading here, since the idea of gas or electric barbecues without charcoal may make them gnash their teeth, but these units are becoming very popular and do give a definite barbecue flavor to the foods cooked on them. In addition, they are more economical to use than charcoal barbecues, and they heat ready to use in just a few minutes. Cleaning is no problem either, since no ash is produced and drips burn away rather quickly.

Although cooking techniques are about the same with gas or electric units, the initial adjustment is critical with gas. Be sure when your unit is installed that the lowest setting produces about 300° of heat with the top down. Your only control is the gas cock, since there are no coals to remove.

All gas barbecues and many electric ones use fuel to heat ceramic or volcanic rock "coals" which then supply radiant energy to cook the food above them. Fat drips onto these coals and flares or smokes to produce a barbecued look and flavor. For stronger smoke flavor, you can sprinkle hickory chips over the coals.

Some electric units do away with the ceramic or rock entirely and use only an electric coil under a heavy metal grill. With these there is still somewhat of a barbecue flavor and a most pleasing appearance, since the grill heats enough to sear strips across the meat. These units are only for grilling or spit roasting.

Gas barbecues may be permanently installed, using natural gas, or they may be portable, using a tank of LP gas. Either way they ignite immediately and heat their ceramic or rock elements in about ten minutes. On units using chunks of volcanic rock to radiate heat, the rock can become discolored by dripping fat. If you want to clean it, just turn it over with the dark side toward the gas burner. The intense heat burns it white as you cook.

Both gas and electricity are excellent for indoor barbecues since they require less powerful ventilating systems than you need for the dangerous fumes of burning charcoal. Electric units require a 220-volt line, as do other major electrical appliances, but can be installed in a protected permanent barbecue area outdoors provided they aren't exposed to the wear and tear of the elements.

Accessories, Practical and Fun

You can equip yourself with mountains of barbecue accessories, some of which are very useful, while others are just amusing gimmicks.

The Basic Basics

First of all, you'll need something to light the fire. Suggestions in detail appear in the following chapter. Once the fire is going, a long pair of tongs with good gripping ends makes fire arranging easy. A stiff metal brush, with or without scraper, keeps your grill free of burned particles.

Once the food is sputtering over the coals, a strong, long-handled fork and a long-handled spatula are necessary. If you're of the don't-pierce-the-meat school, your tongs will do for turning food. For basting, use a long-bristled brush. A pastry brush will do, but there are special barbecue brushes with long handles available.

Mitts are useful for handling hot metal, and a good cotton apron that covers most of you will keep you presentable. For spit cooking, pliers help to tighten screws on spit forks and accessories.

When using covered barbecues, and even for braziers, a grill-temperature or air-temperature thermometer makes cooking much easier. Covered units often have them built in. With a thermometer on the grill, you know the temperature at a glance all through the cooking period and can add or arrange coals as soon as necessary.

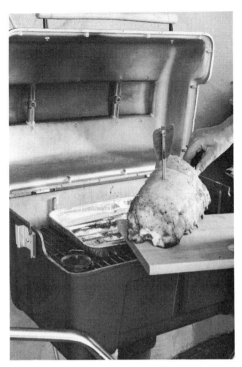

ELECTRIC AND GAS BARBECUES. *Table-top electric unit (shown at left) is for spit roasting or grilling; the grid (not shown) fits over electric coil. A portable gas smoke cooker is shown on right.*

For large cuts of meat, poultry, or fish, a meat thermometer tells you just exactly how done the meat is. This is even more important in barbecuing than in oven cooking, since time is much more variable and dependent on distance from the heat, the wind, and the weather.

Get the best carving knife available, and always use it with a carving board. Have it sharpened by an expert a couple times a year. (A good knife shouldn't require sharpening more often than this, but you can hone it before use to even up any tiny nicks and roughness.)

If you like shish kebab, buy some long skewers. Wooden handles are nice, but your mitt will protect you if you decide on the more practical metal rods. In any event, really long skewers can be placed with the grip well away from the fire so they won't heat up too much.

Some Practical Fantasies

Once you have the basic tools, a few gadgets add spice to outdoor cookery. A tined spatula is good for hamburgers. This looks like a wide flat fork, and if the burgers sag into the spaces between the grill bars you can still reach under to flip them without shaving off a portion of the meat.

The various long-handled toasters and grills are useful for hot dogs, sausages, small steaks, and chicken parts. These toasters range from two simple grids hinged on one side, to pairs of shallow baskets which prevent food from slipping out as you turn them. Toasters are fine for cooking over an open fire at a picnic or on a camping trip.

A fire rake is nice for arranging coals, although the tongs are more precise.

Spit-Roasting Gear

True spit roasting is one of the prime joys of barbecuing. You can find spit assemblies for even small portable barbecues.

The basics of spit roasting consist of a strong motor to turn large roasts and poultry without laboring, a spit that shows no tendency to bend, and a pair of spit forks to hold food in place as it turns.

Basic extras to consider are extra forks for holding rows of small poultry solidly, and a balance weight with which you can adjust the center of gravity while the food is cooking so that it turns evenly. One kind of weight slips over the spit and screws down. Point it toward the lighter side of a poorly balanced roast. The weight is adjustable toward or away from the spit. If there are changes in balance, shift the weight toward the spit to make it lighter, pull it away to make it heavier.

This is all you really need for spit cooking, but you can also buy a rotary shish-kebab attachment that holds and turns six or eight skewers. These look dramatic and, most important, save you the trouble of hand-turning the skewers.

Cylindrical and flat baskets are made to fit over spits for cooking small or hard-to-spit foods. These promise more than they give, since meats tend to tumble around like balls in a bingo basket.

Miscellaneous Accessories

Stores that sell barbecue equipment offer such things as long-handled salt and pepper shakers, branding irons that put your initials on steaks, and decoratively designed popcorn poppers. These are nice for decor but have little practical value.

Somewhat more practical if you like to heat bread and rolls or keep foil-wrapped vegetables hot is an extra grill that stands above the standard grill and covers a quarter to a third of it. In a covered barbecue you can cook on this upper grill. Although it is intended to give you extra space, you may have a hard time fitting anything underneath it. Tall roasts won't fit and steaks or hamburgers are hard to turn.

USEFUL BARBECUE ACCESSORIES include (left to right): wire brush with scraper, hinged wire broiler, skewers, long-handled salt and pepper shakers, basting brush, turning fork, tongs, balance weight for spit.

An Inexpensive Portable Grill

A barbecue for 25 is almost as easy as one for just the family when you cook it on this big portable grill. Not only that, but you can set up anywhere you like and carry off the pieces afterward with ease.

Because the grill can be raised or lowered on its fence-post supports to control the heat, you can cook large meat cuts slowly and evenly. In the photographs below, two 7-rib roasts, about 20 pounds each, cook on the grill; delicate fish fillets can be cooked with the same ease.

For the legs you'll need four 6-foot lengths of lightweight steel fence post that have self-fastening lugs at 6-inch intervals. For the grill, buy a 2 by 3-foot piece of heavy expanded steel, and two 3-foot lengths of punched angle iron for edging.

Fasten the angle irons to the expanded metal, using three bolts on each side. Cut four lengths of heavy wire, each about 12 inches long. Loop a piece of wire through the end hole of each angle iron and fasten it securely.

At the barbecue site, set the grill on the ground and pound in the four posts, each 2 inches out from the corners of the grill, making sure that the lugs on the posts are facing out. Lift the grill, slip the wire loops over the posts, and hang the grill.

Fire Building

Start your fire with 20 pounds of good quality, long burning briquets; when well ignited, rake them evenly over the fire bed.

For long cooking, add 10 pounds of briquets to the fire about every 1½ hours. Start the additional briquets at either end of the fire, and spread them evenly when ignited. To add smoky flavor to meat and to supplement fuel, you can add hardwood logs.

A grill thermometer will help you keep the fire at the right heat. With the grill about 2½ or 3 feet off the ground, the temperature should be kept about 300° to 350°.

Barbecuing Meats

Allow plenty of time for barbecuing. If the meat should cook before you're ready to eat, just raise the grill to stop cooking and keep it hot.

To keep the heat and smoke close around the meat as it cooks, cover it with a blanket of heavy foil. Most meats are better if you basted with oil, butter, or a sauce as they cook.

Chicken Halves or Quarters. About 1 dozen broiler-fryer chickens cut in halves or quarters will cover the surface of the grill. Set grill about 2 feet from the fire; cover chickens with a foil blanket, and cook about 1 hour, turning once. Baste frequently with a mixture of 1 cup soy sauce, ½ cup each salad oil and lemon juice, and 3 cloves crushed garlic.

Fish Fillets. Use sablefish (black cod), lingcod, or salmon. Buy about ½ pound fish per person and have each fish cut into 2 boneless whole fillets with skin left on. Cut pieces of heavy foil the same size and shape as each fillet. Lay foil against skin side of fillet and place, foil side down, on the grill about 2 feet above the coals. Cover loosely with a blanket of foil and baste frequently. Fillets weighing 3 to 4 pounds will take about 1 hour to cook. Fish is done when it flakes easily when tested with a fork. As a baste, use a mixture of 1 cup lemon juice, ½ cup salad oil, ½ teaspoon salt, 1 teaspoon sugar, dash pepper, and ¼ cup chopped green onion.

Standing Ribs of Beef. Barbecued standing rib roasts in full 7-rib sections weigh 15 to 25 pounds. When buying, allow 1 pound to 1½ pounds per person, as there is bone and fat.

For these large roasts, set the grill 2½ to 3 feet above the fire. Start the meat fat side down until nicely browned. Turn rib side down, insert a meat thermometer, and cover with a blanket of foil. Allow about 6 hours total cooking time for a roast of about 22 pounds to reach an internal temperature of 140° (medium rare). No basting is necessary. You will need at least 40 pounds of charcoal.

Barbecued Leg of Lamb. For a barbecued leg of lamb (the grill holds up to six), allow 2½ to 3 hours, and baste with a mixture of 1½ cups lemon juice, 2 teaspoons grated lemon peel, ⅔ cup salad oil, ¼ cup chopped parsley, 2 tablespoons whole oregano, 1 teaspoon each salt and sugar, ¼ teaspoon pepper, 4 drops liquid hot-pepper seasoning.

PLIERS, wrench are tools for grill. Buy parts at builder's supply store.

DINNER is just an hour away as fish is basted, covered with foil to cook.

ROASTS need hours to cook; if there's wind, allow more time.

GET YOUR FIRE GOING. *Once coals are covered with ash, you are ready to cook; in this case, it's turkey roll on the spit. Drippings may cause flare-ups, but a water pistol will douse them.*

BARBECUE TECHNIQUES

BEGIN WITH THE FIRE

Before stoking the charcoal, many barbecue chefs like to line the firebed with foil, or with sand or gravel. The foil, shiny side up, makes cleaning easier and reflects a certain amount of extra heat. Sand or gravel protects the metal of the firebed from overheating; gravel supplies a certain amount of bottom draft and is particularly good with a light metal and solid-bottomed barbecue.

Sand or foil liners can simply be discarded every few weeks when you clean out the barbecue. If you want to save gravel for reuse when it gets really greasy, pour it into a bucket of warm detergent suds; then dry it thoroughly before lighting a fire on it. Wet gravel sometimes pops when heated.

Don't bother to clean a barbecue too often. A layer of ash or some grease won't impede your cooking.

Barbecue Fuels

The oldest barbecue fuels are undoubtedly hardwood and hardwood charcoal. You can still use hardwood —oak, fruit wood—for a large-scale pit barbecue, but you will have a long wait for cord wood to become glowing coals. Never use soft wood such as pine. It burns hot, gives off resinous smoke, and won't develop adequate coals.

Either charcoal or briquets are quicker and briquets have the added advantage of being uniform in size and easy to arrange under the grill.

Briquets vary widely in their composition, but the material used to form them is indicated somewhere on the sack. Most seasoned barbecue cooks prefer briquets with a hardwood or fruit-pit base, although other materials, including anthracite coal, are sometimes used. Whatever the base, the material is first converted into charcoal, then ground, mixed with a binder, and pressed into shape. Each kind burns a little differently than the others, so cooking heats and times depend strongly on the kind of briquet you use. Once you've discovered how long it takes to prepare coals and cook your favorite recipe with one brand, you'll probably prefer to stick to it. In particular, don't try a new brand when guests are coming.

How to Light a Fire

Charcoal briquets can be hard to light. If you already have a favorite method there's no reason to change, but if you're new to outdoor cooking, or not very proficient at fire starting, here are a few ways, old and new, that will enable you to produce glowing embers in the shortest possible time. Whatever method you choose, allow 30 to 45 minutes between lighting up and cooking.

Kindling

The oldest, and probably the slowest way to ignite charcoal is to build a paper and kindling fire to which you add briquets once it's burning well. But the method requires several steps, and the briquets tend to roll around disconcertingly and ignite unevenly.

Inflammable Liquids and Jelly

A number of these are sold specifically for lighting charcoal. (The liquids are petroleum products for which you can substitute paint thinner. The jelly is jellied alcohol like that used for canned heat.)

With the liquids, either douse a pyramid of coals, wait a minute for the liquid to soak in, then light, or place several briquets in a closed can or wide-mouthed jar and cover them with fluid, allowing it to soak in until the briquets stop bubbling. You can keep "marinated" briquets on hand all the time, ready for barbecuing at short notice. Just place two or three at the bottom of the briquet pyramid, cover them up, and light. Using this method of dousing or marinating with a pyramid of 25 briquets, you should have coals ready for cooking in 30 to 40 minutes.

With the jelly, you again prepare a pyramid, then push two or three spoonfuls of jelly into the crevices. Be sure it's well under the briquets or you may not get a good start. If you position it properly, you will have cooking coals in 30 to 40 minutes.

Special Packs and Egg Cartons

Briquets are sometimes sold specially packaged in treated or untreated cartons. You place the whole pack in the firebed and light it. It ignites the briquets inside. Since the packs are more or less flat, the briquets are already spread out for grilling when the fire is hot. Some of these packs resemble egg cartons and are impregnated with an inflammable substance.

You can create a home version by opening an egg carton out flat, filling both top and bottom with a layer of briquets, and dousing carton and briquets with lighter fluid. After waiting a minute, light. With a special pack or egg carton, you wait 30 to 40 minutes for a fire of 25 briquets.

Chimney Starters

A fire chimney, either home-made or bought, creates a strong draft through the coals and decreases the time necessary to ignite them. The simplest version is a two or three-pound coffee can with top and bottom removed. Punch eight or ten holes around the bottom edge with a beer can opener, bending the little triangles straight down to form short legs. Place two wadded sheets of newspaper, a squashed milk carton, or marinated coals in the bottom, fill the chimney with briquets, and light. You'll have coals ready for cooking in 20 to 30 minutes. Lift a coffee-can chimney off the coals with tongs. Ready-made chimneys usually have a handle of some sort.

Electric Starters

Many versions of the electric starter are available, and some barbecues have them built in. You place the resistance coil of the simplest kind in the firebed, pour coals over it, plug it in, and the coals are ready for cooking in 20 to 30 minutes.

Some electric starters are built into a chimney which creates a draft for quicker starting. At least one kind has a small fan built into the handle that blows on the coals as the element heats them. Always put the element under the coals for best results.

Other Methods

Some people start coals by placing them in a wire mesh basket over the burner of a stove. This tends to smoke up the house if you don't have a really efficient ventilator hood. If you have a small gas-pressure torch, you can start coals by playing a hot flame over them for a few minutes.

Firemanship

You don't need too many coals. Charcoal fires are hot, and for grilling under normal circumstances, 25 to 30 coals should be adequate. For roasting thick pieces of meat or whole birds you may have to add more coals in the course of cooking. Allow 15 minutes for them to ignite at the edges of the fire. The more open the barbecue, the more coals you need, since the heat escapes and the charcoal burns more quickly.

Arranging the Coals

When you grill, arrange the coals to cover the entire area under the food. If the fire seems too hot, and the coals flame up because of dripping fat, space them farther apart with tongs, making a checkerboard pattern of coals and empty spaces. If there are still occasional flareups, keep a water pistol or spray bottle on hand and lightly douse the flaming coals. If the coals are easy to reach, you can drop a lettuce leaf over the flame. It quickly burns to ash.

Don't cook over coals that are not completely covered with ash. Coals that are still spotted with black or are flaming a good deal are much more likely to flare and smoke, and the heat they produce is uneven. It's not flame that cooks barbecued foods, but

direct infra-red radiation that comes from completely heated coals.

When you add coals while cooking, place them at the edge of the fire, well away from the food. The smoke won't smudge your dinner, and they'll be ready in 15 minutes.

Grilled foods normally rest directly over the coals. Thick pieces, however, sometimes require such long cooking time that intense heat blackens the outside, while the inside is still raw. For these, arrange the coals in a ring at the outside edges of the food, and place a drip pan in the firebed directly underneath to catch the fat. The pan can be made of heavy aluminum foil so that it's exactly the right size. As an alternate to the ring, arrange the coals in two parallel rows with the drip pan in the center. This arrangement is best when the food is long and narrow.

On a covered barbecue, the cover will trap and reflect heat to cook the top and sides of roasts and poultry. If you have an open brazier, even a simple tent of foil directly over the food will trap some heat, while a complete dome of foil greatly increases efficiency (see chapter on smoke cooking for directions on making a foil dome). A drip pan catches fat and prevents flaring, so food requires less watching.

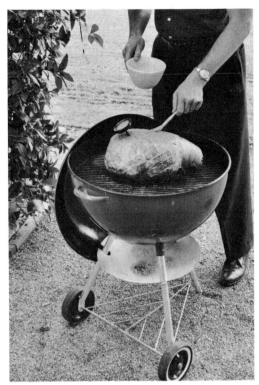

ARRANGING THE BRIQUETS *around a drip pan, as shown at left, keeps fat from dripping on coals and causing flare-ups. In picture on right, upper grid is in place with the meat above the pan.*

When you roast on the spit, arrange it so that the bottom of the spitted roast turns toward you, while the top turns away. Arrange the fire under the back half of the roast, and place a drip pan under the front half. Fat from a turning roast does not fall from the bottom, but from the portion just beginning the up-swing. With a drip pan in front, you can leave the roast to cook itself without fear of flareups.

When you do smoke cooking, place the coals to one side or at the edges of the meat and use a drip pan. You always smoke in a covered unit so that the heat and smoke are trapped as in an oven. With the coals to one side, you get plenty of heat but you won't risk burning the bottom of the food.

You can develop excellent flavor in food by burning something aromatic in the coals, even when your barbecue is not covered. Hickory chips are the most-used flavor additive. Put them on either early or late in the cooking, or keep a few going all the time if you're smoke cooking. A few garlic buds in the fire toward the end of the cooking period add pungency. If there's thyme or rosemary in the garden, or a few bay leaves on hand, throw them on in the last few minutes for a special aroma. Twigs of fruit wood also add aroma and flavor.

Conserving the Coals

When you've finished cooking, you may find that there is plenty of good charcoal only half burned. In a covered unit, just close the dampers and it will go out in a few minutes, ready to be relighted the next time. Half-burned coals light very quickly. In a brazier, transfer the coals with tongs to a tightly covered metal container. Again, they go out in a few minutes, and you can use them to start your next fire. Some people just douse the coals in a pail of water. If you try this, empty the water immediately and let the coals dry or they may dissolve.

If you find that the heat of the charcoal is decreasing rapidly just at the end of your cooking time, you can cause a brief renaissance by tapping the coals to remove the ash. Ash is an insulator, and once you remove it the fire becomes more intense. Don't blow it off, or a cloud of it may settle on your dinner.

One important thing to keep in mind with charcoal briquets is that they absorb moisture rapidly, and once damp, are almost impossible to start. Twist the top of an opened bag tightly shut, and if you live in really damp areas, transfer the charcoal to a plastic bag or tightly covered container.

SAUSAGES IN VARIETY brown on the grill of a small hibachi. Only a few coals are required; with rolls, relishes, and a salad, you can prepare a whole meal indoors or outside. See page 77 for tips on barbecuing sausages.

BARBECUE TECHNIQUES

GRILL COOKING

Straight grill cooking is useful for quickly cooked foods such as steaks, chops, ground meat patties, sausages, small fish, and poultry parts. And skewered foods cook just as well right on a grill as they do on special rotating attachments. With a little ingenuity, you can adapt a grill to cook larger pieces of food, either by covering the whole thing with a foil dome, or by placing a tent of foil directly over the food (directions for making a foil dome are given in the chapter on smoke cooking).

Directions for preparing and arranging a fire for grill cooking appear in the section under firemanship

in the foregoing chapter. Before placing food on a new or freshly cleaned grill, rub the grill with a piece of fat or a little oil so food won't stick to the hot grid. Don't bother to clean the grid after each barbecue. Each time, wait until it is heated by the fire, then scrape and brush it with a metal brush. You remove most of the char this way, and the coating that's left keeps food from sticking. For a thorough cleaning at the end of the barbecue season, spray the grill with one of the pressurized oven cleaners and follow directions for cleaning.

When you cook fatty foods on a grill, tilt the grill

slightly toward you. You can prop it on a brick at the rear. The fat will run to the edge of the grid as it melts, instead of falling straight down and causing flares and smoke. Lean foods are best when basted with a little oil or butter as they cook.

Since cooking time is short on a grill, the flavor of bastes only clings to the surface of the food. For stronger flavor in grilled foods, marinate them several hours before cooking; then baste with the marinade as they cook. Very thick bastes, or bastes containing sugar burn rather easily, so use them over a low fire or use them during the last half of the cooking period.

Don't allow the coals to flame under the cooking food. Either use a drip pan or watch the fire and douse flare-ups. Flames may smudge and burn the food, leaving an unpleasant flavor and appearance.

When turning thin pieces of food such as steaks or poultry parts, many barbecue cooks prefer to use tongs rather than pierce the food, since piercing allows some of the juices to escape. If you use a fork, try to pierce an area of fat so that the seared surface of the meat itself remains intact. This no-piercing rule does not hold true for extremely fat meats or poultry. In fact, duck tastes better and less greasy if you pierce the skin often to let the fat escape.

Meats with a large cut surface such as steaks should be started near the coals to sear the surface and seal in juices, then moved away to finish cooking. Foods that tend to disintegrate, such as ground meat patties or fish, are easier to cook if you use a hinged wire broiler for holding and turning them. Whole fish the size of salmon or albacore should be wrapped in poultry netting or expanded metal so you don't break them when turning.

Protruding bones or fragile parts such as wing tips and the tails of whole fish may be protected from burning with a bit of foil wrapped around them or placed under them on the grill surface. In fact, if food gets too dark before it's done to your taste, slip a sheet of foil under the whole thing and continue cooking.

The grill cooking chart on pages 22 and 23 gives approximate times for cooking most grilled foods. If you use a grill thermometer, you will know the exact temperature. If you have no thermometer, you can estimate temperature with your hand. Hold it palm down near the grill and count seconds. If you're forced to remove it at three seconds, the fire is at about 350° to 400° degrees, right for steaks and chops. If it's hotter than that, wait awhile or space out the coals. If you can keep your hand in place for six to eight seconds, push the coals together, knock off the ash, or add more coals to boost the firepower.

Skewers on the Grill

Skewer cookery is probably the most versatile barbecue method. From the hot dog roast to the most complicated shish kebab and back down to marshmallow toasting, all is skewer cookery.

Skewers also adapt themselves to any size barbecue. A tiny hibachi with just a few coals will grill whole prawns or small chunks of meat, fish, or poultry. On hotter fires, cut the pieces bigger, up to 1½ to 2 inches on a side, and push them more tightly together. Packed skewers cook more slowly and center chunks are pinker and juicier.

If you want vegetables or fruits on the skewer with the meat, use firm ones that cook slowly, or use some of the skewers for meat only, others for the quicker-cooking vegetables.

For appetizers, buy slivers of bamboo in an Oriental store and soak them in water for awhile before use to keep them from burning.

Certain foods, such as pork chunks, should be precooked in the oven before skewering so that they will be cooked when their skewer companions are ready.

When you skewer chunks of fish, leave the skin on. It will help hold the flesh together when the fish is completely cooked.

You can baste skewered foods with butter, oil, or a marinade, or you can create self-basting skewers by threading a bacon slice over and under each food chunk in an undulating pattern.

As you prepare various foods for skewer cooking ahead of time, keep in mind their cooking requirements. Those that just need heating—fruits, canned or pre-cooked foods—can be skewered in larger portions than those that require cooking. Group longer cooking foods, such as meats, together; add foods to be cooked quickly or just heated at the end of cooking time.

Skewer cooking more than any other form of barbecuing lends itself to do-it-yourself parties. Have an assortment of food already cut and arranged on plates. Let guests fill their own skewers with a mixture that pleases them. If you're using one large barbecue, it's best to do the actual cooking yourself, but you can also fire up several smaller ones so that the traffic is divided.

Foods for Skewer Cooking

Here are several food groups to choose from when baiting up your skewers. If you're a veteran skewer-cooker, many of these suggestions will be familiar; some, on the other hand, may surprise and inspire you.

Meats and fish

Chicken
Beef
Lamb
Cocktail sausages or smoky links
Pre-cooked pork
Ham
Beef salami (soft)
Knackwurst
Bratwurst
Frankfurters
Blood sausage
Luncheon meat
Turkey breast
Polish sausage
Chinese sausage
Bacon
Pork sausage (brown-and-serve)
Shrimp
Lobster meat
Albacore (fresh)
Liver
Chicken livers
Oysters
Scallops
Parboiled sweetbreads
Ground meatballs

Vegetables

Zucchini chunks
Cherry tomatoes or quartered unpeeled tomatoes
Cooked sweet potatoes or yams
Corn on the cob (2-inch pieces)
Canned white potatoes or small parboiled potatoes
Onion wedges or small whole onions (canned or parboiled)
Eggplant cubes
Green pepper squares
Green tomato quarters

Fruits

Apple wedges, cored
Bananas, thick slices
Pineapple chunks
Pear quarters, cored
Oranges, thick unpeeled half slices
Papayas, peeled and seeded
Peaches, canned cling halves
Pitted apricots
Cantaloupe

Frills

Kumquats
Dried apricots
Pitted prunes
Dried figs
Pitted ripe or green olives
Mushrooms (fresh or canned)
Canned artichoke hearts
Pickles
Water chestnuts (canned)
Sliced bread
Brown-and-serve rolls or French bread, cut into chunks
Ready-to-bake biscuits
Spiced crab apples
Spiced peaches or pears
Cheese
Anchovies

Shish Kebab Combinations

If you are wondering just what foods complement each other on skewers, here are some tried and true combinations:
■ Pork cubes, pineapple chunks, green pepper squares, sweet potato squares.

■ Steak cubes, brown-and-serve bread chunks, mushroom caps, tomatoes.

■ Prunes, brown-and-serve sausage, small onions, spiced crab apples.

■ Refrigerated biscuit wrapped around cheese cubes, then wrapped in bacon; apple quarters.

■ Ham cubes, thick-sliced banana, sweet potatoes.

■ Figs stuffed with anchovies; ripe olives, salami cubes, brown-and-serve rolls.

■ Polish sausage, cherry tomatoes, eggplant cubes, stuffed green olives.

■ Cheese cubes and luncheon meat, cut in quarters, and threaded alternately with mushrooms or ripe olives.

■ Meatballs, onions, cherry tomatoes, mushrooms.

■ Knackwurst, small onions, potato or zucchini slices.

■ Turkey cubes, pineapple chunks, ripe olives, sweet potatoes.

■ Ham cubes, corn on the cob, cheese wrapped in refrigerated biscuits, stuffed olives.

■ Brown-and-serve sausages, papaya cubes, ripe olives, brown-and-serve rolls.

■ Shrimps, pineapple cubes, green pepper squares, cherry tomatoes.

■ Fresh albacore cubes, stuffed olives, zucchini slices, small onions, potatoes wrapped in bacon.

■ Liver cubes, cherry tomatoes, eggplant cubes, bacon squares, onion slices.

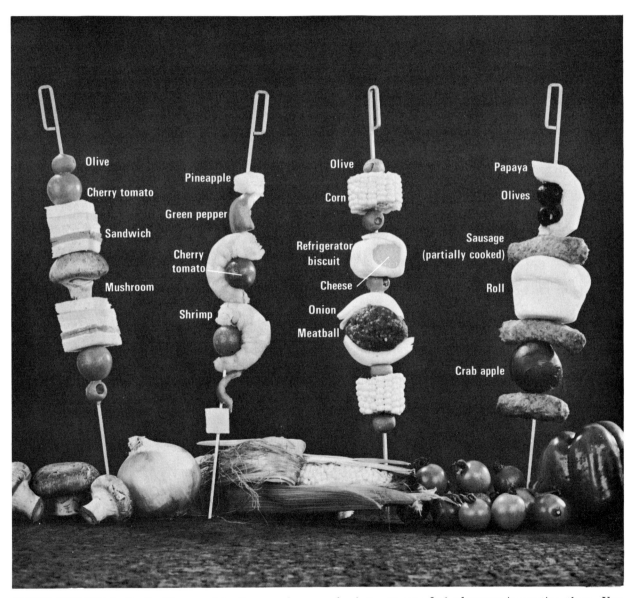

SHISH KEBABS invite limitless combinations, and any cook of any age can find adventure in creating them. You make a good start by skewering a good assortment of your favorite foods.

Variety of Meat	Cut of Meat	Size or Weight	Frozen Meat Warm-up Time		Recommended Heat of Fire ①
			In Refrigerator to 40°	In Room 40° to 70°	
BEEF	**Steak**	1 Inch	8 Hrs.	4 Hrs.	Hot
	Steak	1½ Inches	9½ Hrs.	5 Hrs.	Hot
	Steak	2 Inches	10½ Hrs.	7 Hrs.	Medium to Hot
	Steak	2½ Inches	12 Hrs.	10 Hrs.	Medium to Hot
	Flank Steak	Whole	8 Hrs.	2½ Hrs.	Hot
	Hamburger	1 Inch	8 Hrs.	3 Hrs.	Medium to Hot
	Tenderloin	Whole	12 Hrs.	10 Hrs.	Medium
FISH	**Steak**	½ Inch	———		Medium
	Steak	1 Inch	———		Medium
	Fillets or Split	1 Inch	———		Medium
	Fillets or Split	1½ Inches	8 Hrs.	4 Hrs.	Medium
HAM	**Slice**	1 Inch	8 Hrs.	4 Hrs.	Low to Medium
	Slice	1½ Inches	9½ Hrs.	5 Hrs.	Low to Medium
LAMB	**Chops or Steaks**	1 Inch	8 Hrs.	4 Hrs.	Medium
	Chops or Steaks	1½ Inches	9½ Hrs.	5 Hrs.	Medium
	Chops or Steaks	2 Inches	10½ Hrs.	7 Hrs.	Medium
LOBSTER	**Split**	1 to 2½ Pounds	———		Medium to Hot
PORK	**Chops or Steaks**	1 Inch	8 Hrs.	5 Hrs.	Low to Medium
	Chops or Steaks	1½ Inches	9½ Hrs.	4 Hrs.	Low to Medium
	Chops or Steaks	2 Inches	10½ Hrs.	4 Hrs.	Low to Medium
	Spareribs	Whole	7 Hrs.	3 Hrs.	Very Low
POULTRY	**Chicken**	Split	10 to 12 Hrs.	6 Hrs.	Medium
	Cornish Hen	Split	8 to 11 Hrs.	2 to 3 Hrs.	Medium
	Duck	Split	11 to 12 Hrs.	6½ Hrs.	Medium to Low
	Squab	Split	8 to 11 Hrs.	2 to 3 Hrs.	Medium
	Turkey	Split (3½ to 6 lbs.)	12 to 16 Hrs.	8 Hrs.	Medium
VEAL	**Steaks or Chops**	1 Inch	8 Hrs.	4 Hrs.	Medium
	Steaks or Chops	1½ Inches	9½ Hrs.	5 Hrs.	Medium
VENISON	**Steaks or Chops**	1 Inch	8 Hrs.	4 Hrs.	Hot
	Steaks or Chops	1½ Inches	9½ Hrs.	5 Hrs.	Hot
	Steaks or Chops	2 Inches	10½ Hrs.	7 Hrs.	Medium to Hot

TEMPERATURE CHART

Approximate Time for Cooking (each side)					Comments
Very Rare	Rare	Med.-rare	Medium	Well-done	
4 Min.	5 to 6 Min.	7 Min.	7 to 8 Min.	10 Min. or More②	① Hot fire, 375° and over; medium, 325°; slow 200° to 275°. Check with thermometer.
5 Min.	6 to 7 Min.	8 to 9 Min.	10 Min.	12 to 15 Min.②	
7 to 8 Min.	8 to 10 Min.	10 to 15 Min.	15 to 18 Min.	20 Min. or More②	
10 to 12 Min.	12 to 15 Min.	15 to 17 Min.	18 to 23 Min.	25 Min. or More②	② To ascertain degree of doneness, cut steak near center with sharp knife.
3 to 4 Min.	4 to 5 Min.	5 to 6 Min.	———	———③	
3 Min.	4 Min.	5 Min.	6 Min.	7 Min. or More	
10 to 12 Min.	12 to 15 Min.	15 to 17 Min.	18 to 23 Min.	———④	③ Will not be tender unless very rare or rare.
———	———	———	———	3 to 5 Min.⑤	
———	———	———	———	4 to 6 Min.⑤	④ Should be served rare.
———	———	———	———	20 to 25 Min.⑤	
———	———	———	———	25 to 30 Min.⑤	⑤ Do not overcook lest fish become dry. When fish flakes easily with a fork it is done. Internal temperature will be about 120°.
———	———	———	———	15 to 20 Min.	
———	———	———	———	18 to 23 Min.	
———	4 to 5 Min.	6 Min.	6 to 7 Min.	8 Min. or More⑥	
———	5 to 6 Min.	7 Min.	8 to 9 Min.	10 Min. or More⑥	⑥ Lamb may be cooked rare to med.-rare. However, it is a matter of taste.
———	6 to 7 Min.	8 Min.	9 to 10 Min.	12 Min. or More⑥	
———	———	———	———	15 Min. in All	
———	———	———	———	13 to 18 Min.⑦	⑦ Pork should be well done but juicy. Cook to 180° to 185° internal temperature.
———	———	———	———	15 to 23 Min.⑦	
———	———	———	———	20 to 30 Min.⑦	
———	———	———	———	½ Hr.⑧	⑧ Turn every few minutes.
———	———	(———	———	35 to 45 Min.⑨	
———	———	———	———	15 to 20 Min.	⑨ Do NOT overcook.
———	4 to 6 Min.	6 to 8 Min.	9 to 10 Min.	15 to 25 Min.⑩	
———	———	———	———	12 to 18 Min.	⑩ For wild duck, have very hot fire and cook rare.
———	———	———	———	20 to 30 Min.	
———	———	———	———	9 to 10 Min.⑪	⑪ Veal should be well done but never dry.
———	———	———	———	12 to 15 Min.⑪	
4 Min.	5 to 6 Min.	6 to 7 Min.	7 to 8 Min.	10 Min. or More⑫	⑫ Some hunters prefer venison rare rather than well done.
5 Min.	6 to 7 Min.	8 to 9 Min.	10 Min.	15 Min. or More⑫	
7 to 8 Min.	8 to 10 Min.	10 to 15 Min.	15 to 18 Min.	20 Min. or More⑫	

Salmon Broiled in Foil

STARTING with cleaned salmon, first trim off fins. Protect head and tail from heat by wrapping with oiled waxed paper held in place with foil.

SEASON fish cavity; slip fish inside folded strip of expanded aluminum, with tail in fold. Lace side loosely with wire (fish will expand).

BRUSH the fish lightly with salad oil. Foil-covered wood squares help protect head and tail. Cover with hood or foil, cook slowly, turning as needed.

When a fisherman comes home with his trophy—a fine, fresh Pacific salmon—the next question is how to cook it. Salmon is one of the finest fish to prepare on the barbecue.

If you want to keep the fish whole for serving, there are some problems in handling. The size of your grill sets the size limit for a salmon that can be barbecued whole. Its head and tail, however, may extend 2 or 3 inches beyond the grill edges.

It is easiest to accomplish slow, even cooking of salmon on a barbecue grill that can be raised high above the fire. If you must cook close to the fire, keep the heat low and spread out the coals evenly under the fish. A barbecue with a hood keeps in the smoke and allows for greater heat control, but if your grill doesn't have a hood, you can cover it with foil.

Rinse the cleaned salmon in cold water and pat dry. Remove the dorsal fin (at center of back) by cutting along either side of fin, then pulling it forward to remove it with root bones attached. Cut off the pectoral fins (just back of gills) without disturbing root bones.

You will need to take precautions to preserve the appearance of the head and tail during cooking. Wrap them with oiled waxed paper and then with foil as shown in the photograph. If the fish weighs more than about 6 pounds, put a layer of damp paper towels between the waxed paper and foil.

To prepare the salmon for cooking, sprinkle salt and pepper inside the cavity. Fill the cavity with 1 whole lemon, sliced; 1 medium-sized onion, sliced; and a handful of parsley sprigs. Enclose the fish in a strip of expanded aluminum (sold in hardware stores for covering rain gutters) and lace strip together with wire. If the fish is large, use two strips.

Put the fish on the grill and brush it with salad oil. Cover the barbecue with its hood or a blanket of foil. Cook slowly. Insert a thermometer through opening in the salmon's back into the thickest part when you turn the fish. If possible, add hickory chips or hardwood twigs to fire for extra smoke. Fish is done when it flakes easily or reaches about 120° on the thermometer. This temperature is not indicated on most thermometers, but can be estimated.

TURNING ON A SPIT, *two broiler-fryers cook juicy and brown. Small birds are fairly easy to spit roast; truss them firmly so that wings and drumsticks won't protrude and cook too rapidly.*

BARBECUE TECHNIQUES

SPIT ROASTING

Spit cooking is the only true form of roasting. Our oven "roasts" are actually baked. The advantage to turning meat on a spit as it cooks is that the juices and bastes roll around the surface rather than dripping off into a pan or into the fire. The meat stays moist and flavorful, because it bastes itself.

Excess fat or baste will, of course, drip off the rotat-

ing food, but if you arrange your fire and a drip pan as suggested in the firemanship section of the chapter on fire, you don't need to pay much attention to roasting meat. Constant basting is unnecessary.

The only problem that needs careful attention in rotisserie cooking is the balance of the meat on the spit. The spit must turn evenly or there will be jerks and fast and slow rolls which will cause the meat to cook unevenly and possibly burn the heavier side, leaving the light side pale and unappetizing.

You can spit-roast very well indeed without a speial balance weight, but such a weight makes the occasional problem roast easy to balance. You put the weight on the spit protruding toward the light side of the roast. If there are changes in balance during cooking due to melting fat and contracting meat, the weight can be adjusted easily to compensate. (Further tips on weights for spit roasting are given in the section on accessories in the first chapter of the book.)

The easiest roasts to balance are those of uniform shape and texture. With a rolled roast, judge the center by eye, run the spit through, tighten the holding forks, then pick up the spit, letting the ends rest in your palms loosely. If there's no tendency to roll, give the spit a quarter turn. If it's still stable, give it another quarter turn. It should rest without turning in each of these positions. You can then put it over the coals. If it does turn, respit and try again.

Small birds are fairly easy too. Truss them firmly so the wings and drumsticks stay close to the body. You can stuff the cavity with onion, garlic, celery, or a few herbs if you like. Pull down the neck skin and fix it firmly over the back with a small skewer. Then run the spit through lengthwise, catching the bird in the fork of the wishbone. Center it and tighten the holding forks. Then test the balance as above.

Irregular roasts are harder to balance, and a weight is advisable, but there are tricks to help. A turkey is so much heavier than a chicken that the holding forks need help. Truss a turkey tightly, then run the spit in at the base of the tail and diagonally through the cavity to the fork of the wishbone. Then tighten the holding forks.

Unboned rib roasts should be spitted diagonally through the meaty section. Start the spit on one cut side near the point where the ribs begin to protrude. Run it out diagonally toward the top of the other side and test the balance.

Remember that any piece of meat which is very fat will change its balance as the fat melts. If you have no adjustable weight, you will have to respit a roast that begins jerking on the turns.

Spit-Roasting Techniques

As discussed in the section on firemanship (see chapter, Begin with the Fire), a spit must turn so that the top of the roast moves away from the cook and the bottom comes toward him. This makes placement of fire and drip pan easier since fat drips from the ascending side and the pan can be placed near the cook. If your spit turns in the opposite direction and you can't mount the motor on the other side to correct it, then put the coals in front (the descending side) and the pan in back (the ascending side).

If you find that protruding bones or wing tips are browning too rapidly, cover them with foil.

The chart on pages 28 and 29 gives times and temperatures for spit roasting meats, poultry, fish, and game. You should test the heat near the spit (see chapter on fire for directions). Heat is more variable since there is more air space between the cooking food and the fire than when you grill, so insert a meat thermometer in the center of the roast (don't let it touch bone, fat, or the spit) to be sure it is done as you like it.

Although the spit is best for large chunks of meat or for poultry, you can spit roast nearly anything if you prepare it properly. Spare ribs can be folded back and forth in an undulating pattern and impaled through the folds. A large piece of liver is delicious spit roasted if you tie it into a compact piece before putting it on the spit. Whole fish can be spit roasted without danger of going to pieces if you wrap them in poultry netting or expanded metal first. However, these foods are just as good done on the grill and the effort you save in watching and basting goes into the spit preparation.

Spit-Roasting Accessories

There are numerous accessories that make spit roasting of small pieces of food possible, but they are often less practical than fun. A shish-kebab attachment is good if you want no more than four to eight skewers. These attachments either turn as a whole, or the individual skewers turn separately. Best are those skewers that turn independently, so that the food is evenly browned on all sides.

Another spit-roasting accessory is a cylindrical spit basket, which will take chicken parts or chunks of meat. With chicken parts, the friction of the turning basket tends to rub off the skin, and the pieces may not turn and brown properly. Too few pieces of food in the basket tend to just bump along the bottom. A flat spit basket will take small fish, ribs, or steaks, but the method is likely to produce less barbecue appearance and flavor than grill cooking. And if the pieces are not uniform, they may slip around in the basket.

ONE SPIT-ROASTING TECHNIQUE *confines coals to the back of the firebed, with a drip pan in front. The spit rotates the top of meat away from pan, bottom toward it; fat drips from ascending side.*

Variety of Meat	Cut of Meat	Size or Weight	Frozen Meat Warm-up Time		Recommended Heat of Fire ①
			In Refrigerator to 40°	In Room 40° to 70°	
BEEF	Standing Rib	3 to 5 Ribs	36 to 40 Hrs.	8 Hrs.	Hot-Medium
	Rolled Rib	6 to 7 Pounds	36 to 40 Hrs.	8 Hrs.	Hot-Medium
	Spencer	8 to 10 Pounds	36 to 40 Hrs.	8 Hrs.	Hot-Medium
	Rump	3 to 5 Pounds	24 to 30 Hrs.	6 Hrs.	Medium
	Tenderloin	4 to 6 Pounds	12 to 18 Hrs.	10 Hrs.	Hot
	Sirloin	5 to 7 Pounds	18 to 24 Hrs.	8 Hrs.	Hot-Medium
FISH	Large, Whole	10 to 20 Pounds	30 to 40 Hrs.	12 Hrs.	Slow
HAM	Smoked	We do not recommend roasting cured ham over charcoal. If you wish to do			
LAMB	Leg	4 to 8 Pounds	15 to 40 Hrs.	5 to 7 Hrs.	Medium
	Rolled Shoulder	3 to 6 Pounds	15 to 30 Hrs.	4 to 6 Hrs.	Medium
	Saddle	6 to 16 Pounds	15 to 36 Hrs.	6 to 10 Hrs.	Medium
	Rack (ribs)	4 to 7 Pounds	12 to 24 Hrs.	5 to 6 Hrs.	Medium
	Baby Lamb, Kid	12 to 25 Pounds	30 to 54 Hrs.	12 to 15 Hrs.	Medium
PORK	Loin	5 to 14 Pounds	28 to 36 Hrs.	6 to 10 Hrs.	Medium
	Shoulder	3 to 6 Pounds	24 to 30 Hrs.	6 to 8 Hrs.	Medium
	Fresh Ham	10 to 16 Pounds	30 to 48 Hrs.	10 to 15 Hrs.	Medium
	Spareribs	1½ to 3½ Pounds	4 to 7 Hrs.	2 to 3 Hrs.	Medium to Hot
	Suckling Pig	12 to 20 Pounds	30 to 54 Hrs.	12 to 15 Hrs.	Medium
POULTRY	Chicken	3 to 5 Pounds	10 to 12 Hrs.	4 to 5 Hrs.	Medium
	Cornish Hen	12 oz. to 1 Pound	8 to 11 Hrs.	2 to 3 Hrs.	Medium
	Squab	10 to 14 Ounces	8 to 11 Hrs.	2 to 3 Hrs.	Medium
	Turkey	10 to 25 Pounds	15 to 36 Hrs.	8 to 10 Hrs.	Medium
	Junior Goose	4 to 7 Pounds	13 to 20 Hrs.	5 to 7 Hrs.	Medium
	Goose	8 to 15 Pounds	20 to 30 Hrs.	6 to 9 Hrs.	Medium
	Duckling	4 to 6 Pounds	13 to 18 Hrs.	5 to 7 Hrs.	Medium
VEAL	Leg	8 to 14 Pounds	24 to 36 Hrs.	7 to 10 Hrs.	Medium
	Loin	10 to 13 Pounds	20 to 30 Hrs.	6 to 9 Hrs.	Medium
	Shoulder (rolled)	3 to 5 Pounds	15 to 24 Hrs.	4 to 6 Hrs.	Medium
VENISON	Leg	9 to 12 Pounds	20 to 40 Hrs.	7 to 10 Hrs.	Hot-Medium
	Saddle	5 to 7 Pounds	15 to 24 Hrs.	4 to 6 Hrs.	Hot-Medium
	Shoulder	12 to 18 Pounds	18 to 40 Hrs.	8 to 12 Hrs.	Medium

Approximate Time for Cooking					Comments
Very Rare 120°-130°	Rare 130°-135°	Med.-rare 135°-145°	Medium 145°-155°	Well-done 155°180°	
1½ to 2¼ Hrs.	1¾ to 2¼ Hrs.	2 to 2¾ Hrs.	2½ to 3 Hrs.	3 to 4½ Hrs. ②	① Hot fire, 325° or over; medium, 250 to 300°; slow, 150 to 225°. Check with thermometer.
1¾ to 2½ Hrs.	2 to 2¾ Hrs.	2¼ to 3 Hrs.	2¾ to 3¼ Hrs.	3¼ to 5 Hrs. ②	
1½ to 2½ Hrs.	2½ to 3 Hrs.	2¾ to 3½ Hrs.	3 to 4 Hrs.	3½ to 5½ Hrs. ②	
1¼ to 1¾ Hrs.	1½ to 2 Hrs.	1¾ to 2½ Hrs.	2½ to 3 Hrs.	3 to 4½ Hrs.	② Start with very hot fire; let it burn down to medium.
25 to 40 Min.	35 to 45 Min.	45 to 60 Min.	1 to 1¼ Hrs.	1 to 2 Hrs. ③	
1 to 1½ Hrs.	1¼ to 1¾ Hrs.	1¾ to 2¼ Hrs.	2¼ to 3 Hrs.	3 to 4 Hrs. ④	
Cook to about 120° internal temperature. ⑤					③ If meat is larded (wrapped in fat), it will take somewhat longer to cook.
so, follow timing for fresh ham (below).					
50 to 65 Min.	1 to 1¼ Hrs.	1¼ to 1½ Hrs.	1½ to 2 Hrs.	2 Hrs. or More ⑥	
50 to 65 Min.	1 to 1¼ Hrs.	1¼ to 1½ Hrs.	1½ to 2 Hrs.	2 Hrs. or More ⑥	④ Handle fire as for rib roast, above.
———	¾ to 1¼ Hrs.	1 to 1½ Hrs.	1¼ to 1¾ Hrs.	2 Hrs. or More ⑥	
———	¾ to 1 Hr.	1 to 1¼ Hrs.	1¼ to 1½ Hrs.	2 Hrs. or More ⑥	
———	———	———	2 to 2½ Hrs.	2½ to 3½ Hrs.	
———	———	———	———	2 to 4 Hrs. ⑦	⑤ Thawing time varies, depending upon shape of fish.
———	———	———	———	2 to 3½ Hrs. ⑦	
———	———	———	———	4 to 6 Hrs. ⑦	
———	———	———	———	1 to 1½ Hrs. ⑦	
———	———	———	———	3 to 4 Hrs. ⑦	⑥ Some believe lamb is tenderer and more flavorsome when cooked rare.
———	———	———	———	1 to 1½ Hrs. ⑧	
———	———	———	———	¾ to 1 Hr. ⑧	
———	———	———	———	¾ to 1 Hr. ⑧	⑦ Pork should be cooked to 180° to 185° internal temperture.
———	———	———	———	2 to 4 Hrs. ⑧	
———	———	———	———	1¾ to 2½ Hrs.	
———	———	———	———	2 to 3 Hrs.	
———	———	———	———	1 to 2 Hrs. ⑨	⑧ Eviscerated weight. Use leg joint test to determine doneness.
———	———	———	———	2 to 3 Hrs.	
———	———	———	———	1½ to 2½ Hrs.	
———	———	———	———	¾ to 1½ Hrs.	
1 to 1¼ Hrs.	1¼ to 1½ Hrs.	1½ to 1¾ Hrs.	1¾ to 2¼ Hrs.	2 Hrs. or More	⑨ Whole wild duck cooks in 20 to 30 minutes to very rare stage.
50 to 65 Min.	1 to 1¼ Hrs.	1¼ to 1½ Hrs.	1½ to 2 Hrs.	2 Hrs. or More	
———	1¼ to 1½ Hrs.	1½ to 1¾ Hrs.	1¾ to 2¼ Hrs.	2 Hrs. or More	

An Argentine Barbecue

Patterned after the cooking method of gauchos on the Argentine pampas, meat for an asado (ah-*sah*-do) is fastened on a long stick (asador) that's driven into the ground at an angle above a pile of hot coals.

A temporary asador can be made by lashing three metal coathangers (preferably unpainted) to a 5-foot-long metal fence post with fine wire; then wire meat to hangers. To make more permanent asador, weld iron rod crossbars to fence post as shown in diagram below. Dig a shallow firepit and drive asadors into ground alongside so they lean over pit at about a 60° angle. Build a fire in firepit.

Most important in this barbecue is the meat and its slow cooking. Serve just shortribs or a mixed grill chosen from meats listed below. Cook meat over low heat—just hot enough for slow cooking and light browning; it will take about twice as long as usual.

While meat is cooking, serve guests your favorite vegetable-potato salad on small plates as an appetizer. Then have them select meat from the asador and serve themselves green salad, French bread, and red wine. Traditional Argentine dessert is corn pie and coffee; ice cream or fruit might be substituted.

The distinctive seasoning for the meats is the *chimichurri* sauce. Use half of it as a baste, the rest as sauce with cooked meat.

Chimichurri Sauce

Chop very fine 2 medium-sized carrots, 1 large tomato, 1 stalk celery, 1 clove garlic, ½ seeded green pepper, and 1 whole lemon, sliced and with both ends trimmed off; whirl in electric blender a few pieces at a time. Add 1½ teaspoons salt, ½ teaspoon crushed red pepper, and ½ teaspoon black pepper. Stir in ¼ cup red wine, ¼ cup vinegar, and 1½ cups salad oil (half may be olive oil). Cover; refrigerate 2 to 5 days. Makes approximately 1 quart.

Meats For Asado

Allow about 1 pound of meat for each person; either all short ribs or ribs plus other meats. Cook ribs on the asador, other meats on the grill over medium low heat.

Short Ribs. Ask your meatman to prepare triangle cuts of shortribs weighing 4 to 5 pounds each; cut each bone in two places. Hang meat on hooks with bone sides toward fire. Cook about 2½ hours; then turn and baste. Cook about 2 hours longer, basting 2 or 3 times. To serve, carve bottom pieces first, using sharp knife.

Skirt Steak. Buy 1 for 2 to 3 servings. Cook 20 to 30 minutes per side, basting 2 or 3 times with sauce.

Chicken Breasts. Buy ½ breast for each serving. Grill skin side down over medium-low heat for 45 minutes per side, basting frequently with the sauce.

Lamb Chops. Buy 1 small chop per serving. Cook over medium-low heat about 30 minutes on each side, basting frequently with sauce.

Italian Sausages. Buy 1 per serving. Barbecue about 15 minutes on each side without basting.

Sweetbreads. Buy 1 pound for 8 servings. Cut into 8 pieces. Cook 12 to 15 minutes on each side, or until browned, basting often.

ASADOR, shown in drawing at right, will hold enough short ribs for a large scale barbecue. Other meats can cook on the grill underneath. Meat which is cooked this long and slow way is particularly juicy and tender.

COVERED SMOKE COOKER has large grill area; prune-stuffed rack of pork (page 83) is basted occasionally while cooking. Meat thermometer gives internal temperature; thermometer on hood gives oven temperature.

BARBECUE TECHNIQUES

SMOKE COOKING

Smoke cooking and smoking are really quite distinct, although in the Chinese smoke oven, where the meat cooks in a chimney well away from the coals, the two approach each other. When foods are smoke cooked, the heat does the job, and the smoke imparts flavor. Smoking is more a curing process than a cooking process, in that the smoke causes certain chemical changes in the meat which render it edible. You can do smoke cooking in any covered barbecue in about

the same time as it takes to oven cook the same things. But true smoking takes days and uses little heat.

The greatest advantage of smoke cooking over spit roasting or grilling is in the definite smoky flavor. There's no doubt that smoke-cooked food was cooked over a fire of coals, for even the outside slices of a roast often take on a characteristic red coloring.

A second advantage to smoke cooking, mainly evident in cool or windy weather, is that covered cooking maintains temperature and you don't have to worry about lengthened cooking times when the breeze comes up.

Yet another advantage is that you can cook the rest of your meal in a covered barbecue at the same time you are doing a roast. Potatoes and onions will bake, and you can heat a covered casserole or roast corn. Leave the cover off already-baked beans for a smoky, crusty surface.

For the strongest smoke flavor, you must add chips or twigs of aromatic wood to your charcoal. You can even throw in small quantities of damp sawdust, but be careful not to use pine sawdust or any other soft resinous wood. You'll get an unpleasant, tarry surface on the food and a turpentine flavor. Suggestions for fire additives appear in the section on firemanship (see chapter on fire).

Whatever you add, you have considerable choice about when to add it. For strongest flavor, put in your chips or twigs at the beginning and add more when the smoke dies down. For mild surface flavor, put in chips during the last 15 or 20 minutes.

As a rule, covered smoke cooking is sparing of charcoal. You need to maintain a temperature of 300° inside the cover, but heat doesn't escape as it does with open barbecuing, so a small amount of fuel goes a long way. Start with about 25 to 30 briquets in a kettle or kamado, up to 50 in a box or cylinder-shaped wagon. Be prepared to add more if cooking times are very long, but the initial amount should supply adequate cooking heat for two hours or more. You should have an air temperature thermometer for accurate checking of the inside temperature.

As discussed under firemanship, you should place

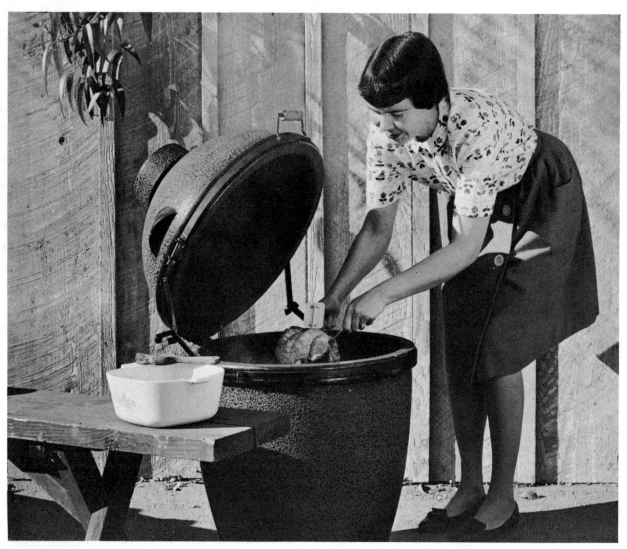

JAPANESE EARTHENWARE SMOKER used here to roast marinated turkey roll (see page 118 for recipe). Heat is regulated by opening and closing the cap on lid and the draft door on bottom.

the coals to one side of the roast rather than underneath, and use a drip pan to prevent flaring. You use direct heat only for those foods you would normally grill, such as chicken parts or steaks. Watch these grillable items carefully since they are cooking top and bottom in a covered unit and therefore cook more quickly.

A commercially made covered barbecue, with its efficient dampers and rather deep firebed, is ideal for covered cooking; but if you'd like to try out the method on a brazier or tabletop barbecue, any cover will do. The most quickly made cover consists of a frame of 22-gage galvanized steel wire covered with foil. Make a ring of wire the diameter of your brazier, then bend three equal half hoops of wire, attach the ends on opposite sides of the ring, and whip them together where they cross at the top. To cover the frame, run strips of foil from bottom to top, folding the vertical seams together tightly.

For small barbecues or hibachis, use a similar dome, or overturn a large kettle or Chinese wok to serve as a cover. Don't worry too much about a perfect fit since an air-tight cover will snuff out the coals.

One specialized smoker is the Chinese smoke oven. In this unit the fire is built in a fire box toward the front while the food is hung on a hook in a chimney at the back. You generally build a fire of hardwood an hour or so before you begin cooking, then stoke it with more wood from time to time during the cooking. Flames don't matter since the food is well away from the fire. Commercial units may have a thermometer on the chimney so that you can judge cooking times accurately. Dampers help control the heat. With a very slow fire, you can approach real smoking.

CHINESE SMOKE OVEN *burns any hardwood. Here, leg of lamb is hung on hook in chimney, and meat takes on a wood-smoked flavor. The barbecue also has a rack for holding meats that cannot be hung.*

An Indian-Style Salmon Bake

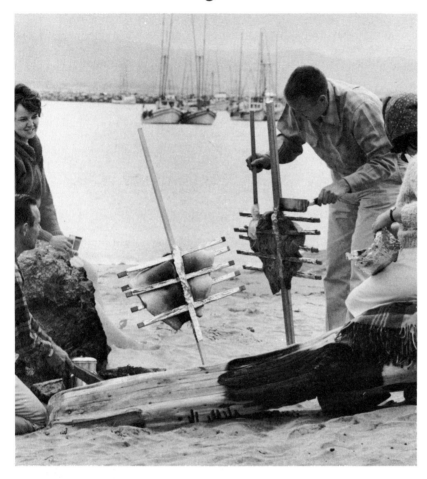

SALMON is almost ready to eat as cook bastes fish with lemon butter while friends tend coffee and wrap the bread for last-minute heating.

The salmon barbecue rack and method illustrated here originated with the Indians of the Pacific Northwest. Indians traditionally use alder to make the frame; if you have access to green alder (or fruitwood branches) use it. If you must use milled lumber, any non-resinous wood will do. To keep the wood from burning, you can soak the pieces in water overnight.

For each frame you'll need two 6-foot stakes, ¾ by ¾ inch; five to eight crosspieces (depending on the size of the fish) of ¼ by ¾-inch stock, 18 inches long; and 2 feet of 22-gage (or heavier) wire.

To prepare the salmon, butterfly it by removing head, tail, backbone, and main rib bones, then spread it flat. Immerse the fish in a saline solution (¼ cup salt to 1 gallon of water) for about an hour to enhance flavor and firm the meat. Wrap the wood with foil and affix salmon to the frame as shown in the photos.

Once the salmon is secured, sharpen the lower end of the double main stake and hammer it into the sand at an angle until the fish is about two feet above the fire. Cook about 25 minutes a side, turning once (you'll probably have to pull out the stake and pound it in again). Baste frequently with a lemon butter made of ¼ pound melted butter and the juice of 2 lemons.

To insure adequate heat, build a driftwood fire against a rock or cliffside that will reflect some heat. Let it burn down to a bed of coals before cooking.

CROSSPIECES alternate, and are pinched together by wired uprights.

HAMMER in sharpened uprights, angling salmon over bed of coals.

SERVE yourself right from the frame as soon as fish flakes easily.

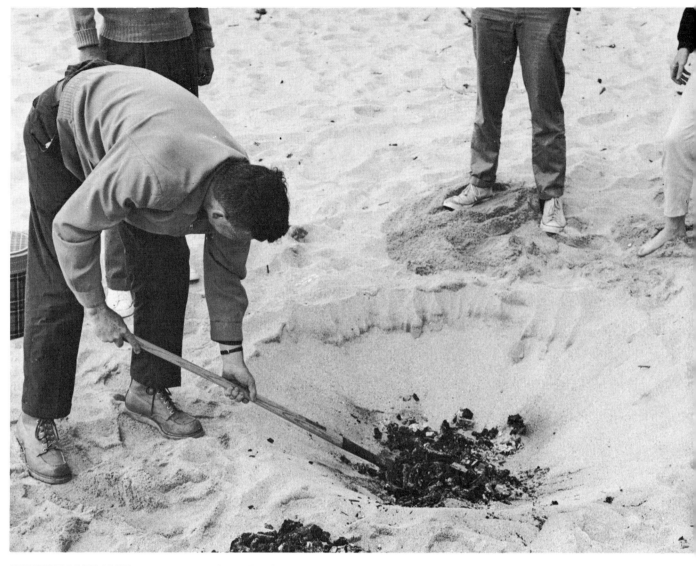

FIREPIT PREPARED at beach to cook whole salmon. Sand has been heated for two hours by burning wood down to coals. Coals are shoveled out, leaving hot sand for cooking (sequence continues on pages 36-37).

BARBECUE TECHNIQUES

FIREPIT COOKING

Cooking underground is a method of cooking that was practiced many years ago by the Indians and by the white scouts, hunters, and trappers who roamed the country. This method of cooking beef is still favored by many barbecuers, especially at such all-out community occasions as round-ups, rodeos, fairs, and farmers' picnics. You can do pit cookery in a small way just as successfully as you can with a whole side of beef.

Essentially, cooking underground is a primitive version of roasting meat in an oven, with two important exceptions: 1) You can't peek into your "oven" to see whether the meat is done, or you may destroy the effectiveness of your coals. 2) Because the meat is tightly wrapped, it is really steam-cooked under pressure rather than roasted.

Steam-cooking keeps the meat moist while it is in the pit but is no guarantee against overcooking. It doesn't prevent overcooked meat from drying out and losing its flavor as soon as it is exposed to the air. In pit barbecuing, meat doesn't get the kind of searing that seals in juices when you roast it in the oven or cook it over an open fire.

How do you control the process? You can't read dials on the oven or on a meat thermometer. You have to control the cooking by the way you handle the fire and by your timing. The important elements are these: size of the pit; kind of wood; length of time the fire burns before you put on the meat; size, weight, kind, and preparation of the meat used for cooking underground; covering of the meat and the fire; cooking time.

The Pit and the Fire

The experts on pit barbecuing don't agree among themselves as to the proper size of the pit. Actually, you can figure out the best size for your own operation if you understand the method.

As for the length and width obviously these dimensions should be large enough so you can spread the meat out on the coals, in one large package or several small ones. In addition, there should be a little extra space all around the meat, so that heat from the outer coals will cook the outside edges of the meat. On a small-scale job, you might cheat a little on the outside edge and make the pit about 1½ feet wide. For easy handling of the meat and general convenience, a 3-foot width is about maximum. Length can be anything required by the quantity of the meat.

To determine the depth, just add up the thickness of each layer you intend to put in the pit.

Many experts like to line the bottom (and sometimes part way up the sides) with bricks or with large round stones, which should be hard and dry, without crevices or porous sections holding water that might later make the rock explode under steam pressure.

When the pit is ready for cooking, the first thing you must add is the bed of coals; recommended depths range from 1 to 2 feet (depends on cooking time you favor). Next comes the meat; some put it right on the coals, and others bank the fire and protect the meat from possible burning with about an inch of pre-heated dry sand. Finally comes the layer of dirt (right on the meat package or on a cover of

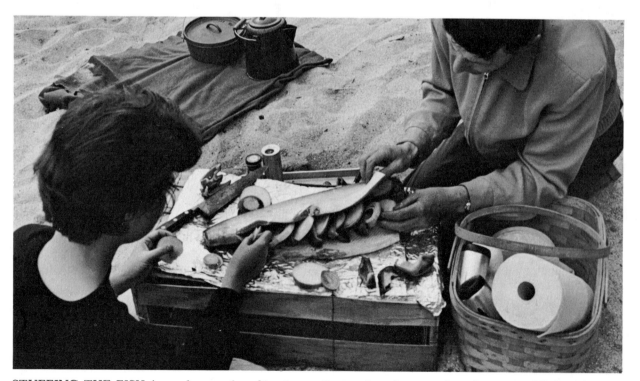

STUFFING THE FISH for underground cooking is easy (instructions for preparing pit on page 35). Just alternate enough slices of onion and green pepper to fill salmon cavity without overloading.

metal or canvas); recommended depth is 1 foot.

Add up these figures and you get a depth of about 2½ to 5 feet. It varies according to the depth of the bed of coals, the size of the meat packages, and, if you use a cover, whether you put it right on the meat or a few inches above it. (If you use galvanized iron, burn off the coating beforehand so it won't add an undesirable flavor to the meat.)

If you cook a pot of beans underground, you can use a smaller, shallower pit. The bed of coals may be as little as 6 inches deep, although a little extra depth won't matter.

Kind of Wood

With the pit dug, the next step is to prepare the fire. The aim is to prepare a bed of coals of the approximate size and consistency of charcoal. All the pieces of wood should be burning or be thoroughly charred. Any uncharred pieces should be removed before the meat is placed on top.

Wood has to be fairly hard if it is to burn slowly enough to pile up a bed of coals. Anything as soft and fast-burning as pine is likely to leave ashes and very little else.

Favorite woods for this purpose include oak, alder, hickory, mesquite, ironwood, and the wood from most orchard trees—walnut, pecan, apple, orange, lemon. Needless to say, the wood should be thoroughly dry. It burns best if pieces aren't more than about 4 inches thick.

Timing the Fire

When you stoke your preliminary fire, you are really heating up an oven—the bottom and sides of your pit—so that the stored heat will continue to cook for the next several hours. The principle is very much like that of the igloo-shaped Mexican oven, in which you build your fire, then scrape it all out and do your cooking with the heat stored in the walls.

In the pit barbecue, you should keep replenishing

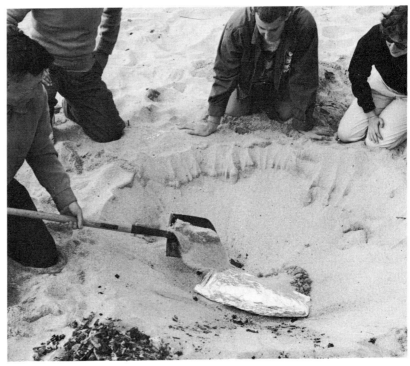

WRAPPING AND BURYING SALMON are final stages after stuffing it (see page 36). Triple-turn edges of heavy-duty foil; then cover packages with hot sand. Place coals and more fuel over sand and cook one hour.

the fire until the bed of coals reaches the desired depth. Each expert has his own timing on this step, but the majority would agree that 3 to 6 hours should be enough to develop a 1 to 2-foot depth of coals. Less than 3 hours may not pre-heat your "oven" enough; more than 6 hours may get it too hot.

Preparing the Meat

Standard practice is to wrap the chunks of meat in one or more layers of closely woven white cloth, parchment, or foil, and tie with twine; then wrap in one or more thicknesses of burlap and secure with wire. Each package is sprinkled or doused quickly in water before it goes on the coals.

Before wrapping, you can use any of the seasonings you might use with a roast. You can sprinkle the meat with liquid and dry seasonings or you can inject marinades with a syringe.

The traditional large-scale barbecue calls for whole quarters or whole sides of beef. But without a whole corps of meat cutters on duty, it is difficult to carve such huge pieces fast enough to serve the meat while it is still hot. For this reason many now prefer to bone the meat beforehand and tie it in reasonably small rolls than can be carved fast and easily. You can keep each piece wrapped until the cutter is ready to go to work on it. This method is definitely best for any family-size pit barbecue.

Covering the Pit

The most primitive method is to pile the layer of dirt right on the meat packages—and do it fast before they have a chance to burn. A good idea here is to wrap a length of thick but soft wire around each package and let it stick up above the layer of dirt; you'll have no trouble pulling out each piece of meat and won't have to grapple for it with either a shovel or pitchfork.

For a more sanitary job, and especially if you'd like to use your burlap again for the same purpose, put a cover over the meat before throwing on the dirt. Canvas is used occasionally, but by far the most popular covering is thick sheet iron or corrugated galvanized iron (with the coating well burned off).

Some improvise a frame inside the pit in order to get the cover close to the meat. Others put pipes or rods across the top of the pit to support the cover; then they mound up the dirt on top.

In either case, work fast. Shovel dirt until you see no smoke or steam escaping. Some prefer to stamp on the dirt as it is being piled up. Others use a little water and seal the top with mud.

About every half hour, make an inspection to see that no steam is escaping. If it is, cover with dirt and stamp it down.

Cooking Time

Here is the supreme test of artistry. You have to know your fire and what it will do. You also have to gauge time by the size of your pieces of meat, much as you gauge oven cooking times by the size of your roast. Generally, meat in 6 to 10-pound pieces will require about 5 hours cooking time; in 20-pound pieces, 8 to 10 hours; hindquarters of beef (100 to 150 pounds, dressed), 15 to 18 hours; pots of beans, 4 to 6 hours.

The theory is that if your preliminary firing is right, the heat will subside after the first few hours of cooking is done. You do have some latitude, but don't trust this theory too far.

On your first trial, you'll have to do some experimenting and adjusting to fit these directions to your cooking job.

It's worth noting that most reliable experts in this field are not improvisers at all. After trial and error, they've learned exactly what to do (pit, fire, and timing) with a certain quantity of meat. They have developed a set routine and they know it well, and they don't mind repeating it over and over again.

CUTTING SHORTRIBS Korean style for grilling makes good eating. This technique is one of many you can use in preparing meat for the barbecue. The cooked ribs are pictured on page 47; recipe on page 69.

BARBECUE TECHNIQUES

MEATS FOR BARBECUING

Today's meat markets offer a wide choice of meats, poultry, and fish for cooking on your barbecue. Look beyond traditional tender beef steaks and roasts to an interesting variety of lamb and pork cuts, sausages, many sizes and kinds of poultry, and many different fish.

The use of commercial meat tenderizing products with some of the less tender beef cuts makes them quite suitable for barbecue (or dry heat) cooking. Most cuts of lamb can be cooked deliciously tender on a barbecue. The flavor of beef, lamb, and pork is gen-erally enhanced by the smoke of a barbecue fire.

Once people worried about being able to cook pork thoroughly enough on a barbecue. There is much less need for concern today with improved quality of pork meat. Any pork roast may be cooked in a covered bar-becue if you use a meat thermometer.

Of all the meats, veal is the least satisfactory to bar-becue. It is an especially lean meat that tends to be-come dry when barbecued; the smoky flavor imparted by the fire doesn't complement its delicate flavor.

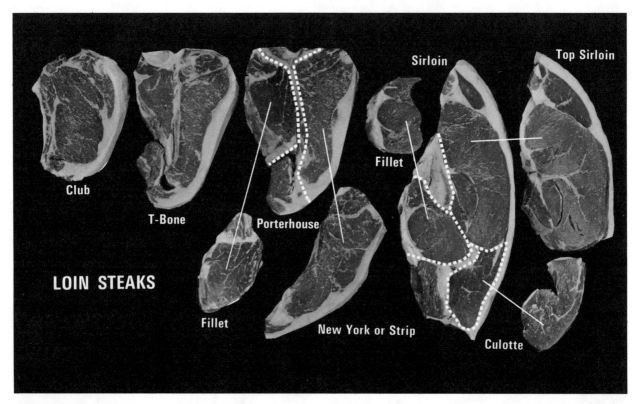

BEEF LOIN STEAKS are tasty and tender; these represent about 1/6 of all retail cuts. Some may be cut in slightly different ways, or sold under various names, but terms given here are ones commonly used.

Beef Steaks

Choosing a beef steak (see also page 41) wisely from the variety offered at meat counters isn't easy. That steaks vary widely in size, shape, price, and even name, is plain to see. What you can expect from each in terms of tenderness and flavor is less obvious.

Loin Steaks: The muscles of the short loin and sirloin yield very tender steaks with generous marbling of fat for flavor. All are excellent barbecued.

Club, smallest of loin steaks, is cut from the end of the loin next to ribs. A generous single serving— 1½-inch-thick steak—weighs about 1¼ pounds.

T-Bone is named for the easily recognizable bone. Muscles are a continuation of those in club steak, plus slice from small end of fillet. Steak 1 inch thick weighs about ¾ pound.

Porterhouse, one of the choicest steaks, serves at least two persons when cut 1½ inches thick for barbecuing (about 2 pounds). New York or strip, the large muscle, is continuation of club steak muscle and is often sold as separate boneless steak. Smaller muscle is a slice from center fillet; restaurants also term this piece filet mignon or beef tenderloin.

Sirloin is largest of loin steaks. Its largest muscle is often sold separately as boneless top sirloin steak. Fillet slice is from large end of fillet. Small tail-end of this steak may be sold separately as culotte steak. A 1½-inch-thick piece with bone weighs 3¼ pounds.

Rib Steaks. There are two different steaks cut from the rib section (not shown). Some meat experts consider these the most flavorful of all beef cuts because of the generous streaking of fat.

Rib steak is cut through entire rib section and contains rib bone, tender rib eye, less tender top muscles (often called beef lifters when sold separately for stew). A 1-inch-thick steak weighs about 1 pound.

Rib Eye, Market, or Spencer steak is choice central muscle of rib steak. A 1-inch-thick steak weighs about ¾ pound.

Steaks from Other Muscles: The chuck or shoulder of steer, the round, and other muscles also yield steaks suitable for barbecuing. They are generally less tender than loin or rib steaks, more economical.

Round steak is very compact, lean, with little marbling to add flavor; largest muscle in round—top round —is most tender part. First two cuts of top round, be-

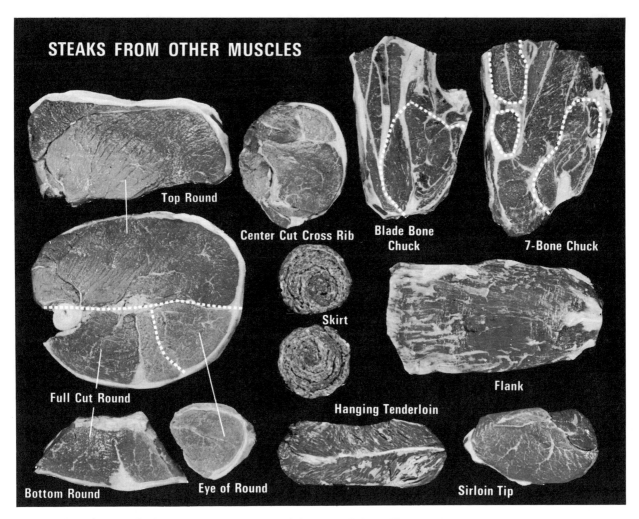

STEAKS FROM OTHER MUSCLES

Top Round

Center Cut Cross Rib

Blade Bone Chuck

7-Bone Chuck

Full Cut Round

Skirt

Bottom Round

Eye of Round

Hanging Tenderloin

Flank

Sirloin Tip

ECONOMICAL STEAKS are shown in a variety of shapes and sizes. Flavor and tenderness vary considerably, even within a single steak. Most are best when marinated or tenderized before cooking; best barbecued rare.

cause they are most tender, are sometimes labeled London broil and sold at a higher price. Bottom section—bottom round (often labeled Swiss steak) and eye of round—are less tender. All are best tenderized for barbecuing.

Center-Cut Cross Rib steak is a slice cut from the larger roast sections. It has good flavor, is best tenderized for barbecuing. A 1-inch-thick steak weighs about 1½ pounds.

Blade Bone Chuck steak should be cut about 1½ inches thick, then boned. Outlined area in picture is most tender part of this steak—a continuation of muscles in rib section. Flavor is good; marinate or tenderize, if you wish. Best cooked to rare stage, thinly sliced. A 1½-inch-thick boneless steak weighs about 2½ pounds.

7-Bone Chuck steak is cut next to the blade bone; 7-bone contains smaller portion of rib-area muscles

(outlined area at right) plus slices of lean chuck fillet (center) and flatiron (top left). Cooking size is the same as blade bone chuck.

Skirt steak is similar to flank, only smaller, weighing about ¾ pound. It's from inside rib cage; each carcass has two. Each steak is usually rolled, cut in two pinwheels.

Flank steak is quite lean, with coarse fibers; it's usually scored before cooking or sliced diagonally to serve. There are only two on each steer, each weighing about 1½ pounds. Has robust beef flavor; marinate if you wish. Cook it flat, stuffed, or cut in pinwheel.

Hanging Tenderloin is named for its shape and position (part of it actually hangs free). There's only one to a carcass and it weighs about 1½ pounds. It's often ground, but it barbecues well.

Sirloin Tip steak is best tenderized for barbecuing. A 1-inch-thick steak weighs about ¾ pound.

LOIN, RIB, AND SIRLOIN ROASTS

Fillet

New York or Strip

Top Sirloin

Club

Standing Rib

Rolled Rib

Rib Eye

TENDER, FLAVORFUL beef roasts shown here are best you can buy. Fillet is most tender, very lean; top sirloin and New York roasts have heavy fat cover. Bottom row shows three variations of rib roast; latter two are boneless.

Beef Roasts

All the beef roasts shown on this and page 43 are suitable for barbecuing. The flatter ones can be placed directly on the grill; round, compact roasts are best for rotisserie cooking.

Loin, Rib, Sirloin Roasts: Beef Tenderloin or Fillet, a most tender and expensive roast, has excellent flavor with little waste. A whole fillet weighs about 6 pounds, but it can be cut in smaller roasts. For barbecuing, it should have an even fat covering tied around it.

Top Sirloin roast is quite flat, boneless, tender, and has good flavor. Barbecue a whole 8 to 10-pound roast or a smaller cut directly on the grill covered with a barbecue hood or blanket of foil.

New York or Strip roast is cut from the porterhouse area of a beef loin. It's quite flat and very tender with generous marbling of fat for good flavor. Grill, covered with barbecue hood or foil. The whole piece weighs 10 to 12 pounds.

Club roast, almost a miniature standing rib roast, is cut from the end of the loin, next to the rib section.

Rib bones provide a natural rack for this 3½ to 4-pound roast; there's good fat covering on top and it's tender with good flavor.

Standing Rib roast, with its generous marbling and layers of fat, has excellent flavor and tenderness. You can buy a small 2-rib roast weighing 4 to 5 pounds or a whole rib section weighing up to 25 pounds.

Rolled Rib roast contains the same muscles as standing rib, only the bones have been removed and the meat and fat rolled and tied. You can purchase this boneless roast in any size up to about 16 pounds.

Rib Eye, Market Roast, or Spencer Roll is choice, tender eye muscle of the rib section, best done on a rotisserie. It can be purchased up to 10 to 12 pounds.

Roasts from Other Muscles: Sirloin Tip or Ball Tip roast is easy to carve because it is just one muscle tied with a fat covering. Lean, tapering, it's best done on a spit; meat is similar in texture to round, has marbling and flavor like sirloin. Weighs 10 to 14 pounds.

Eye of Round is least tender area of the round. The lean, mild-flavored meat must be tenderized for barbecuing and should be tied with a fat covering. Whole roast weighs 4 to 6 pounds.

ROASTS FROM OTHER MUSCLES

Sirloin Tip

Top Round

Eye of Round

Rolled Rump

Flatiron

Cross Rib

Chuck Fillet

NOT AS TENDER, but still good eating, these boneless roasts are best marinated, barbecued to rare stage, served thinly sliced. Top-row roasts cut from round, rump areas; bottom row shows chuck or shoulder roasts.

Top Round roast is compact enough for rotisserie cooking, however it needs to be tenderized. It has mild flavor, compact meat structure, and the whole roast weighs 16 to 20 pounds.

Rump roast is sold in several shapes: as a flat, boneless triangular piece weighing 4 to 6 pounds; the same piece rolled and tied (shown above); or a rectangular section that's often called a watermelon roast. You'll notice a variation in the grain of the meat as you slice it; the muscle turns a corner, you might say. For barbecuing, rump needs a fat covering.

Flatiron or Triangle roast is one of the most tender muscles in the chuck. Usually cut as part of blade bone chuck roasts, it may be cut separately and sold as a small, flat, boneless piece weighing about 2½ pounds. It has robust beef flavor and is distinguishable by the small piece of gristle running horizontally through the center. Barbecue it quickly on the grill, with fat side on top. Good flavor.

Cross Rib, Shoulder Clod, and English Cut roasts are all made from beef shoulder, cut just over the chuck ribs. While the names differ in various cities, the meat is basically the same. Roasts have good fat marbling; best marinated or tenderized for barbecuing. A whole roast weighs 12 to 16 pounds.

Chuck Fillet or Scotch Tender is a slim, tapering muscle in the chuck that's usually cut as part of a blade bone roast. However, it may be sold as a single muscle weighing 2 to 3 pounds, as two fillets tied together, or one fillet tied with a layer of fat and other muscle. (Its only resemblance to the tenderloin is its shape.) Good flavor, with or without a marinade.

Lamb

Lamb roasts (not illustrated here) will vary in size, shape, and amount of bone and meat—and each may be cut in several different ways. Barbecue relatively flat roasts on a grill; more compact rolled roasts on a rotisserie.

Lamb Shoulder has a large proportion of bone to meat and isn't a good choice for barbecuing as a square-cut, bone-in roast (4 to 6 pounds). However, it may be precut into serving-sized pieces, tied, then barbecued.

LAMB CHOPS *vary widely in size, shape, amount of meat, and amount of bone. Those in top tow and first one in second row are cut from shoulder. Two small chops are from rib area; next is small loin chop.*

Lamb Breast contains rib bones covered with layers of fat and lean. Breast section weighs about 2 pounds and is often barbecued flat and basted with a sauce. For lamb riblets, bones are separated. Sometimes breast is boned, rolled, and tied; or then sliced apart in pinwheels.

Rack of Lamb or Lamb Rib roast has fine texture, delicate flavor. Weighing about 2 pounds, it's just right for two. When the tips of the bones are cleaned of meat and fat and decorated with paper frills, it's called a French rack. For a crown roast, two rib roasts (with backbones removed) are shaped into a crown and sewn with string.

Loin roast contains loin, tenderloin, and flank muscles, along with the backbone. It has fine texture, delicate flavor, and more meat in proportion to bone than does a rib roast. Weighing about 2 pounds, one roast is enough for two persons. Loin may be boned and tied for spit cooking.

Sirloin roast comes from the upper part of the leg. Muscles are continuation of those in loin. Whole roast weighs 1 to 2 pounds and may be cut as part of a full-cut leg of lamb.

Leg of Lamb has large proportion of meat to bone. Most common form is the short-cut leg weighing 5 to 6 pounds. A full-cut leg includes the sirloin and weighs 7 to 8 pounds. Cut in half, it's sold as shank half (lower) and butt or sirloin portion (upper). The leg can be boned and halves laid open butterfly-fashion. If you don't have a covered barbecue or a rotisserie, this is a good way to do leg of lamb directly on the grill. Boned, rolled, and tied, it's best for the rotisserie.

The identifying pictures on this and page 45 show common lamb chops as well as some that are more difficult to find. All are tender enough to barbecue. Choose chops about 1½-inches thick; those with a minimum amount of bone are best.

Round Bone chop is cut from shoulder and has a small bone with a large portion of meat.

Saratoga chop, usually made from shoulder meat, is boned, rolled, and skewered.

Boneless Blade chop is cut twice as thick as regular blade chop; it's sometimes labeled "shish kebab."

Blade Bone chop, cut from shoulder, has more bone than round bone chop.

Shoulder Block is a double-thick blade chop with bone left in. Forward cuts have less bone.

Rib chop is best known of all lamb chops. It has one small eye muscle that is fine textured and very tender.

French Rib chop is the same as the rib described above except a paper frill is put on the cleaned end of the bone after cooking.

Small Loin chop is also finely textured and very tender. It has more meat in proportion to bone than a rib chop.

ENGLISH, SADDLE CHOPS *are variations of small loin chop. Pinbone, hip block are cut from large loin, followed by sirloin and leg chops. Chops from hindquarter are considerably larger than forequarter chops.*

English chop is a small loin chop, boned, with half or slice of lamb kidney skewered in center. Kidney should be thinner than chop for even cooking. Chop can be wrapped in bacon and is sometimes termed a Saratoga chop.

Saddle chop is two small loin chops cut together across the backbone of the carcass to make a large double chop. Sometimes pieces of lamb kidney are inserted as shown.

Pin Bone chop, often labeled a leg chop even though it is cut closer to the large loin, has less of the large round muscle so prominent in the leg chop and more bone than the sirloin chop.

Hip Block is a double-thick pin bone chop.

Sirloin or Large Loin chop is cut between the small loin section and the leg.

Leg chop or steak is the largest chop with a large proportion of meat to bone.

Pork

Today's pork is leaner, meatier, and more tender than before; these qualities make it quite suitable for the barbecue. Though not illustrated, here are some good choices:

Pork Shoulder weighs 4 to 6 pounds. For barbecuing, have it boned and butterflied or spread open; or it can also be boned, rolled, and tied for rotisserie cooking. Use a covered barbecue. This cut can also be cubed for kebabs.

Loin roast has rib bones to provide a natural rack and is excellent barbecued. Whole roast, weighing 12 to 14 pounds, is usually cut into chops plus several roasts. The choice center-cut roast weighs 4 to 5 pounds. Loin is tender, has delicate pork flavor.

Fresh Pork Leg roast, weighing 10 to 12 pounds, can be barbecued whole; or boned, rolled, and tied; or cut in leg chops or steaks. Use a covered barbecue for roasts. There's a large proportion of meat to bone. Smoked, cured legs (hams) may be purchased partially or fully cooked; follow cooking directions on label.

Spareribs are probably the most popular pork cut for barbecuing. Choose either regular cut ribs (rib sections from more tender young hogs weigh 3 pounds or less) or have your meatman cut them in 2-inch lengths for appetizers. Country-style ribs are cut from the shoulder end of the loin and have more meat on the bones than regular spareribs. Spareribs are usually precooked and some of the fat is discarded before they are barbecued.

Pork Steaks and Chops may simply be barbecued until well browned, but still tender and juicy.

Pork Sausages may require precooking before final heating on the barbecue. Other precooked pork cuts such as Canadian bacon, and fully cooked ham, need to be just heated and perhaps basted.

Cooking Underground

PIT 4 by 7 by 3½ feet is lined with brick; oak fire burns for 6 hours.

MEAT ROLL flavored with herbs, salted, is wrapped in foil to cook.

ONTO THE COALS, rolls are wet, covered quickly with sheet iron, earth.

An underground barbecue can be adapted to a whole side of beef or a single pot of beans. In the pictures at left, the pit is large enough for 155 pounds of beef, enough for 250 people, but the same principle is at work in the recipe below for one 20-pound beef roll, or in the recipe for bean hole beans.

Beef For a Crowd

2 or more shoulder clod (cross rib) roasts (about 20 pounds meat)
  Salt
  Garlic salt
3 large onions
2 tablespoons Worcestershire
2 or 3 bay leaves
  Pinch of oregano

To Prepare the Pit

Dig a pit 2 feet wide, 3 feet long, and about 2½ feet deep. Have enough hardwood on hand to fill the pit at least 3 times. Start the fire about 15 hours before serving time. Keep adding wood as it burns until the fire has been burning 3 hours.

Salt the meat generously, then add a few dashes garlic salt. Cut up the onions and scatter them around meat. Dash the meat with Worcestershire and add bay leaves and oregano.

To cook the meat, you need aluminum foil, a 10-foot length of butcher paper, heavy twine, 2 burlap sacks, wire, 1 or more sheets galvanized iron (wide and long enough to cover the pit), and 2 pipes about 3 feet long.

Put the roasts together on a large sheet of foil and wrap them carefully so juices cannot escape. Wrap in 3 or 4 thicknesses of paper and tie with twine. Place the package in one sack, wrap the other sack around, and wire.

When the fire has burned down to a foot of glowing coals, wet the meat package, drop it onto the coals, then quickly lay the pipes across the hole, cover it with galvanized iron, and shovel at least a foot of dirt over the top. Wet the surface lightly. Escaping heat will produce dry spots. Shovel more dirt onto these. The meat will be ready in 10 to 12 hours.

Bean Hole Beans

3 pounds dried beans (any kind you prefer)
  Water
¾ pound bacon or salt pork
½ cup brown sugar
2 cans (8 oz.) tomato sauce
1 tablespoon salt

Dig a hole twice as wide as your kettle and deep enough so the top will be at least 6 inches below the surface. Line the hole all around—bottom and sides—with pieces of rock until you have a rock lining at least 1½ inches thick. Now build a fire in the hole and keep it going for at least 2 hours.

Wash beans, or drain if you have previously soaked them overnight (optional). Add enough water to fill the kettle about ¾ full. Bring to a boil and boil 15 minutes. Now cut up bacon or salt pork, add pieces to the pot, and boil for another 15 minutes. Stir in the brown sugar, tomato sauce, and salt. Mix well.

To Bury Beans

Remove all burning embers from the hole. Put a lid on the bean kettle, wrap it thickly in newspaper, and then wrap the whole package in two thicknesses of wet burlap. Spread the hot coals out in an even bed, then cover with about ½ inch of dirt or sand. Set the wrapped kettle of beans in the hole and cover with dirt or sand until the top is buried at least 6 inches.

Leave the bean pot alone for at least 6 hours. Then dig it out and serve beans with hot, buttered French bread. Serves 12 generously.

If you plan this at home, bury pot in the morning for late supper or late evening buffet. On a camping trip, cover up the pot before the day's activities begin and the beans are done for dinner.

You can use a large Dutch oven, or any other big container that will stand up to heat. If you plan the beans to go with the meat in the recipe above, don't bury them together. Prepare a smaller hole to one side for the beans since they take less cooking time.

KOREAN-STYLE SHORTRIBS *grill to a crusty brown over hibachi coals, making savory picnic finger food. A special way of cutting the ribs distinguishes this robust barbecue (see page 69).*

BARBECUE RECIPES

STEAKS, CHOPS, AND ROASTS

Indoors or outdoors, the tantalizing aroma of barbecuing meats is hard to beat for appetite appeal. Choose thick steaks, chops, or flat roasts for grill cooking; more compact roasts for the rotisserie.

The best way to determine doneness, especially in thick roasts, is to use a reliable meat thermometer. Insert it into the center of the thickest muscle so it doesn't touch bone, fat, or the spit, if used. Roasts are best cooked covered, either in a barbecue with a hood or on a grill with a blanket of heavy foil over the meat. A special grill thermometer registers grill level temperature to help you maintain optimum cooking temperature—usually 250° to 325°.

While some cuts of beef are extremely tender and flavorful, others are best tenderized or marinated for additional flavor. Use your favorite marinade with an acid base (vinegar, wine, citrus juice), use a commercial powdered meat tenderizer, or use a packaged flavored meat marinade and follow the directions on the package.

Beef

There's drama in a steak sizzling over a barbecue fire or a succulent roast turning on a rotisserie. While you don't need to be an expert to barbecue beef, it is important to understand some of the basic facts. (See buying guides on pages 40-43.)

You'll notice that the internal temperatures suggested for beef in this book are lower than those formerly considered standard. This is due to the ever-improving quality of beef in our markets, as well as the increasing popularity of less well done meat. Use a good meat thermometer to test the doneness of a roast or even a thick steak. When properly placed in the center of the thickest muscle, 130° indicates the meat is rare—pink throughout, yet firm; at 140°, the meat is brown part way through, yet pink in the middle and still juicy; by 150°, most roasts will be evenly browned throughout, well done, yet still fairly juicy.

Remove meat from the barbecue when it's several degrees below the temperature you prefer; retained heat will cause the temperature of a large roast to rise.

Tournedos Héloïse

GRILL-COOKED

½ pound small mushrooms, washed
2 tablespoons butter or margarine
 Salt and pepper to taste
1½ tablespoons lemon juice
¼ cup heavy cream
1 teaspoon cornstarch or arrowroot
6 artichoke bottoms, 3 inches in diameter (cooked or canned)
2 cans (4 oz. *each*) pâté de foie, chilled
6 beef tournedos, cut ¾ inch thick
 Truffles or ripe olives for garnish
 Madeira sauce (recipe follows)

This is a prize steak entrée of many Western restaurants and one that benefits from barbecue cooking; the smoky flavor that permeates the meat as it grills over charcoal is excellent with the other choice ingredients.

Ask your meatman for tournedos, the small tenderloin steaks cut from the fillet. Visit a delicatessen or the gourmet section of your food store for the canned artichoke bottoms, pâté, and truffles.

Using a large frying pan, sauté mushrooms in melted butter. Season with salt and pepper to taste and sprinkle with lemon juice. Blend cream with cornstarch, and stir in; stirring constantly, cook until thickened. Set aside.

Heat artichoke bottoms in their own liquid. Open both ends of each can of pâté, and push out ¾ inch and slice; continue to slice the pâté, making 3 rounds from each can. Place pâté on foil, and heat in a 325° oven for 10 minutes.

Meanwhile, barbecue beef over hot coals (allowing about 2 to 3 minutes on a side for rare). Place artichoke bottoms at either end of a platter, top each with a hot tournedo, and arrange a slice of pâté and truffle on top.

Spoon Madeira sauce over (recipe follows), and arrange sautéed mushrooms in center of plate. Makes 6 servings.

Simple Madeira Sauce

Put 1 teaspoon beef extract in a small pan; add ¼ cup Madeira and simmer until slightly reduced. Blend ½ teaspoon cornstarch with 3 tablespoons water and stir in; cook until thickened.

👉 *Porterhouse with Béarnaise*

12 large mushrooms, approximately
    2½ inches in diameter, washed
½ pound small mushrooms, about
    ¾ inch in diameter, washed
3 tablespoons butter or margarine
    Salt and pepper to taste
1½ tablespoons lemon juice
¼ teaspoon crumbled dried tarragon
2 large porterhouse steaks, cut
    1½ inches thick
    Béarnaise sauce (recipe follows)
    Parsley

Here's a steak that's both good and good looking; the meat is topped with sautéed mushrooms, and Béarnaise sauce in mushroom caps is served alongside.

Remove stems from the large mushrooms and slice the stems. Leave small mushrooms whole. Melt the 3 tablespoons butter in a large frying pan and quickly sauté the large whole mushroom caps; season with salt and pepper to taste and remove from pan. Add the small whole mushrooms and the sliced stems to the pan; season with salt and pepper to taste and sprinkle with the lemon juice and crumbled tarragon. Sauté until mushrooms are just tender; set aside.

Grill steak to desired degree of doneness, allowing about 8 minutes to a side for rare, and place on a carving board. Surround with the large mushroom caps and spoon some Béarnaise sauce (recipe follows) into each one; garnish each filled mushroom cap with a parsley sprig. Spoon the sautéed small mushroom caps over grilled meat. Pass remaining sauce to spoon over the meat. Makes 4 to 6 servings.

Béarnaise Sauce

1½ teaspoons crumbled dried tarragon
1½ teaspoons chopped green onions
    or chives
3 tablespoons white wine vinegar
½ cup (1 cube) butter
3 egg yolks

Place tarragon and green onions or chives in a small saucepan. Add vinegar and cook until liquid is reduced by half. Heat butter until bubbly; reserve. Place egg yolks in a blender container (preheated with warm water), add the herb and vinegar mixture, and blend well. With the blender turned on, gradually pour in the melted butter in a steady stream and blend until smooth. Fill mushroom caps; spoon remaining sauce into serving bowl.

👉 *Oyster-Topped Beef Fillet*

A slice of onion, a slice of lemon, and a large smoked oyster top each of these juicy fillets.

Grill 1½-inch-thick beef fillet steaks (1 for each serving) over charcoal fire (allow 5 minutes on each side for rare steaks; sear 1 minute on each side, then cover with a hood or foil to finish smoke-cooking). Place thin crosswise slices of onion, thin crosswise slices of lemon, and drained large oysters (one each per serving) on a sheet of heavy foil. Brush with melted butter. Place on grill to heat and smoke as steaks cook. Stack on each steak an onion slice, a lemon slice, and a smoked oyster; grind black pepper over top.

Whole Fillet with Blue-Cheese Log

For the steak that climaxes all, barbecue a whole fillet. It can be cooked right on the grill or on the spit. You can purchase the whole fillet (about 4 to 6 pounds) or a center cut fillet roast (about 2½ to 3 pounds). For a less expensive fillet barbecue, it is sometimes possible to get two tails of the fillet (the end portion of the tenderloin muscle which tapers toward the rib section) tied together securely, and handle them as a whole fillet. If you plan to do this, place an order at your market ahead of time.

If you prepare the fillet on the grill, turn it quite often, exposing all sides to the heat. It's a lean cut, so brush frequently with a mixture of half melted butter and half oil. Or you may choose to have your meatman lard the fillet, wrapping a layer of fat around the meat so it self-bastes as it grills; this costs more, of course. It will take about 30 minutes to grill a whole fillet if you like it rare. Timing will be about the same when you spit roast.

For the most dramatic serving, place the charcoal-browned whole tenderloin on a handsome platter or board and garnish with the sprigs of watercress and a log of blue-cheese butter (recipe follows). Then carve generous, thick slices and serve as individual steaks. Place a pat of the butter on each serving of steak and let it melt.

To serve this superior meat to a larger number of people, slice thin and offer as sandwiches on crusty buttered hot French bread. For a beautiful serving, cut a long thin loaf of French bread in half lengthwise. Spread cut surfaces generously with plain or seasoned butter. Heat. Arrange thin slices of the savory grilled steak on one half of the bread, thin slices of onions, tomatoes, and radishes or cucumbers on the other. Arrange the bread halves side by side, and cut diagonally across both to make 12 to 15 servings from a whole fillet.

Blue-Cheese Butter Log

1 cup (2 cubes) soft butter
¼ pound blue cheese
1 tablespoon finely chopped green onions, fresh rosemary, or basil
Finely chopped parsley
Watercress

Blend butter and cheese with onions, fresh rosemary, or basil. Place on a sheet of waxed paper, shape into a log, and roll in parsley. Wrap with waxed paper; refrigerate until firm. Serve on watercress.

FOR THE OUTDOORSMAN

There are many barbecue methods and recipes that have originated as on-the-spot inventions, when and where equipment is at a minimum. If you like a meal pioneer-style, try this planked porterhouse, which is cooked on a plank in front of an open fire.

Buy a 2-inch-thick porterhouse steak, and let it stand until it reaches air temperature. Sear one side of the steak to a rich brown (a hinged broiler is helpful). Lace the steak with stainless steel wire (available in sporting goods stores) against a well-oiled hardwood plank (don't use pine or redwood). Prop the plank upright, about 18 inches from a fire, and arrange the fire in a line along the length of the board. Add fuel to maintain a low flame. Cook in a sheltered spot where wind won't be a problem.

Allow about 20 minutes for a rare steak, 25 to 30 minutes for medium, and about 35 to 40 minutes for well done. If the board begins to char, brush it with water. To serve, unlace the steak and carve it on the plank.

As materials, you'll need the hardwood plank, large enough to allow a 3 to 5-inch margin around the meat. Nail an evenly spaced row of upholstery tacks, about 5 in each row, along the wide sides of the board, and about 1 inch in from the edge. Center the steak on the plank; lace it with wire back and forth across tacks.

Filet Mignon Aubergine

GRILL-COOKED

If you like your beef rare, put the eggplant slices on the grill before starting to cook the beef.

For each serving allow a 1-inch-thick steak cut from the small end of a beef fillet, and one crosswise slice of eggplant cut about ¾ inch thick. With olive oil or melted butter, generously brush the cut sides of the eggplant slices and lightly brush the beef fillets; sprinkle with salt.

Prepare this sauce while coals heat: For 4 servings, whip ½ cup heavy cream until stiff and blend in 1 tablespoon prepared Dijon mustard, 3 tablespoons tomato catsup or purée, and salt to taste. Chill until ready to use.

Place eggplant on grill about 5 inches above medium-hot coals. Cook for 10 to 12 minutes, turning occasionally with a spatula and basting with more oil or melted butter. Cook the beef on the same grill, allowing 4 minutes to a side for rare meat, 7 minutes to a side for medium, and 9 or more minutes to a side for well-done.

To serve, place a fillet on a slice of eggplant, top with sauce and a thin slice of tomato. Dust with coarse ground black pepper and serve immediately.

Tenderloin Steak Casanova

The next time you feel like splurging, try this voluptuous dish on your non-dieting friends. Serve the sauced steaks with crusty rolls and a simple salad.

Sprinkle 6 tenderloin steaks (cut 1 inch thick) with salt and pepper; then brush with olive oil. Let stand while you ready a charcoal fire and the sauce. For the sauce, heat 4 ounces pâté de foie gras with ¼ cup cream sherry or Marsala in a large frying pan, stirring until smooth. Grill the steaks to your liking; then put them in the frying pan on top of the sauce. Add ¼ cup warm cognac; then flame. As the burning cognac blends with the sauce, spoon it over the steaks and serve at once. Makes 6 servings.

Rib Eye Steaks with Seasoned Butters

For added flavor, top each tender rib eye steak with a pat of seasoned butter. See page 147 for flavored butters.

Have the rib eye (market) steaks cut about 1 inch thick. Barbecue about 5 inches from the heat for 4 to 6 minutes on each side for rare to medium doneness. Sprinkle with salt and pepper and serve, sizzling hot, topped with a ¼-inch pat of seasoned butter.

BARBECUE BONUS

STEAK ON THE COALS

For dramatic effect and delicious meat, try cooking a steak right on the coals. This method of cooking steak cannot be done altogether satisfactorily by rote. You have to practice it a time or two before you can count on reasonably consistent results. It's so much fun, though, that you'll probably consider it worth the risk.

Build up your fire until you have about 2 to 3 inches of coals. Use a hard charcoal or hardwood that gives off a very fine ash after it burns.

Use any good steak, cut 1 to 1½ inches thick. Have steak at room temperature and throw it directly on the coals. Turn it when the juices show on top and place on an area of coals not previously covered by the steak. Actually the steak doesn't burn; it damps down the fire a bit, unless you get your bed of coals too thick and hot. The cooking process should take about 10 to 15 minutes. It is a good idea to whisk any surplus ash off the top of the coals with a brush or blow it off with a bellows.

👉 *Honolulu Steak*

6 rib eye steaks (also called market
    steaks), about 1 inch thick
1 cup soy sauce
1 clove garlic, crushed
¼ cup salad oil
¼ cup dry red wine
    Dash monosodium glutamate
    Juice from small piece celery
      (about ¼ medium-sized stalk)

This version of teriyaki steak from Honolulu may prove one of the finest flavor combinations you've tasted.

Arrange the steaks in a baking dish or bowl. Combine the soy sauce with the garlic, salad oil, wine, monosodium glutamate, and celery juice. (Cut up the small piece of celery and put through the garlic press to obtain juice—a small but important part of this recipe.) Pour this marinade over the steaks and let stand for 30 minutes only. Remove from marinade, drain, and barbecue to doneness desired. Makes 6 servings.

If you wish to use this same marinade on larger steaks, score the steaks lightly and marinate for 45 minutes to 1 hour, but no longer or the marinade flavors will be overpowering.

👉 *Oyster-Stuffed Market Steaks*

It may be gilding the lily, but for superlative steak, try stuffing market steaks with a luscious oyster and herb-flavored filling before they're grilled.

Have market steaks cut 1 inch thick. Slash horizontal pocket in inner curve of each of these slightly crescent-shaped steaks. Leave enough rim around outer edge of meat so filling won't break through. Lightly fill pocket with oyster stuffing (recipe below). Each steak will take ⅓ to ½ cup stuffing. Skewer edges together with strong toothpicks or little metal skewers. Grill over hot coals (about 5 minutes on each side for rare steak).

Oyster Stuffing

¼ cup finely sliced celery
2 tablespoons chopped onion
¼ cup (½ cube) butter or margarine
    Water, stock, or white wine
1 can (8 oz.) small oysters, drained,
    liquid reserved
½ package (8-oz. size) herb-seasoned
    stuffing mix
    Salt

Sauté sliced celery and chopped onion in butter or margarine until soft. Add water, stock, or white wine to oyster liquid to make ½ cup liquid. Add to sautéed celery and onions along with oysters, stuffing mix, and salt to taste. Mix lightly. Makes stuffing for 4 to 6 steaks.

Steak au Poivre (Pepper Steak)

GRILL-COOKED

2 teaspoons whole black peppers
4 club steaks or small New York
   steaks, cut ¾ inch thick
2 large tomatoes
3 tablespoons butter or margarine
⅛ teaspoon sweet basil
⅛ teaspoon garlic salt
   Salt to taste
4 tablespoons brandy

Hot, herb-scented tomato slices adorn this classic pepper steak. It gains flavor from barbecue smoke; then you flame it. Complete this menu with a Caesar salad, buttered crookneck squash, and a platter of fruit and cheese.

Crush whole black peppers coarsely with a mortar and pestle or rolling pin. Sprinkle both sides of the meat with the crushed peppers. Let meat stand at room temperature for at least 30 minutes to absorb flavor. Barbecue over hot coals (allow about 5 minutes on a side for rare). Transfer to a hot, heatproof serving platter. Slice the tomatoes ⅓ of an inch thick and sauté in melted butter in a frying pan, just until slices are hot through. Season with crumbled basil, garlic salt, and salt to taste. Arrange tomato slices on top of the steak. Warm brandy, ignite, and spoon flaming over the meat. Makes 4 servings.

Ginger Beef Teriyaki

SKEWER-COOKED

2 pounds sirloin steak, sliced ¼ inch
   thick
½ cup soy sauce
1 tablespoon grated fresh ginger or
   1 tablespoon ginger juice
¼ cup sake or sherry
1 clove garlic, puréed
1 teaspoon to 3 tablespoons sugar

Ginger lovers will savor this version of the popular teriyaki treatment for barbecuing steak.

Marinate steak for about 1 hour in a mixture of soy sauce, fresh ginger or ginger juice (available now in some markets), sake or sherry, garlic, and sugar (according to taste). Drain; weave meat on skewers, using one skewer for each strip of meat. Cook quickly, 1 to 2 minutes on each side, over hot coals, basting with the marinade. Do not overcook. Makes about 6 servings.

Pizza-Style Cube Steaks

GRILL-COOKED

Have sirloin tip steaks cut thick enough so that when they're run through the tenderizer to make cube steaks, they'll be a bit less than ½ inch thick. Each steak should weigh not less than 6 ounces; plan on one per person.

Brush steaks with a mixture of half salad oil and half lemon juice. Broil quickly on one side, very close to hot coals. Turn and sprinkle browned side with dill weed, oregano, rosemary, or a favorite herb blend. Top each steak with a thin slice of natural jack cheese and a slice of tomato. When brown on the under side, lift steak to a hot crusty buttered bun or slice of French bread to serve.

👉 Japanese-Style Steak

2 pounds boneless beef steak, not
    more than 1 inch thick
¾ cup olive oil or other salad oil
½ cup wine vinegar
1 large slice raw onion
3 tablespoons soy sauce
2 whole cloves
2 bay leaves
    Juice of ½ medium-sized lemon
¼ teaspoon freshly ground black pepper
3 tablespoons brown sugar

Choose top round, sirloin, or sirloin tip steaks for this mildly flavored variation of the classic teriyaki steak. If your meat is less tender, first tenderize it as directed on the package of meat tenderizer.

Remove the fat from the steaks and cut into serving-sized pieces. Combine the olive oil, wine vinegar, onion, soy sauce, cloves, bay leaves, lemon juice, pepper, and 1 tablespoon of the brown sugar. Pour over the steak and marinate at room temperature for about 1 hour; turn the steaks once. When you are ready to barbecue, remove steaks from the marinade and rub with the remaining 2 tablespoons brown sugar. Broil over charcoal until it is done to your liking. Makes 4 servings.

👉 Sirloin à la Mirabeau

1 sirloin steak, cut 1½ inches thick
    (approximately 2½ lbs.)
1 tablespoon butter
1 teaspoon anchovy paste
    Freshly ground pepper
1 can (2 oz.) anchovy fillets
½ cup stuffed olives

Latticed anchovy fillets and pimiento-stuffed olives make a decorative, flavorful topping for barbecued sirloin.

Barbecue steak over hot coals for about 8 minutes. Turn, and spread the grilled side with butter blended with the anchovy paste. Barbecue the other side about 6 to 8 minutes, or to desired doneness. Remove to a carving board and season with pepper to taste. Arrange anchovy fillets, crisscross fashion, over the top, and fill each square with a sliced stuffed olive. Carve in 1-inch slices to serve. Makes 4 servings.

👉 Rosemary Barbecued Sirloin

2 tablespoons fresh rosemary or
    2 teaspoons dried rosemary
1 boneless top sirloin steak, cut 2 inches
    thick (about 4½ lbs.)
    Salt
    Pepper

This steak is a simple one to serve for a barbecue gathering of several families.

Press rosemary into the meat, coating both sides. Place over medium barbecue coals and cover with barbecue hood (if barbecue doesn't have a hood, make one with heavy aluminum foil as directed on page 33). Barbecue about 15 minutes on each side for rare meat, or until the meat thermometer registers 135° for rare. (You can insert a meat thermometer into meat after barbecuing one side.) Place on a carving board and season with salt and pepper; then slice on the diagonal. Makes 10 to 12 servings.

SKEWERED BEEF-OYSTER APPETIZERS

¼ *cup oyster sauce*
2 *tablespoons salad oil*
2 *tablespoons soy sauce*
1 *clove garlic, mashed*
2 *green onions, chopped*
¼ *teaspoon sugar*
1 *pound beef sirloin, cut into bite-sized strips or cubes*
½ *pound fresh mushrooms, washed and drained*
1 *can (6½ oz.) whole water chestnuts, drained*
3 *green onions, cut into 1-inch pieces*

Oyster sauce (bottled like soy sauce) is a necessary ingredient for this hot appetizer. The sauce may be purchased in most Oriental markets.

Combine the oyster sauce, salad oil, soy sauce, garlic, chopped onion, and sugar in a bowl. Marinate the beef and mushrooms in this mixture for 1 to 2 hours in the refrigerator. Then string meat, mushrooms, water chestnuts, and pieces of green onion on skewers. Barbecue about 5 inches from the heat for 5 minutes, turning once. Serve hot.

Western Barbecue Steak

GRILL-COOKED

1 cup bacon drippings
½ cup finely chopped onions
⅓ cup lemon juice
2 tablespoons catsup
1 tablespoon Worcestershire
1 tablespoon prepared horseradish
1 teaspoon paprika
½ teaspoon salt
⅛ teaspoon pepper
1 large clove garlic, minced or mashed
2 bay leaves
   Steaks at least 1 inch thick for
      broiling (weight should total
      about 4 pounds)

Try this barbecue treatment on costly or economical cuts. Bacon-onion overtones from a marinade-baste penetrate the steak.

Melt bacon drippings in a saucepan. Add chopped onions, lemon juice, catsup, Worcestershire, horseradish, paprika, salt, pepper, garlic, and bay leaves. Stir thoroughly. Place steaks in a single layer in a shallow pan. Pour sauce over meat. Allow to stand 30 minutes at room temperature. Turn steaks once during marinating time to be sure sauce reaches all surfaces of meat. Lightly grease barbecue grill. Drain excess marinade from steaks. Place on grill over hot barbecue coals. Broil on each side to your liking, basting with remaining marinade during grilling. Makes 6 generous servings.

Steak Sandwiches with Mushroom Sauce

1½ pounds top sirloin, cut about ½
   inch thick
   Red wine marinade (recipe follows)
   Salt
¾ pound mushrooms, sliced
3 tablespoons butter or margarine
6 slices light rye bread
   Chopped parsley

Served on rye toast, these small steak sandwiches are covered with a red wine-mushroom sauce.

Cut sirloin into 6 equal-sized servings. Place meat in bowl; cover with red wine marinade (recipe follows). Cover and refrigerate for 1 to 2 hours. Drain meat, reserving marinade. Barbecue quickly to desired doneness; sprinkle lightly with salt. Keep steak warm while preparing sauce.

Sauté mushrooms in butter or margarine. Pour marinade into pan with mushrooms and cook quickly until reduced to sauce consistency. Toast bread. Place meat on toast; spoon sauce and mushrooms over each sandwich. Sprinkle with chopped parsley to garnish. Makes 6 servings.

Red Wine Marinade

½ cup dry red wine
½ medium-sized onion, cut in chunks
2 tablespoons lemon juice
¼ cup olive oil
1 clove garlic, sliced
½ teaspoon salt
   Dash pepper

Place in blender container the red wine, onion, lemon juice, olive oil, garlic, salt, and pepper; whirl until ingredients are well blended.

Smoked Sirloin Tip

3 to 4 pounds sirloin tip, cut in
   1¼-inch-thick slices

Marinade

4 tablespoons salad oil
2 tablespoons paprika
1½ teaspoons salt
¼ teaspoon coarsely ground pepper
¼ teaspoon monosodium glutamate
1½ teaspoons onion salt
¼ teaspoon garlic salt
1 tablespoon soy sauce
½ teaspoon whole oregano, crumbled
½ teaspoon liquid hot-pepper
   seasoning (or less, to taste)
2 tablespoons white port wine
½ teaspoon dry mustard

If you have a Chinese smoke oven, fire it up and try this recipe for smoked sirloin tip.

Combine marinade ingredients and marinate steaks about 2 hours, turning occasionally. Hang from top of smoke oven. Cook about 11 minutes at 450°—or longer as necessary, depending on the efficiency of your oven. Steaks will be a little on the rare side. Makes 6 to 8 servings.

☛ *Giant Beef-Lobster Kebabs*

1½ to 2 pounds top sirloin or top
     round steak, cut in 2-inch cubes
     Unseasoned meat tenderizer
     (optional)
3 frozen lobster tails (about 1½ lbs.),
     split lengthwise and thawed
⅓ cup dry white wine
⅓ cup salad oil
1 tablespoon lemon juice
     Lemon wedges
     Tomato Bearnaise (recipe follows)

Meat for six cooks on two skewers when you use this giant shish kebab combination. If you like, you can also skewer parboiled vegetables and continue cooking them over the hot coals (see page 144). There's also a special Béarnaise sauce.

If you use round steak, you may want to prepare it with instant meat tenderizer, following the directions given on the package. Wrap a lobster tail around a piece of beef and thread the skewer through the thick end of lobster tail, the beef cube, then the end of the lobster tail. You can put three of these combinations onto each of two long skewers. To make the basting sauce, combine the wine, salad oil, and lemon juice. Grill the kebabs over hot coals for 8 to 12 minutes, or until lobster flakes when tested with a fork and beef is done to your liking. Baste while cooking. Serve hot with lemon wedges and Tomato Béarnaise (recipe follows). Makes 6 servings.

Tomato Béarnaise

3 egg yolks
1½ tablespoons tarragon vinegar
¾ cup butter
½ teaspoon salt
½ teaspoon tarragon
3 tablespoons finely chopped parsley
2 tablespoons tomato purée

Combine the egg yolks and tarragon vinegar in an electric blender container. Melt butter; turn blender on high speed and immediately pour in the hot butter in a steady stream. Add salt, tarragon, and finely chopped parsley; whirl until blended, about 30 seconds. Mix in tomato purée. Makes about 2 cups sauce.

☛ *Steak Kebabs*

¾ cup dry red wine
3 tablespoons olive oil
3 tablespoons lemon juice
2 cloves garlic, minced
½ teaspoon salt
¼ teaspoon rosemary
¼ teaspoon thyme
3 pounds top sirloin steak, cut into
     1½-inch cubes

Tender cubes of sirloin steak marinate in a flavorful wine-herb sauce. If you wish, use a plastic container to carry the meat in its marinade to a picnic site, where it can then be skewered for barbecuing.

To make the marinade, mix together the wine, olive oil, lemon juice, garlic, salt, rosemary, and thyme. Let meat marinate in this mixture for several hours or overnight, turning meat occasionally. Skewer the meat and barbecue over moderately hot coals, turning once, for about 8 minutes for rare meat. Makes 8 servings.

MAKING BEEF JERKY ON THE BARBECUE

If family and friends enjoy the chewiness of good beef jerky, you can make it for them right on your barbecue grill. Besides the barbecue, the only things you need are: a piece of light-weight screen to keep flies off the meat, a cover for the grill to keep out moisture at night, 3 or 4 days of warm summer sun, and very lean beef.

Preparing Meat for Jerky. When making a batch of jerky, start with a minimum of 3 to 5 pounds of very lean beef; this will yield less than 1 pound of jerky. Round steak, flank steak, or other very lean beef will make good jerky. Have your meatman cut the beef into steaks about 1½ inches thick. Then trim away all the fat (this is important because the fat can become rancid) and cut the meat into strips ⅛ to ¼-inch wide. Make the strips as long as possible.

The seasoning of beef jerky is entirely a matter of taste. If the meat is to be used on a hiking or camping trip, you'll want to leave it unseasoned or simply sprinkle both sides lightly with salt and pepper. (Eating salty jerky on a hike may make you thirsty.) For appetizers, make the jerky more highly seasoned.

Appetizer Jerky. To make jerky for appetizers or snacks, soak meat in the following marinade:

Combine 1 tablespoon onion powder, 1 tablespoon seasoned salt, 1 teaspoon garlic powder, 1 teaspoon black pepper, ½ cup Worcestershire, and ½ cup soy sauce. Pour this mixture over the strips of meat, mix gently, and let stand in the refrigerator several hours or overnight, stirring occasionally. Then drain the meat and dry as suggested.

Drying the Meat. For drying the meat, your barbecue grill should be as clean as possible. It is a good idea to line the bottom (the charcoal box) with foil, shiny side up, so the bottom is clean in case any meat falls into it. This also increases the reflection from the sun. Place the grill on the barbecue about 2 inches below top. Place the lightly seasoned, unseasoned, or marinated and drained meat across the grids: Do not let the strips overlap or touch each other. Then fasten a canopy of light-weight screen over the barbecue to keep out flies, bugs, and leaves (do not let the canopy touch the meat).

Put the meat out to dry in the morning. When the sun goes down you'll want to cover the barbecue or put it under a shelter to keep the meat from absorbing any moisture from the air. The meat will dry on one side in 1 to 2 days, depending on the heat of the sun and the dryness of the air. Turn the meat and let it dry another 1 to 2 days. When the jerky is dry and ready to eat, it is rather brittle and chewy. You can serve it immediately or store it in a covered container (or wrapped in foil or plastic film) in a dry place.

Beef Skirts-Kebab

SKEWER-COOKED

2 whole skirt steaks
¼ cup salad or olive oil
1 cup dry red wine
1 clove garlic, crushed
1 medium-sized onion, minced
    or grated
½ teaspoon pepper
2 tablespoons soy sauce
2 tablespoons prepared mustard
    Fresh mushroom caps, quartered;
        onions, green peppers, and
        tomatoes as desired

Skirt steaks resemble flank steaks, but are smaller. Two will adequately serve four persons.

Cut each skirt steak in half lengthwise. Combine salad oil, wine, garlic, onion, pepper, soy sauce, and mustard. Marinate the steaks in this mixture for at least 5 hours—the longer the better.

When the charcoal fire is ready, thread the meat on metal skewers in a ribbon style, alternating with mushrooms and other vegetables used.

The fire should be 6 to 8 inches from skewers. Barbecue steaks about 5 minutes on each side. When you serve, give each of your guests a skirt-kebab, sliding it deftly off the skewer. Makes 4 servings.

👉 Skirt Steak with Burgundy Sauce

GRILL-COOKED

6 rolled skirt steaks, secured
    with wooden picks
1 small onion, chopped
¼ pound chicken livers, chopped
1½ cups sliced fresh washed
    mushrooms
¼ cup butter or margarine
½ teaspoon salt
    Dash freshly ground black pepper
⅓ cup Burgundy
    Parsley for garnish

Here is a recipe that calls for grilling rolled skirt steaks, then serving them immediately with a special sauce of chopped chicken livers, mushrooms, onion, and Burgundy.

Grill the steaks 5 to 6 inches from the source of heat for 7 to 9 minutes on each side. While the steaks are grilling, sauté the onion, chicken livers, and mushrooms in the butter until tender. Add the salt, pepper, and wine; boil rapidly for 3 to 4 minutes to reduce the liquid. To serve, arrange the steaks on a warm serving platter; pour the sauce over all and garnish with parsley. Makes 6 servings.

👉 Skirt Steaks Teriyaki

GRILL-COOKED

1 teaspoon unseasoned meat tenderizer
6 to 8 skirt steak pinwheels
¼ cup sherry
¼ cup soy sauce
¼ teaspoon ground ginger
¼ teaspoon garlic powder
    Dash pepper

Many meat markets sell skirt steaks rolled jelly-roll fashion and fastened with wooden skewers. Two of these pinwheels are made from each skirt steak.

Rub tenderizer into both sides of each steak; place in a shallow container that can be tightly covered. Combine sherry, soy sauce, ginger, garlic powder, and pepper; pour over meat. Cover and chill for several hours or overnight; turn once or more, if possible. Barbecue for 6 to 8 minutes on each side, or until steaks are well browned. Makes 6 to 8 servings.

👉 Barbecued Hanging Tenderloin

GRILL-COOKED

1 hanging tenderloin (butcher steak),
    about 2 pounds
¼ cup olive oil
1½ tablespoons wine vinegar
2 cloves garlic, minced or mashed
1 teaspoon rosemary
¼ teaspoon salt
¼ teaspoon pepper

This surprisingly tender piece of meat is similar to flank steak in size and coarseness of grain. It should be barbecued rapidly to your liking (preferably rare), then sliced on the diagonal in thin slices.

Brush hanging tenderloin with a mixture of olive oil, wine vinegar, garlic, rosemary, salt, and pepper. Allow steak to marinate for 1 hour. Basting with remaining marinade, barbecue steak over hot coals to your liking (about 8 minutes on each side for rare). Turn only once. Slice across the grain, on the diagonal from the top to the bottom of the steak. Makes 5 or 6 servings.

☞ Cumin Steak Strips and Cheese

SMOKE-COOKED

1 flank steak (about 1½ lbs.)
  Hot bread slices
½ pound Meunster cheese, sliced thin
  Powdered cumin

Thin slices of smoked flank steak and Meunster cheese are layered on warm bread for hot open sandwiches.

Place flank steak on grill over very hot coals; cover and grill 5 minutes on each side. Place on carving board and slice very thinly, on the diagonal. Arrange hot steak strips on top of hot bread slices as an open sandwich, alternating and overlapping steak with thin slices of Meunster cheese. Sprinkle with powdered cumin. Makes 4 servings.

☞ Tender Teriyaki Steak Strips

GRILL-COOKED

1 whole flank steak (about 1½ lbs.)
1 cup undiluted beef consommé
    (use half dry red or dry white
    wine, if desired)
⅓ cup soy sauce
1½ teaspoons seasoned salt
¼ cup chopped green onions with tops
1 clove garlic, minced or mashed
3 tablespoons lime juice
2 tablespoons brown sugar or honey

These flank steak strips are exceptionally tender when you slice the steak diagonally, marinate it, then barbecue it quickly close to very hot coals just to the rare or medium-rare stage. You can grill the strips in any of three ways: Lay them flat on the grill; string them on skewers; or place them in a hinged wire broiler.

Slice meat into ¼-inch-thick strips, cutting diagonally across the grain. Refrigerate overnight in a marinade made by combining the beef consommé, soy sauce, seasoned salt, green onions, garlic, lime juice, and brown sugar or honey. Drain meat and save marinade. Grill strips quickly over hot coals (about 2 minutes on each side), basting with marinade. Turn only once. Makes 5 or 6 servings.

☞ Steak with Roquefort Butter

GRILL-COOKED

1 flank steak (about 1½ lbs.)
  Well seasoned French dressing
¼ cup (½ cube) butter or margarine
½ cup Roquefort or blue cheese
1 clove garlic, minced
1 tablespoon chopped chives
2 tablespoons brandy

The tangy chive-and-cheese spread melts into this steak and mixes with the meat juices.

Marinate flank steak in your favorite well seasoned French dressing for several hours. For Roquefort butter, cream butter and cheese until blended; mix in garlic, chives, and brandy; turn into a bowl. (You may prepare this ahead and refrigerate; warm to room temperature before using.)

Remove flank steak from marinade and barbecue over hot coals, allowing five minutes on each side for rare. Transfer to a hot platter and slice on the diagonal into ⅛-inch-thick slices. Spoon Roquefort butter over meat. Makes 4 servings.

THREE SNACKS OVER THE COALS

Toasting a snack over the fireplace flames or campfire is always fun, especially for children. Here are three ideas to add variety to fireside refreshments.

Ham-Broiled Holiday Cherries. Cut boiled ham into strips about ½ inch wide. Wrap around red or green glacéed cherries; spear onto long skewers and broil over flame until ham is crisply browned.

Frank and Cheese Roll-Ups. Trim crusts from an unsliced sandwich loaf of bread; cut into thin slices, lengthwise. Spread with a creamy cheese spread made as follows: Combine 1 small package (3 oz.) cream cheese with 1 teaspoon chicken stock base (or 1 bouillon cube)

dissolved in 2 teaspoons warm water, and 1 tablespoon pickle relish.

Plump up cocktail frankfurters by letting them stand in hot water for 5 minutes; then dry (or use canned cocktail frankfurters, thoroughly drained). Arrange, lengthwise, at edge of bread slice. Roll up and wrap in waxed paper or foil; refrigerate for several hours. Slice between frankfurters; spear with skewers and toast.

Toasted Bacon and Bread Poles. Cut unsliced, ready-to-bake French bread into poles about 1 inch across and 4 or 5 inches long. Spiral strips of bacon around each pole, securing the ends with toothpicks. Cook on grill over hot coals.

 # *Beefsteak Jalisco*

GRILL-COOKED

You squeeze the juice of a fresh orange over this thick-cut barbecued top round steak. Since this recipe is Mexican in origin, you might serve it with your favorite cheese or sour cream enchiladas, a green salad with sliced onions, oranges, and cucumbers, and fresh fruit for dessert.

Have your meatman make the first cut of beef top round about 2 inches thick (this is the part next to the sirloin); you should have about 3 pounds or more.

Trim off all fat and gash the surface of the steak in a diagonal pattern, making ⅜-inch-deep cuts about 1 inch apart. Rub the meat lightly with salt. Grill about 5 to 6 inches over medium-hot coals for about 10 minutes on a side for rare meat; or cook to degree of doneness you prefer. Transfer meat to carving board and squeeze the juice of 1 cut orange over the meat. Slice meat vertically and make sure some of the accumulating juices moisten each piece. Makes 8 to 10 servings.

Barbecued Beef Stroganoff

2 medium-sized onions, sliced,
    each slice cut in half
3 tablespoons butter
2 pounds barbecued round steak, cut
    into slices about 3 inches long,
    ½ inch wide
½ pound fresh mushrooms, sliced
½ cup regular strength beef broth
    (may be half dry wine)
2 cups commercial sour cream
  Salt
  Pepper
  Prepared mustard
  Hot steamed rice

When midsummer barbecuing becomes a frequent family routine, it's sometimes a good idea to barbecue an extra quantity for the next day. On an evening when you're having steaks, broil an extra piece of round steak so that you'll have smoke-flavored meat to make into Beef Stroganoff.

Sauté onion slices in butter until wilted. Add the meat and mushrooms. Pour in beef broth and cover. Simmer until meat is tender and liquid has almost evaporated, about 40 minutes. Remove from heat and stir in sour cream. Season to taste with salt, pepper, and prepared mustard. Serve with hot steamed rice. Makes 6 servings.

Grilled Eye of Round Steaks

Instant meat marinade or teriyaki
    marinade (recipe follows) plus
    unseasoned meat tenderizer
6 eye of round steaks, cut ½ inch thick
  Marinated or freshly cooked artichoke
    hearts for garnish

These lean, firm-textured steaks require tenderizing before you barbecue them. Use an instant meat marinade (available in market meat departments) or your favorite meat marinade plus an unseasoned commercial meat tenderizer.

When using the instant meat marinade, follow package directions exactly. If you use another marinade, allow the meat to marinate for 1 to 2 hours; then use an unseasoned meat tenderizer as directed on the package.

Grill steaks 5 to 6 inches from heat for 3 to 4 minutes per side for medium doneness. Serve on a heated platter, garnished with marinated artichoke hearts and barbecued fruit or vegetables, if you wish. Makes 4 servings.

Teriyaki Marinade

1 cup beef broth
⅓ cup soy sauce
2 tablespoons lime juice
1 clove garlic, mashed
1 green onion with top, chopped
1 tablespoon firmly packed brown
    sugar

Combine the beef broth, soy sauce, lime juice, garlic, green onion, and brown sugar.

Family Round Steak Barbecue

GRILL-COOKED

First cut of top round (3 to 4
    lbs.), cut 2 inches thick
⅓ cup wine vinegar
3 tablespoons salad oil
2 tablespoons honey (or use syrup
    from sweet pickles)
2 tablespoons chopped green onions
    with tops
1 clove garlic, minced or mashed
¼ teaspoon dried oregano or
    1 teaspoon fresh oregano
¼ teaspoon dried rosemary or basil
    (or 1 teaspoon of fresh rosemary
    or basil)
¾ teaspoon salt
¼ teaspoon paprika
    Butter
    Finely chopped parsley or
      watercress
    Avocado slices
    Lemon juice

Ask your meatman to slice the first cut of the top round for this recipe; this is the tenderest portion of the round section, the part closest to the sirloin section.

If you buy high quality aged meat (such as U.S.D.A. graded choice beef), you won't need to tenderize this cut for the barbecue. If you're not sure of the meat's tenderness, however, it is a good idea to treat top round with meat tenderizer. The marinade also helps tenderize the steak.

Score both sides of top round on the diagonal, about ¼ inch deep. Marinate 4 to 5 hours or overnight in a mixture of the wine vinegar, salad oil, honey or syrup from sweet pickles, chopped green onions, garlic, oregano, rosemary or basil, salt, and paprika. Drain and save marinade. Grill over hot coals (about 10 to 12 minutes on each side for rare meat), basting with remaining marinade. As meat comes from the grill, place on slicing board, spread lightly with butter, and sprinkle with chopped parsley or watercress. Arrange avocado slices, dipped in lemon juice, down center of steak. Slice across the grain. Makes 6 to 8 servings.

Top Round Steak with Artichoke Hearts

SMOKE-COOKED

Marinated artichoke hearts season and garnish this thick-cut top round steak. To prepare it, ask your meatman to cut a 2-inch-thick steak off the top of the round. Depending on the size of the animal, you will have 3 to 5 or more pounds of solid lean meat. Best results can be obtained on a covered barbecue. You can use a meat thermometer to ensure having it done just the way you like it.

If you wish, use unseasoned meat tenderizer (follow package directions). Drain the marinade from 1 jar (6 oz.) marinated artichoke hearts into a measuring cup; add salad oil if needed to make ¼ cup (reserve artichokes). Add ½ cup dry red wine. Trim fat from steak and put meat in a baking dish; pour over the marinade; let stand about 1 hour.

Lift out the meat (reserving the marinade), and place on the grill over low bed of coals. Cover the barbecue with a hood and cook slowly. When well browned on one side, about 25 to 30 minutes, turn steak over and baste with reserved marinade. Insert a meat thermometer, if you have one, into the center of the meat. Also arrange the reserved artichoke hearts on top. Cover the barbecue again and continue cooking until done. (If you like meat quite rare, remove this cut from grill at 135°.) The total time required to cook a 4-pound steak rare is about 35 minutes. Slice diagonally across the grain to serve. A 4-pound steak makes about 8 servings.

Chuck Steak with Anchovy Butter

1 chuck steak, cut 1 inch thick
Unseasoned meat tenderizer
Lemon-anchovy butter (recipe follows)

At serving time, each guest tops his serving of this grilled steak with a slice of lemon-anchovy butter cut from a butter ring garnish.

Prepare chuck steak with unseasoned meat tenderizer according to package instructions. Grill over hot coals until done to the stage you prefer (about 5 minutes on each side for rare). Cut into serving portions and serve immediately, topped with lemon-anchovy butter.

Lemon-Anchovy Butter Ring

Combine ½ cup (1 cube) soft butter, 1 teaspoon lemon juice, and 1 can (2 oz.) anchovy fillets. Press into small ring mold (about 3 inches across), oiled and sprinkled with finely chopped parsley. Chill until firm. At serving time, dip into warm water and unmold on a bed of parsley. Makes enough butter to top 6 to 8 steak servings.

Garlic Steak in a Crust

Unseasoned meat tenderizer
Boneless chuck steak, 1 inch thick,
    cut into 6 pieces each about
    3 by 4 inches
Salad oil
Garlic salt
4 cups all-purpose flour
2 teaspoons salt
1 cup shortening
    About ¾ cup cold water

Barbecue a steak inside a pastry crust and you get a tender, well-browned, extra-juicy steak. It's worth using the pastry wrap just to get such a good steak, but your eating audience will probably eat the crispy, near-charred pieces of the crust right along with the steak, as a steak turnover.

Follow directions with unseasoned meat tenderizer to prepare steaks for cooking. Rub all sides of meat with salad oil; sprinkle generously with garlic salt.

To make pastry, sift flour and measure; add salt. Cut in shortening and stir in cold water to make a soft dough. On lightly floured board, roll out dough about ⅛ inch thick. Cut into six ovals, each about 6 inches wide, 8 inches long. Place a piece of steak on one half of a pastry oval; fold over pastry, moisten and seal edges together. Prick crust several times with a fork. Place steak turnovers on grill above low coals. Cook about 45 minutes, turning to brown crust on all sides. Makes 6 servings.

👉 *Lazy Holiday Roast*

SPIT-ROASTED

1 boneless beef cross-rib roast (4 to
    5 lbs.), rolled and tied
⅓ cup catsup
¾ cup dry red wine (or ½ cup water
    and ¼ cup red wine vinegar)
½ cup salad oil
1 tablespoon instant minced onion
1 tablespoon Worcestershire
1 teaspoon crumbled rosemary
1½ teaspoons salt
¼ teaspoon monosodium glutamate
¼ teaspoon pepper
5 drops liquid smoke seasoning
    (optional)

Once the marinade for this cross-rib roast is assembled, you're ready to enjoy a leisurely holiday. Marinate the meat overnight and, when the day of celebration dawns, just put the roast over the fire and sit back until time to carve.

Set roast in a deep, close fitting bowl. Blend together catsup, wine (or water and red wine vinegar), salad oil, instant minced onion, Worcestershire, crumbled rosemary, salt, monosodium glutamate, pepper, and liquid smoke seasoning. Pour this mixture over the roast; if it does not cover meat, turn roast over several times while marinating. Cover and refrigerate 12 to 24 hours. Lift meat from marinade and insert a meat thermometer into the center.

Cook roast on a rotisserie or in a covered barbecue, basting frequently with marinade. On a rotisserie, place meat 6 inches above medium-hot coals; in covered barbecue have medium coals. Both methods of cooking require about 1½ hours for rare to medium-rare meat. The meat thermometer should register 130° for rare or 140° for medium-rare to medium. (This is lower than most recommendations for beef, but because the cross-rib is so lean, the lower temperature is better.) Let roast stand about 20 minutes, then slice thinly and serve with meat juices. Makes 8 to 10 generous servings.

👉 *Chef's Chuck Roast*

GRILL-COOKED

2 cloves garlic, finely minced
2 tablespoons olive oil
¼ teaspoon dry mustard
1 teaspoon soy sauce
½ teaspoon rosemary, crushed, or
    1 sprig of the fresh herb
2 tablespoons wine vinegar
¼ cup sauterne
    Chuck roast, 2½ to 3 inches thick
2 tablespoons catsup
½ teaspoon Worcestershire
1½ teaspoons meat seasoning sauce

When served, the chef's chuck roast will be charred outside, rare in the middle.

Sauté garlic gently in olive oil, add mustard, soy, and rosemary. Remove from fire and stir in vinegar and wine. Place roast in a bowl and pour sauce over it. During the next 24 hours, turn the meat frequently in the sauce.

Prior to barbecuing, remove the meat and to the remaining sauce add the catsup, Worcestershire, and meat seasoning sauce. Stir well and apply some of the mixture to meat before barbecuing; continue using as a basting sauce during cooking. If the sauce appears too thick, add more olive oil.

The meat should be turned frequently and basted often. A piece of meat 2½ inches thick should be cooked over hot coals for 40 minutes to be charred outside and rare in the center. Makes 4 to 6 servings.

☛ *Savory Chuck Roast*

5-pound chuck roast, cut about 2 inches
  thick
Unseasoned meat tenderizer

Sauce

1 onion
4 tablespoons olive oil
1 clove garlic, chopped
½ cup finely sliced celery
¾ cup chile sauce
¾ cup catsup
½ cup water
2 tablespoons Worcestershire
2 tablespoons wine vinegar
1 teaspoon horseradish
1 teaspoon prepared mustard
2 tablespoons lemon juice
2 teaspoons hickory smoked salt
  Liquid hot-pepper seasoning to taste
½ teaspoon freshly ground black pepper
3 tablespoons brown sugar, firmly
  packed
½ cup sherry, or white or dry red wine

The sauce for this chuck roast may be used either hot or cold. It keeps well in the refrigerator and may also be frozen for use later.

Treat meat with tenderizer according to package directions. Slice onion finely and break into rings. Put olive oil in skillet; add chopped garlic and the onion; sauté until onion is golden brown. Blend in celery, chile sauce, catsup, water, Worcestershire, vinegar, horseradish, mustard, lemon juice, smoked salt, liquid hot pepper, black pepper, and sugar. Bring to a boil and continue simmering slowly for 20 minutes. Add wine, increasing amount if necessary, so the mixture will have a moderately thick consistency and will be just right for applying with a brush. Simmer for an additional 10 minutes.

With the sauce, thoroughly baste the tenderized chuck roast. Place roast on grill close to a hot barbecue fire and brown on both sides. Then raise the grill so the roast will get only moderate heat; cover and cook until done (1 to 2 hours, depending on heat of fire and degree of rareness you wish), turning once. Baste very frequently. Cut in thin slices across the grain. Makes 4 to 6 servings.

☛ *Herbed Beef Shanks with Summer Squash*

4 slices meaty beef shank, each cut
    1 inch thick
2 cups water
½ medium-sized onion, sliced
1 carrot, sliced
1 bay leaf
8 whole black peppers
1 teaspoon salt
6 tablespoons butter or margarine
½ teaspoon basil
2 teaspoons prepared mustard
½ teaspoon prepared horseradish
½ to ¾ cup fine dry bread crumbs
4 medium-sized crookneck or zucchini
    squash, cut in half lengthwise
  Salt
  Prepared mustard

As a slight departure from usual barbecuing, you might like to grill precooked beef shanks, coated lightly with seasoned crumbs, along with colorful sections of summer squash.

First cook the beef shanks: Place them in a wide shallow pan. Add water, onion, carrot, bay leaf, whole black peppers, and salt. Bring to a boil, cover, and simmer very slowly for about 1½ hours or until tender. Let cool slightly in stock, then gently remove shanks (save stock for soup) and cut away the bone.

Melt butter or margarine; blend in basil, mustard, and horseradish. Dip meat in butter, then coat with fine dry bread crumbs. Dip squash in the butter mixture. Sprinkle with salt.

Place vegetables, cut side down, and beef on a grill about 5 to 6 inches above medium-hot coals. Cook about 10 minutes, turning as needed, or until meat is brown and squash is tender and brown. Brush squash with the butter; it may take a little longer (up to 15 minutes) to cook. Pour remaining butter over meat and vegetables before serving. Pass additional mustard to eat with the hot beef. Makes 4 servings.

👉 Barbecued Rib Bones

GRILL-COOKED

Purchase about 6 pounds meaty rib bones (about 16 ribs) and let stand several hours or overnight in your favorite barbecue sauce or oil-vinegar marinade, turning occasionally to coat the bones and meat evenly.

To barbecue the bones, drain and place over medium-hot coals (about 5 inches from heat), bone side up. Turn ribs to brown on all sides, basting with the sauce or marinade. Cook a total of approximately 20 minutes. Makes about 6 servings.

👉 Marinated Beef Shortribs

GRILL-COOKED

6 pounds beef shortribs, cut about
    3 inches long
2½ cups tomato juice
1 tablespoon sugar
1 teaspoon Worcestershire
¼ teaspoon ginger
¼ teaspoon allspice
1 teaspoon celery salt
½ cup vinegar
1 onion, finely chopped
1 clove garlic, cut
    Basting sauce (recipe follows)
    Serving sauce (recipe follows)

After these shortribs have been marinated, the marinade is used to make two sauces, one for basting the meat, and another to serve with the meat.

Marinate the meat for 48 hours in a mixture of the tomato juice, sugar, Worcestershire, ginger, allspice, celery salt, and vinegar. Place in the refrigerator and turn the meat frequently. For the last 4 hours, remove from the refrigerator and add the chopped onion and garlic.

Remove the meat from the marinade and put in a Dutch oven with a little water. Cover and cook over low heat. When almost tender, take out and complete cooking on the barbecue grill. Baste with basting sauce (recipe follows) until brown and slightly crisp. Serve with serving sauce (recipe follows). Makes 8 servings.

Basting Sauce

While meat is cooking, strain marinade; discard onion and garlic. Mix ½ cup of marinade with ¼ cup of olive oil or drippings. Baste the meat with this mixture while barbecuing.

Serving Sauce

Use the rest of the marinade to make the following sauce to serve with the meat. Sauté a finely chopped onion until brown; add the marinade, 1 teaspoon powdered oregano and 1 teaspoon cumin. (If these are not available, substitute 2 teaspoons chile powder.) Boil the sauce down until it is about half the original volume.

👉 HAWAIIAN BAMBOO-BEEF APPETIZERS 👈

2-inch piece fresh, peeled ginger, sliced
2 cloves garlic, mashed
2 small onions, chopped
1 cup soy sauce
4 tablespoons sugar
8 small dried, hot chile peppers
2 tablespoons red wine vinegar
4 teaspoons cornstarch
½ cup water
2 pounds beef sirloin, cut into bite-sized pieces

These Hawaiian beef cubes are simple to make and can be cooked over a tiny hibachi.

In small pan, combine ginger, garlic, onions, soy sauce, sugar, chile peppers, and wine vinegar. Cook over medium heat until slightly thick, about 20 minutes. Blend cornstarch and water. Gradually stir into sauce and cook, stirring until clear and thickened. Pour mixture through a wire strainer, pressing out all the juices, and discard the pulp; cool. Add beef pieces to marinade and allow to stand, covered, for 2 hours. Thread 2 or 3 pieces of meat on each skewer; barbecue over hot coals. Makes about 4 dozen appetizers.

👉 *Korean Shortrib Barbecue*

GRILL-COOKED

4 pounds well trimmed beef shortribs, sawed through bone at 2½-inch intervals
½ cup soy sauce
½ cup water
¼ cup sliced green onions with tops
2 tablespoons sesame seed
2 tablespoons sugar
2 cloves garlic, minced or mashed
½ teaspoon pepper
¼ teaspoon monosodium glutamate

Barbecued shortribs, Korean style, make good eating for a picnic outing. You charcoal-grill these meaty pieces of beef to a crusty brown and eat them with your fingers like chicken.

A special way of cutting shortribs and a savory marinade distinguish the Korean barbecue. When you buy the shortribs, ask your meatman to saw through the bone at 2½-inch intervals so you can dice-cut the meat chunks as directed below.

With bone side down, dice-cut the 2½-inch shortrib cubes as follows: Cut meat halfway to bone every ½ inch in one direction; at right angles, cut every ½ inch, but go only ½ inch deep. To make marinade, combine the soy sauce, water, onions, sesame seed, sugar, garlic, pepper and monosodium glutamate. Put scored pieces of meat into marinade and chill, covered, in refrigerator for 4 to 5 hours.

Place meat, bone side down, on barbecue grill over high heat. When brown, turn and cook on meat side. Lift and turn meat throughout cooking time (about 15 minutes) to expose all surfaces to heat. Cook until crisply browned and done to your preference. Have plenty of napkins on hand and eat while hot. Makes 4 servings.

☛ *Skewered Veal Barbecue*

⅓ cup soy sauce
1 large onion, chopped
2 tablespoons salad or olive oil
1 tablespoon dried oregano
2 or 3 veal steaks, ½ to ¾ inch thick
  Dry red wine
1 can (1 lb., 13 oz.) sliced pineapple

When making these kebabs, if you have any pineapple left over drain it well; then sauté the pieces in a small amount of butter until lightly browned and serve as an accompaniment.

Mix together the soy, onion, oil, and oregano. Cut the veal steaks into 1 to 1½-inch squares, depending on the thickness of your skewers. Put the veal squares in a bowl, pour in the marinade, then add enough wine to cover the meat. Let the meat marinate all day and turn it in the marinade from time to time. Cut the pineapple slices into quarters.

About 2 hours before time to barbecue, string the meat on the skewers with a piece of pineapple between every two pieces of meat. You'll have to work carefully as the pineapple might split if skewers are too large. Arrange the skewers on a shallow pan, pour over the sauce and marinate, turning occasionally, until time to barbecue over coals. Barbecuing takes about 20 minutes in all, turning 4 times. Baste with the marinade when you turn skewers. This fills 6 good-sized skewers.

☛ *Chef's Ground Beef*

1½ pounds ground lean beef
1 teaspoon salt
¼ teaspoon pepper
½ teaspoon monosodium glutamate
2 tablespoons butter or margarine

Sauce

1 tablespoon butter or margarine
1 tablespoon chopped parsley
1 tablespoon lemon juice
⅛ teaspoon salt
  Pepper
  Paprika

For unqualified success, make certain that those on the receiving end of this loaf like rare meat, and that the sauce is ready before the meat is put on the flames.

Blend the ground beef, salt, pepper, and monosodium glutamate and form into a loaf about 3 inches wide and 1½ inches thick. Spread the butter over the loaf.

For the sauce, melt butter, and add parsley, lemon juice, salt, and a sprinkling of paprika and pepper. Set aside.

Broil meat over coals, lowering grill so that the meat is close to the coals. (Extinguish serious conflagrations immediately.) Count on 5 or 6 minutes for each side, carefully turning the meat only once with a broad spatula. The result should be a loaf crusty brown on the outside, deliciously rare inside.

Place the loaf on a sizzling hot platter the instant it comes from the fire, and pour over it the lemon-butter sauce. Slice into individual servings and serve on warm plates without further delay. Makes 3 or 4 servings.

Hamburger Steak in the Round

1 round loaf French bread, cut in
    half horizontally
½ cup (1 cube) soft butter
½ teaspoon prepared mustard
½ teaspoon chile powder
3 pounds ground beef chuck
2 teaspoons seasoned salt
½ cup finely chopped green onions
    with tops
2 tablespoons chile sauce
1 tablespoon soy sauce or
    Worcestershire
    Thin cucumber half-slices
    Small tomato half-slices

Rich meat juices mingle with a mustard and chile-seasoned butter, then sink into the French bread as you grill these giant hamburgers over hot coals.

Spread cut surfaces of French bread with seasoned barbecue butter made by blending the soft butter, mustard, and chile powder.

Combine ground chuck with seasoned salt, chopped green onions, chile sauce, and soy sauce or Worcestershire. Shape into 2 round patties each a little larger than the bread (the meat shrinks slightly when cooked). Place bread, crust side down, at back of grill (away from hottest coals) to heat slowly. Barbecue meat patties on one side until browned and partially done. Turn patties, and place bread, buttered side down, on top of them. Continue grilling patties until undersides are browned and meat is cooked to degree desired.

To serve, turn meat and bread onto serving platter with bread on bottom, meat on top. Garnish with alternating cucumber and tomato half-slices on top of meat patties, marking individual portions. Cut each round into wedges to make 10 to 12 servings.

Stretched Hamburger

1 pound ground beef
2 carrots, grated
2 stalks celery, finely chopped
1 sprig parsley, finely chopped
1 green pepper, finely chopped
1 onion, finely chopped
1 clove garlic, finely chopped
1 tablespoon steak sauce
1 egg
    Dash salt and pepper
2 tablespoons cooking oil or shortening
8 hamburger buns
½ cup (1 cube) melted butter or
    margarine
8 large tomato slices
    Sliced unpeeled cucumber

One pound of ground beef will make eight hamburgers when prepared according to this recipe.

Mix together the ground beef, carrots, celery, parsley, green pepper, onion, garlic, steak sauce, egg, salt, pepper, and oil. Roll into patties the size of the hamburger buns and grill. Split hamburger buns into halves and toast cut sides; then brush with melted butter. Cover each hamburger with one slice of tomato and several slices of fresh, crisp, unpeeled cucumber. A little prepared mustard may be added, if desired. Makes 8 servings.

☞ *Soy-Dipped Hamburgers*

GRILL-COOKED

½ cup soy sauce
½ cup water
1 clove garlic, crushed
2 teaspoons grated fresh ginger
2 tablespoons Worcestershire
6 tablespoons brown sugar
3 pounds lean ground beef
8 sourdough French rolls
  Thinly sliced tomatoes
  Sliced green pepper

You can shape these hamburgers and place them in their marinade (with a tight cover) just before leaving home for a family picnic. Take along a small hibachi, or use a deep cakepan and cake rack for grilling the hamburgers. You might complete a picnic menu with a marinated bean salad, fresh fruit, and beverages.

Combine soy, water, garlic, ginger, Worcestershire and brown sugar. Shape ground beef into 8 log-shaped meat patties (to fit the long French bread rolls). Pour marinade over the meat, cover, and marinate for 1 to 1½ hours. Cook meat over hot coals until done to your liking. Split and toast rolls on the grill and fill with the meat patties, thinly sliced tomatoes and sliced green pepper. Makes 8 servings.

☞ *Mushroom-Filled Hamburger Cups*

GRILL-COOKED

1½ pounds ground chuck
  1 egg
  3 tablespoons fine dry bread crumbs
  ½ teaspoon salt
  ¼ teaspoon pepper
    Sautéed mushrooms (recipe follows)
    About ½ cup shredded Cheddar
      cheese

You can make these individual hamburger cups by molding ground beef over the bottoms of foil muffin cups. Then barbecue them over hot coals and fill with mushrooms and cheese. Serve with corn on the cob, green salad, and sourdough French bread.

To shape the cups, buy foil muffin pans. Use kitchen shears to cut the muffin cups apart; trim the edges of each cup to make it round.

Mix together ground chuck, egg, bread crumbs, salt, and pepper. Divide meat mixture into 6 equal portions, forming each portion into a patty about ½ inch thick and 4 inches in diameter. Mold each patty evenly over the bottom of a foil muffin cup. Place on grill, with the inside of the muffin cup facing down.

Cook until bottom edges are browned and the top part of the mound is still slightly pink. (Meat next to cup should be cooked enough that it will hold its cup shape when turned.) Turn; remove foil cups carefully. Fill meat cups with sautéed mushrooms (recipe follows); top each with about 1 tablespoon cheese. Return to barbecue and cook only until cheese melts. Makes 6 servings.

Sautéed Mushrooms

2 tablespoons butter or margarine
1 tablespoon chopped green onion
1 tablespoon chopped parsley
½ pound mushrooms, quartered
¼ teaspoon salt
⅛ teaspoon pepper

In a small pan, melt butter or margarine, add green onion, parsley, mushrooms, salt, and pepper. Cook slowly until mushrooms are tender, stirring occasionally.

☛ Cheeseburgers with Guacamole

GRILL-COOKED

Broiled cheeseburgers appear in a new guise topped with guacamole. You might serve these with a mixed green salad, green beans, toasted French rolls, fresh apples, and brownies for an easy family supper.

Mix together 1½ pounds lean ground chuck, ½ teaspoon salt, ½ teaspoon garlic salt, ½ teaspoon onion salt, and 1 teaspoon Worcestershire. Mix in 1½ cups shredded sharp Cheddar cheese. Shape into 4 patties, 1 inch thick. Grill over hot coals 3 to 4 minutes on a side for rare meat. Top with guacamole sauce, made by blending 1 can (7¾ oz.) thawed frozen avocado dip (guacamole) with 1 tablespoon lemon juice and 3 drops liquid hot-pepper seasoning. (Or substitute 1 fresh avocado, peeled and mashed, for the frozen dip.) Makes 4 servings.

☛ Crunchy Onion-Beef Burgers

GRILL-COOKED

1½ pounds lean ground beef or
    ground chuck
1½ teaspoons salt
⅛ teaspoon pepper
1 tablespoon catsup
1 can (3½ oz.) French-fried onions
6 hamburger buns or English
    muffins, split
    Butter

Canned fried onions contribute crunchy texture as well as robust onion flavor to the grilled meat.

In a bowl combine meat, salt, pepper, and catsup; mix until well blended. Add half of the can of French-fried onions to the meat mixture; use a fork to gently mix the onions with the meat. Shape the meat into 6 patties, about ½ inch thick. Barbecue the patties as rare or as well done as you prefer. Sprinkle remaining French-fried onions over tops of the meat patties after they are cooked. Or pass a bowl of the remaining onions along with relishes at the table. Serve inside the hamburger buns or English muffins, which have been lightly toasted and buttered. Makes 6 sandwiches.

☛ Beef and Cheese Stacks

GRILL-COOKED

2 pounds lean ground beef
2 tablespoons minced dried onions
2 teaspoons Worcestershire
2 teaspoons prepared mustard
1 teaspoon salt
½ teaspoon pepper
1½ cups shredded sharp Cheddar cheese
    Melted butter

Fit these ground beef and cheese stacks between split toasted buns for a husky sandwich or serve the stacks without buns, if you wish.

Thoroughly mix together the ground beef, onions, Worcestershire, mustard, salt, and pepper. Divide into 12 portions, and form each into a thin patty. Put ¼ cup cheese in a mound on top of each of 6 of the patties; top each with another meat patty and press edges together to seal. Grill over hot coals to your liking (about 5 minutes on each side for medium). Baste with melted butter; turn only once. Makes 6 servings.

👉 *Individual Meat and Spinach Loaves*

GRILL-COOKED

Ground pork, beef, and chopped spinach are the principle ingredients in these small meat loaves.

Crumble ½ pound ground lean pork into a frying pan; add ½ medium-sized onion, finely chopped, and sauté until pork loses its pink color and onion is soft. Crush 15 round butter crackers to make ½ cup fine crumbs. Beat 1 egg slightly; blend in cracker crumbs. Add pork mixture, 1 pound ground beef chuck, 1 cup chopped fresh spinach (or ½ cup well drained, thawed, frozen spinach), ¼ cup dry red wine (optional), and a dash pepper. Mix gently to blend, using your hands if you wish. Shape mixture into 6 oval loaves about 2 inches thick.

Place on grill over slowly burning coals and barbecue about 45 minutes, turning carefully several times and brushing frequently with tomato-soy sauce (recipe below), until loaves are well browned. Makes 6 servings.

Tomato-Soy Sauce

Blend ½ cup canned tomato sauce, ¼ cup dry red wine, 2 tablespoons soy sauce, 1 tablespoon salad oil, and 1 bay leaf in small pan. Warm at edge of grill while loaves cook.

👉 *Pizza-Flavored Meat Loaf*

SMOKE-COOKED

- 2 medium-sized onions, finely chopped
- 3 tablespoons olive oil or salad oil
- 1 large can (6 or 8 oz.) sliced mushrooms, drained
- 2 eggs
- 1½ cups soft bread crumbs
- 1 can (10½ oz.) pizza sauce
- ½ cup chopped parsley
- 1 teaspoon dried whole basil
- ¾ teaspoon salt
- ⅛ teaspoon pepper
- 2 pounds ground beef chuck
- 2 slices jack cheese, cut in strips

Cheese strips melt on top of this meat loaf that's cooked in a 9-inch foil pan on the grill of a covered barbecue.

Sauté onions in oil until soft and lightly browned; add mushrooms and cook for about 3 minutes longer. Beat eggs slightly; blend in bread crumbs. Measure ¼ cup of the pizza sauce; reserve it for basting. Add remaining pizza sauce, parsley, basil, salt, pepper, onion mixture, and ground beef to egg mixture; mix lightly. Pat meat mixture into a 9-inch foil pie pan placed inside another foil pan, to give double thickness.

Place pan on grill above glowing coals (coals should be arranged in a circle around edge of barbecue, or at sides, so meat isn't directly over fire). Cover barbecue, and cook loaf for 45 minutes, adjusting drafts so fire burns slowly. Brush surface of meat with reserved pizza sauce, cover again, and continue cooking for 15 to 30 minutes longer until meat in center reaches preferred doneness (insert a small knife to test). Arrange cheese strips on top, and cover again until cheese melts. Cut in wedges and serve directly from pan. (Or you can cut edges of foil pan in several places with kitchen scissors; flatten pan edge. Using 2 broad spatulas, place loaf on a warm serving plate.) Makes 6 to 8 servings.

👉 *Barbecued Bologna*

Barbecued bologna with a special baste makes a hit with teenagers. Try it for an outdoor late breakfast with fresh fruit and warm coffee cake.

Buy a 3-pound roll of bologna and cut it in half lengthwise. Remove casing from the bologna. Score the entire surface making cuts 1 inch apart and ¼ inch deep and stud it with 24 whole cloves. Skewer both halves or set them on a piece of foil (if cooking on a covered barbecue), and grill over hot coals or on a rotisserie. Turn and baste bologna with a mixture of ½ cup red currant jelly and 2 tablespoons prepared hot mustard.

If you cook the meat in a covered barbecue, turn it once to baste both top and bottom evenly, and cook with barbecue cover on. Cook for 30 to 45 minutes or until well glazed and hot. Makes 10 to 12 servings. (Leftovers make excellent sandwiches.)

BARBECUE BONUS

👉 GRILLED CHEESE APPETIZER 👈

1 to 1¼ pounds jack cheese, cut in ¼-inch-thick slices
3 medium-sized tomatoes
About ¼ cup diced canned California green chiles
3 tablespoons minced onion
½ teaspoon salt
About 2 minced chiles jalapeños (or other hot chiles)
About 1 dozen frozen or fresh corn tortillas

Grill this cheese over *very slow* coals—if your fire is too hot, the cheese will burn on the bottom and boil over. When cheese has completely melted, remove from fire; return to heat occasionally to keep warm and melted as it is served.

Place a single layer of cheese slices in an 8-inch pottery or heatproof dish or cake or pie pan to ½ to ¾-inch depth. Cover and set aside. To make the tomato and green chile sauce, peel and finely chop the tomatoes. Mix with the canned California green chiles, onion, salt, and chiles jalapeños. Heat tortillas by placing on a medium-hot griddle or in a heavy frying pan over medium-high heat; heat about 30 seconds on a side, or until soft. Stack tortillas and cut in quarters. Wrap in a tea towel and keep warm until you are ready to serve.
Place plate of cheese over very slow coals to melt. Have your guests make their own appetizers by spreading some of the softened cheese on a tortilla wedge, spooning on a little of the hot sauce, then folding tortillas to enclose filling. Makes about 48 appetizers.

☞ *Spit-Roasted Meat Logs*

If you're serving hot meat to a crowd, you can speed up the meal by roasting lunch meat loaves on a spit. The meat logs are basted with a seasoned sauce and roasted just long enough to heat through. When hot, simply slice the loaves and serve. These loaves are ideal for a teen-age sandwich party, a patio brunch, or served with thin slices of French bread for appetizers.

Lunch Meats

Firm-textured, mild-flavored lunch meats suitable for spit-roasting include: bologna, boiled ham, cooked Canadian bacon, boiled salami, beef salami, mortadella, the olive-flavored loaves, mildly seasoned coppa, chopped ham, mettwurst, and beef loaf. The loaf should be at least 4 inches long.

Roasting

Allow ⅛ to ¼ pound for each serving; skin meat logs that have casings. For maximum flavor penetration of the baste, score the meat lightly on all sides before roasting. Boiled ham and Canadian bacon work best if tied with heavy cord at about 3-inch intervals. Place spit 6 inches from hot coals. Secure meat on spit with holding irons. Roast, basting as suggested below, until heated through or internal temperature registers about 120°. Meat logs that are 4 to 5 inches in diameter will take 40 to 50 minutes; those less than 4 inches take 20 to 30 minutes.

Basting Sauce

French dressing baste: Use a bottled French or Italian dressing with any of the meat logs suggested above. Baste meat three or four times while cooking.

Herb butter: Add ¼ teaspoon oregano, ⅛ teaspoon thyme, or ½ clove crushed garlic to each 4 tablespoons melted butter. Use butter with any of the meat logs suggested above. Baste meat three or four times while cooking.

Brown sugar glaze: Combine 2 tablespoons brown sugar, 2 tablespoons melted butter, 1 teaspoon prepared horseradish, and 1 teaspoon prepared mustard. Use with cooked Canadian bacon, boiled ham, bologna, or chopped ham. Baste meat frequently while cooking. Makes enough baste for 6 to 8-inch meat log.

HOW TO BARBECUE SAUSAGES

A trip to your local supermarket or delicatessen can yield an assortment of interesting sausages, which make fine eating for a picnic or supper. Here are suggestions for sausages you might try and the cooking that each type requires:

Swiss sausage (bratwurst)—Cover with cold water, bring slowly to just under the simmering point (the water must never boil or the sausage will burst), cover pan, remove from heat, and let stand for 10 minutes. Heat slowly on the grill just until lightly browned and hot.

Italian simmering sausage (coteghino)—Cook in simmering water to cover for 45 minutes. Reheat and brown on grill.

Blood sausage (French boudin or Italian biroldo Toscano)—Heat through slowly on the grill.

Cocktail sausages—String on skewers to heat on grill.

Frankfurters, exposition frankfurters—These need no precooking; just grill slowly until heated through.

German garlic sausage (knackwurst)—Cook slowly on the grill just until brown and heated through.

Italian garlic sausage (salsiccia) — Simmer gently in water to cover for 30 minutes. Grill slowly until heated and browned.

Smoked Polish sausage (kielbasa or kolbassy)—Barbecue slowly until browned and heated through.

Foie de Veau en Brochette

SKEWER-COOKED

Sauce Bercy for Grilled Meats
(see page 151)
2 pounds calf liver, sliced ½ inch thick,
then cut in 1-inch squares
½ cup (¼ lb.) hot melted butter
½ pound sliced bacon, cut in squares
Fine dry bread crumbs

Serve these French-style calf liver squares plain, or with Sauce Bercy for Grilled Meats.

Stiffen liver by dipping it in the hot melted butter. Cook bacon in the butter for 2 or 3 minutes. Thread the liver on skewers, alternating with the bacon. Dip in the melted butter, roll in fine dry bread crumbs, then grill over hot coals until lightly browned. Makes 6 servings.

Mi'Laaf Mashivi

SKEWER-COOKED

1 clove garlic, puréed
¼ cup olive oil
2 teaspoons salt
¼ cup chopped fresh mint
1 tablespoon lemon juice
⅛ teaspoon freshly ground black pepper
2 pounds beef liver, sliced ½ inch thick
3 to 4 tablespoons olive oil

This liver recipe from Lebanon is so simple that it might well become a family standby. Serve it with lemon wedges and hot rice.

Mix together garlic, the ¼ cup olive oil, salt, mint, lemon juice, and pepper. Spread this mixture on both sides of the liver and let stand for 2 hours. Cut into 2-inch squares. Thread liver on two skewers, keeping meat flat. Grill quickly over hot coals, 1½ to 2 minutes on each side, basting with the remaining marinade mixed with the 3 to 4 tablespoons olive oil. The meat should be pink and juicy inside. Makes about 6 servings.

👉 *Marinated Liver Steak*

1½ cups dry red wine
¾ cup chicken stock
2 tablespoons olive oil
1 tablespoon vinegar
1 tablespoon lemon juice
½ medium-sized onion, chopped
½ cup minced parsley
1½ bay leaves, crushed
1 teaspoon whole thyme
½ teaspoon whole basil
¼ teaspoon whole oregano
¼ teaspoon whole tarragon
¼ teaspoon whole rosemary
2-pound piece beef liver,
    2 to 2½ inches thick

If you always cook liver sliced, this recipe may surprise you, for the liver is the size and shape of a thick steak.

Combine in a pan the wine, chicken stock, oil, vinegar, lemon juice, onion, parsley, bay leaves, thyme, basil, oregano, tarragon, and rosemary. Bring to a boil, reduce heat, and simmer 2 minutes. Cook 5 to 10 minutes; then pour over liver. Cover and refrigerate for 24 hours to 3 days.

To cook liver, drain and place over medium-hot coals, 10 to 12 minutes per side (for rare); turn once and baste often with marinade. (To see if done, make a small cut in center of meat.) To serve, carve crosswise slices, ¼ inch thick. Makes about 6 servings.

👉 *Whole Liver with Salt Pork*

Serve this delicious meat sliced fairly thin, with parsley-buttered new potatoes and foil-wrapped onions roasted in the coals. Corn on the cob is also a good accompaniment.

Select a whole calf or lamb liver and tie it into a compact piece. Lard it or tie strips of salt pork on the outside. Insert spit and cook liver over a medium-hot fire for about an hour, or until a meat thermometer reads 150° for juicy pink, 160° for well done.

👉 *Liver Superb*

Liver is at its best when cooked over charcoal. Serve it with bacon and fried onions, broiled tomatoes, or eggplant.

Use beef, veal, or lamb liver, and have it sliced at least 1 inch thick. Brush well with melted butter, oil, or bacon drippings. Grill over a medium-hot fire, allowing the meat to become crisply brown on the outside, pink and juicy but not dry in the middle. (Most people prefer liver grilled medium-rare.) Make a slit in the meat with a sharp knife to test degree of doneness.

👉 *Liver 'n Bacon Grill*

2 pounds calf liver (about
    4 pieces, cut 1 inch thick)
1 teaspoon monosodium glutamate
8 strips lean bacon

Marinade

½ cup olive oil or salad oil
⅛ teaspoon pepper
⅛ teaspoon garlic salt or ¼
    teaspoon onion salt

Bacon drippings that fall on the coals and make the fire flare up give the liver a wonderful barbecue smoke flavor. Ask your meatman for thick-sliced liver to make these liver and bacon rolls.

Have the meatman cut liver into 1-inch-thick slices and trim off veins and outer skin. Soak liver in a mild salt-water solution (1 teaspoon salt to 2 cups water) for 30 minutes. Remove from water and dry surfaces of liver. Sprinkle each side with monosodium glutamate. Put a strip of bacon under each piece and another on top of it; then roll up and secure with a skewer.

Combine salad oil, pepper, and salt in a shallow dish or pan. Turn liver in marinade and marinate in the refrigerator for 2 or 3 hours, turning twice during that time.

Place liver on grill over medium charcoal fire. Grill on each side, turning only once (approximately 15 minutes total cooking time). *Do not overcook.* The meat should be slightly pink on the inside with a mild brown crust on the outside. Makes 4 to 6 servings.

👉 *Sweetbreads and Steak Brochette*

1 pound sweetbreads
1 quart water
1 tablespoon lemon juice
1 teaspoon salt
1 pound top round steak, cut ¾
    inch thick in 1-inch squares
2 strips bacon
6 fresh mushrooms (1½ inches in
    diameter, preferably)
½ cup (¼ lb.) butter or margarine
½ teaspoon grated lemon peel
2 teaspoons lemon juice
¼ teaspoon salt
1 tablespoon finely chopped parsley
¼ teaspoon dried tarragon, crumbled

This French skewer combination of top round steak and poached sweetbreads is enlivened with tarragon-lemon butter in two ways: first, to brush over the meat while it grills, and second, to spoon over the kebabs at the table.

Wash the sweetbreads in cold water, then soak for 2 to 3 hours, changing the water several times. Drain, cover with about 1 quart cold water (enough to cover them) and add the 1 tablespoon lemon juice and 1 teaspoon salt. Bring to a boil and simmer for 15 minutes. Drain and plunge into cold water for 5 minutes to cool; drain again.

With a sharp knife and your fingers, remove as much white connecting membrane as possible. Then cut sweetbreads into pieces similar in size to the steak squares.

Cut bacon crosswise into ¾-inch pieces and precook partially under the broiler, just until limp. Using 6 skewers, alternate steak squares, bacon, and sweetbreads on a skewer and end with a mushroom cap (cut off stems and use in another recipe).

For tarragon butter, cream butter until light and fluffy. Blend in lemon peel, the 2 teaspoons lemon juice, ¼ teaspoon salt, the parsley, and tarragon. Spoon into a sauce bowl.

Place skewers over medium barbecue coals and grill for about 10 to 12 minutes for rare meat, turning to brown all sides. While grilling, brush meat several times with the seasoned butter. Serve with the herb butter to spoon over as desired. Makes 6 servings.

👉 Broiled Tongue

SPIT-ROASTED

1 beef tongue
½ cup melted butter
½ cup dry white wine
1 teaspoon chopped chives
1 teaspoon chopped parsley
1 teaspoon whole tarragon

Tongue needs precooking, but it is very good barbecued until crusty outside.

Cook tongue in a pressure cooker or in boiling water until tender. Drain, skin, and trim. Put tongue on a spit and cook over charcoal for about 45 minutes, basting with a mixture of the melted butter, wine, chives, parsley, and tarragon.

👉 Hickory-Smoked Tongue

SMOKE-COOKED

Smoked beef tongue is delicious hot or cold. Here it can be served in sandwiches or as hors d'oeuvres.

Cook a medium-sized beef tongue in simmering water until tender; skin and trim. Place on grill, cover, and smoke-cook with hickory smoke over very low indirect heat for 2 hours. After an hour's smoking, baste occasionally with mixture of 2 tablespoons tomato purée, 2 tablespoons melted butter, ¼ teaspoon crumbled whole basil, and ⅛ teaspoon crumbled whole tarragon. Slice thinly and serve either hot or cold for sandwiches. Serve cold for hors d'oeuvres.

👉 Thick-Sliced Beef Heart

GRILL-COOKED

If you like rare beef, you will like beef heart sliced ½ inch thick and grilled quickly over charcoal. The slices should first be marinated in equal parts wine and olive oil, or in melted butter. If cooked lightly, the heart will be tender. Do not attempt this method if you like your beef well done, for longer grilling will make the beef heart tough.

👉 Peruvian Anticuchos

SKEWER-COOKED

1 beef heart (about 3 lbs.)
1½ teaspoons salt
1½ teaspoons chile powder
½ teaspoon freshly ground pepper
2 cloves garlic, puréed
½ cup vinegar
¼ cup water
½ cup olive oil

Beef heart cubes marinated in this spicy sauce and cooked to perfection are tender and flavorful. If you wish, skewer meat alternately with mushroom caps.

Trim beef heart of all hard fat; remove the tubes. Cut into 1-inch cubes. Marinate overnight in a mixture of salt, chile powder, pepper, garlic, vinegar, water, and olive oil. String cubes well apart on thin skewers. Grill over hot coals about 3 minutes on all four sides (12 minutes in all), basting 3 or 4 times with the marinade. Don't overcook. Makes 6 servings.

☞ *Tripe Strips in Butter*

You might serve fried onions and green pepper, and roasted potatoes with this tripe for supper.

Like tongue, tripe needs pre-cooking until fork-tender. Do it in a pressure cooker or by boiling in salted water. Cut in strips, dip in melted butter, and grill on both sides until brown. Serve with individual dishes of melted butter and wedges of lemon.

☞ *Butter-Broiled Brains*

Beef, veal, or lamb brains may be grilled over charcoal. Since they vary in size, here's a serving guide: a beef brain serves three, a veal brain serves two, and a lamb brain serves one. Unless you are a master at fire control and charcoal cookery, it is best to parboil the brains first.

Soak brains in cold water, then simmer for 15 minutes in water to cover. (Add 1 tablespoon lemon juice and 1 teaspoon salt to each quart of water.) Drain, and cover with ice water; remove discolored spots. Drain again. Split brains and dip in melted butter, then roll in fine dry bread or cracker crumbs.

Grill over a low charcoal fire, turning so that both sides will brown. Cook about 10 minutes, basting occasionally with a little more butter. Serve them with lemon wedges, crisp bacon, and drawn butter or tartare sauce.

☞ *Barbecued Kidneys*

Beef, veal, lamb, and pork kidneys may all be successfully cooked over charcoal. Split the kidneys and remove cores; brush with oil or melted butter, seasoned, if you wish, with garlic or with bacon drippings. Grill over a medium hot fire 5 to 15 minutes, depending on size. They are done when brown on the outside but still juicily pink inside; don't overcook. Slice and serve with melted butter.

Kidneys may also be cut in pieces, wrapped in bacon, and then charcoal-broiled. In this case it is not necessary to brush them with oil. Cook until bacon is very crisp. Serve with broiled tomatoes or, if desired, as part of a mixed grill with broiled sausage and lamb chops or liver.

Pork

A smoky flavor is a natural addition to pork. To accent the richness of barbecued pork, add fruit or spice flavors with a marinade or baste.

A barbecue with a hood is needed for cooking large cuts of pork such as a leg or boned shoulder roast. Recent testing has shown that bone-in pork loin roasts and boneless leg and shoulder roasts can be safely roasted to an internal temperature of only 170°; they were found to be juicy and flavorful.

When barbecuing pork chops or steaks, choose thick cuts—preferably 1 to 1½ inches thick. Cook them slowly over moderate heat until browned, but still moist and juicy.

Spareribs, a barbecue favorite, can be barbecued by several methods. Brown them first over hot coals, then simmer in a flavorful sauce. Or, partially cook ribs in water and finish them on the barbecue.

See page 45 for pork buying guides.

 Rolled Leg of Pork, Hawaiian-Style

SPIT-ROASTED

A rolled leg of fresh pork looks impressive coming off the barbecue spit. It compares to that dramatic moment at a luau when the pit is uncovered and the whole cooked pig is removed.

Order a whole leg of fresh pork (about 12 lbs.) and have the meatman bone and roll it. Prepare the pork marinade (recipe follows) and marinate the pork for at least 1 hour. Place meat on spit, and roast over medium coals until well done, about 6 hours for a 12-pound roast (internal temperature on meat thermometer should read 170°). Baste frequently with the marinade as meat roasts. When done, remove from spit, slice and serve on a large platter. Add 1 cup applesauce (left from making the marinade) to the remaining marinade; heat and serve with the sliced meat. Makes 12 servings.

Apple-Soy Marinade for Pork

Combine half of a 1-pound can of applesauce (about 1 cup) with ¾ cup dry white wine, ½ cup soy sauce, 2 tablespoons salad oil, 1 cup chopped onion, 1 clove garlic, minced or mashed, and 1 teaspoon ground ginger; mix well.

Pork Loin with Prunes

A prune-stuffed rack of pork can be smoked even when the weather is brisk, for it requires little tending. It acquires a rich smoke flavor and deep brown color in about two hours.

Buy a loin of pork that weighs about 6½ to 7½ pounds. Have your meatman cut through the meaty portion, making cuts about 2 inches apart to the bone (you will stuff these cuts with prunes before roasting the meat). Have the loin bones cracked to make serving easier.

Soak ½ pound large pitted prunes in 1 cup sherry, port, or orange juice for 2 hours. Stuff prunes into cuts in the pork loin—2 or 3 prunes in each pocket. Tie the whole loin lengthwise to keep the pockets from opening while cooking. Insert a meat thermometer into the center of the meat. Place meat on the grill, cook over an even bed of coals in medium heat (300° to 350°) about 2 hours, or until thermometer registers 170°. Baste meat occasionally with liquid in which prunes were soaked. Makes 6 servings.

Venezuelan Barbecued Pork

1 large onion, chopped
1 can (4 oz.) pimiento,
    drained and chopped
2 cloves garlic, minced or mashed
⅓ cup chopped parsley
½ cup white vinegar
¼ cup salad oil
1½ teaspoons salt
¼ teaspoon pepper
1 fresh pork butt (about 6 lbs.),
    boned and butterflied

A surprisingly compact rectangular steak, about 1½ inches thick, results when you buy a fresh pork butt and ask your meat man to remove the bone and butterfly it. The chopped vegetable marinade is typical of Venezuelan barbecuing.

To make the marinade, combine in a bowl the onion, pimiento, garlic, parsley, vinegar, salad oil, salt, and pepper. Set aside.

Place meat, fat side down, on working surface. With a sharp knife, score top of meat with about three lengthwise and five crosswise cuts, each about ½ inch deep. Put meat in baking dish and pour the marinade over it. Let stand 2 hours.

Scrape marinade off meat and reserve. Place meat, scored side down, over low coals. Barbecue slowly (with or without a hood on the barbecue) for 1 hour. Turn meat over and continue cooking slowly for 1 to 1½ hours, or until the meat is cooked through. (You can insert a meat thermometer into the center after the meat is turned; recommended internal temperature for this cut of pork is 170°.) Baste meat several times with the marinade after turning.

To serve, cut through score lines into individual portions. Heat remaining marinade and serve as a sauce. Makes 12 to 15 servings.

Roast Pork Loin on Melon Ring

SMOKE-COOKED

Here's a mouthwatering combination: Thick slices of smoked pork atop smoked cantaloupe rings with whipped cream cheese and chives over all.

Place a 4-pound rolled pork loin roast over moderate coals (grill thermometer should read about 300°). Cover and roast for 2 hours or until meat thermometer registers 170°. Peel cantaloupe; cut one ½-inch thick ring for each serving. Brush with butter and place on sheet of foil; put on grill to heat and smoke for 10 minutes (while you slice pork roast). Have ready 2 small packages (3 oz. *each*) cream cheese with chives, beaten with ½ cup heavy cream until fluffy. To serve, place a thick pork slice atop a melon ring. Top with a spoonful of whipped cheese. Makes about 12 servings.

Spicy Ham Steak

GRILL-COOKED

¼ cup melted butter
1 cup sherry
1 cup pineapple juice
2 teaspoons ground cloves
¼ cup dry mustard
¼ cup firmly packed brown sugar
2 teaspoons paprika
1½ cloves garlic, minced
1 center-cut slice ham, 1 inch thick

Barbecue this ham steak at home or carry it to a picnic in its marinade. You might accompany it with a hot or cold vegetable appetizer soup, sweet potato salad, cherry tomatoes, fruit tarts, and beverage.

Combine the melted butter, sherry, pineapple juice, cloves, mustard, brown sugar, paprika, and garlic. Slash edges of ham and marinate in this mixture for 3 hours, turning several times. Grill over low to medium coals for 20 minutes, basting frequently with marinade and turning occasionally. Carve ham into individual portions and serve hot. Makes about 4 servings.

Ham Steak with Cantaloupe

GRILL-COOKED

4 tablespoons melted butter
¼ to ½ teaspoon curry powder
1 tablespoon syrup drained
   from chutney
1 center slice (about 1¾ lbs.)
   precooked ham steak, 1 inch thick
1 medium-sized cantaloupe,
   peeled and seeded
   Chutney

Total cooking time is short for this ham and fruit entrée. The precooked ham steak takes less than 20 minutes to heat through and brown on the surface; the cantaloupe takes about half that time to become hot and glazed. Hot buttered rice and a tossed green salad are ideal accompaniments.

Blend the butter with curry powder and syrup drained from chutney; brush on both sides of the ham steak. Place steak on grill 5 to 6 inches above medium-hot coals. Cook for 16 to 20 minutes, turning occasionally and basting frequently with the seasoned butter.
   Cut cantaloupe into 6 to 8 wedges; brush with the prepared butter. About 10 minutes before ham is done, place melon on grill. Let each wedge heat for about 3 minutes on each side and the back. Serve ham and cantaloupe with chutney. Makes 5 to 6 servings.

HOW TO SPIT ROAST SUCKLING PIG

It is the ambition of every barbecue chef to try his hand at a roast suckling pig. If you have decided that the time has come for you to undertake this cooking venture, ask your meatman to provide you with a cleaned, tender suckling pig about 15 to 20 pounds in weight. A young pig any smaller would be nothing but skin and bones when cooked.

Stuff the pig with a sage or fruit dressing. Don't stuff too tightly, as the dressing will expand. Sew it in with heavy string and lace it closely and tightly.

Leave the skin on. Head and feet can be cut off either before or after cooking; it is more easily done before, but it won't look much like a pig. Insert a piece of wood in the mouth to simplify adding an apple later. Truss the legs with cord in a kneeling position and place the pig on a spit over a deep bed of hot coals.

The coals should be arranged in such a way to allow for a pan to be placed in the center to catch drippings from the roasting meat; drippings should be used for basting. The pig can be basted with oil, but it will lose some of its flavor. Cooking time about 6 to 10 hours.

When done, remove pig from the spit; place a red apple in the mouth and cranberries or cherries in the eye sockets; then place pig on a bed of watercress. Various garnishes of vegetable flowers, radish roses, stuffed stewed apricots and prunes, or holly berries may be added.

Bring the roast pig to the table with the head separated from the body and the cut ringed with a wreath of watercress and flowers. In carving, first separate the shoulder from the carcass and remove the legs. This will leave the ribs open to the knife. Cut down the backbone; remove the loins and serve the tender chops from the sliced loins.

Smoky Ham Steaks

GRILL-COOKED

Smoke from the barbecue fire and a catsup marinade add flavor to this canned ham supper entrée. To complete the meal you might serve buttered green beans, sliced tomatoes and cucumbers sprinkled with French dressing, buttered bread heated on the barbecue, and ice cream or sherbet.

Combine ½ cup catsup, ½ cup water, and ½ cup salad oil with 4 small crushed cloves garlic. Cut a 3-pound fully cooked canned ham into approximately 8 slices, each about ¾ inch thick. Pour part of the marinade into a large shallow pan, arrange slices in pan, and pour remaining marinade over them; cover and refrigerate several hours, turning slices occasionally in the marinade. Barbecue ham slices about 3 minutes on each side or until hot and lightly browned. Strain marinade and discard garlic; heat and serve with the ham. Makes about 8 servings.

Honey-Glazed Ham

You'll need a covered smoke cooker, or a barbecue with a cover that encloses the grill for this ham. (See page 33 for directions on making a foil cover.)

Place a drip-catching pan in center of grill beneath ham. If you don't have a suitable ready-made pan, you can make one of heavy-duty foil folded double. Make it about 3 inches longer and 2 inches wider than the ham, with sides about 2½ inches high.

Start two charcoal piles (one on each side of the drip pan) of 20 briquets each, 30 to 45 minutes before you plan to start the ham (the briquets should burn down to an even gray). After each hour of cooking time, add about 6 briquets on each side.

Start the ham on the grill 3 to 5 hours before serving time, depending on the size and type of ham you buy. Plan on 15 to 20 minutes per pound if you buy a "tenderized" ham (or cook to 160° on meat thermometer); or 10 to 15 minutes per pound for a fully cooked ham (or 130° on meat thermometer).

As an added precaution to keep ham fat away from the barbecue fire, shape a "pan" of double heavy-duty foil loosely around lower half of ham. Sides should be about 4 inches high and should stand away from ham about 1 inch all around. This pan will catch most of the ham drippings—and the drip pan below will catch the rest. Insert the meat thermometer in thick portion of ham.

Set ham on the barbecue, centered over drip pan. For slow heat, keep any draft opening small. Check the ham every half hour; if it begins to brown too quickly, lower heat by making draft openings smaller (but don't completely close them). If drippings accumulate excessively in the pan directly under the ham, remove them with a meat baster. One hour before ham is done, remove from barbecue, drain off drippings, skin, score, and brush with honey glaze (recipe follows). Return to barbecue and brush with glaze about every 15 minutes. When ham is done, it will be easier to slice if you let it stand 15 to 20 minutes.

Honey Glaze

Combine 3 tablespoons honey, 1 tablespoon Worcestershire, 1 tablespoon dry mustard, ¾ teaspoon ground ginger, and a dash of black pepper; mix well.

Hickory-Smoked Ham for a Crowd

SMOKE-COOKED

A whole ham is rubbed with a mustard-clove mixture and basted with sherry as it cooks. Hickory chips are added to the fire during the last hour of cooking to give the ham a hickory-smoked flavor.

Buy a precooked ham, about 16 pounds. Score with a sharp knife, rub with a mixture of 3 tablespoons prepared mustard and 2 teaspoons ground cloves. Build barbecue fire about an hour before you start cooking. Arrange ham over foil drip pan (you can make a foil pan or use an old metal cake pan, about 9 by 12 inches). Insert a meat thermometer into the thickest portion of the ham. Cover barbecue with its lid or a blanket of foil and cook over medium heat (300° to 350° grill temperature) until the meat thermometer reaches 145°; it takes about 3½ hours. Baste while cooking with 1 cup sherry or orange juice. Before last hour of cooking, sprinkle fire with a handful of damp hickory chips. Makes approximately 20 generous servings.

Garlic Spareribs

SPIT-ROASTED

About 6 pounds spareribs
4 large cloves garlic
1 tablespoon salt
1 cup chicken broth
1 cup orange marmalade
¼ cup vinegar
¼ cup catsup

Those who favor garlic will approve these spit-roasted spareribs.

Figure on at least 1 pound of spareribs per person. Leave the side whole so you can thread them on a spit later. Combine the garlic, with the salt, broth, marmalade, vinegar, and catsup. Marinate the spareribs for at least 12 hours in this mixture, turning several times. Weave the whole strips on a spit, and cook over low coals for 1 to 1½ hours, or until shiny brown and fork tender. Baste with the marinade during the cooking. Makes 6 servings.

Chinese Ribs

SMOKE-COOKED

About 6 pounds spareribs
¼ cup soy sauce
1 teaspoon pepper
4 tablespoons honey
¼ cup sherry
2 teaspoons monosodium glutamate

The trick of drying the honey-marinated meat before cooking plays about the most important part in the resulting crispy surface texture of these spareribs.

Marinate whole sides of the spareribs in a mixture of the soy, pepper, honey, sherry, and monosodium glutamate for at least 30 minutes. Remove the ribs from the marinade and allow to dry thoroughly.

Hang the ribs from the top of a moderate (300° to 400°) Chinese smoke oven for 1¼ to 1½ hours. The closer you place the ribs to the actual fire, the more carefully you have to watch for charring. Makes 6 servings.

☞ Ginger-Barbecued Spareribs

GRILL-COOKED

1 can (8 oz.) tomato sauce
1 can (about 1 lb.) tomato purée
¼ cup wine vinegar
¼ cup brown sugar
1 tablespoon Worcestershire
1 lemon slice
1 medium-sized onion, finely chopped,
   or 1 tablespoon dried minced onions
1 clove garlic, crushed
1 teaspoon salt
½ teaspoon chile powder
½ teaspoon celery salt
½ teaspoon dry mustard
⅛ teaspoon pepper
   About 6 pounds country-style
    spareribs
2 tablespoons finely chopped or
   slivered candied ginger

Slivers of candied ginger are sprinkled onto the red glaze of the barbecue sauce at serving time. Try salted pine nuts as a side dish.

Make this barbecue sauce: Combine in a saucepan the tomato sauce, tomato purée, wine vinegar, brown sugar, Worcestershire, lemon, onion, garlic, salt, chile powder, celery salt, dry mustard, and pepper. Cover and simmer 20 minutes, stirring occasionally.

Barbecue spareribs over low coals for about 1½ hours. Turn frequently, basting with sauce. When ready to serve, sprinkle spareribs with ginger. Makes 8 servings.

☞ Pineapple Spareribs

GRILL-COOKED

10 pounds spareribs
   Water
12 whole black peppers
6 whole cloves
2 bay leaves
2 cloves garlic
   Sweet-Sour Pineapple Baste
   (recipe on page 155)

Pineapple is the special touch in these spareribs, proportioned to serve a holiday crowd of ten to twelve people. You can precook these ribs at home and finish them on the barbecue at your picnic site. Brush with Pineapple Baste or another favorite barbecue sauce.

Place spareribs in water that almost covers; season with black peppers, cloves, bay leaves, and garlic. (If you don't have a pan large enough, cook half the ribs at a time, using half the seasonings each time.) Simmer for 30 minutes, or until almost tender. Drain, then refrigerate, covered.

To finish cooking, arrange spareribs on the barbecue grill over hot coals; cook about 30 minutes turning occasionally. During the last 15 minutes of cooking, baste with your favorite barbecue sauce. Cook until ribs are glazed and tender. Remove ribs to warm platter. Makes 10 to 12 servings.

Smoked Ribs in Barbecue Sauce

SMOKE-COOKED

1 cup catsup
1 cup water
1 cup dry white wine or sherry
¼ cup Worcestershire
1 medium-sized onion, sliced
1 whole lemon, thinly sliced
1 clove garlic, sliced
2 tablespoons butter or margarine
4 pounds country-style spareribs
  Salt
  Pepper

A covered barbecue is recommended for cooking these thick, meaty country-style spareribs. Use part of the sauce to baste the meat; then put the cooked meat into the sauce to simmer for 20 to 30 minutes.

To make the barbecue sauce, combine in a pan (one that's large enough to hold the spareribs) the catsup, water, wine, Worcestershire, onion, lemon, garlic, and butter or margarine. Bring to boiling, reduce heat, cover, and simmer slowly for 30 minutes. This much can be done ahead.

To grill the meat, first sprinkle both sides of spareribs lightly with salt and pepper. Place, fat side up, on the grill over slowly burning coals. Put lid on barbecue and adjust drafts, if any, to keep fire burning slowly.

Cook about 1 hour to 1 hour and 20 minutes, turning several times and basting often with part of the barbecue sauce (put about 1 cup of the sauce into a small pan to use for basting). Reheat the rest of the barbecue sauce in the pan; as the rib pieces are cooked, remove from grill, cut into individual servings, and put into the sauce. Cover pan and simmer 20 to 30 minutes. Spoon some of the sauce over each piece as you serve it. Makes about 6 servings.

Pork Satés Bali

SKEWER-COOKED

½ cup chutney
¼ cup catsup
1 tablespoon soy sauce
4 drops liquid hot-pepper seasoning
2 tablespoons salad oil
2 pounds boneless pork loin, cut ¾ inch thick in 1-inch squares
¾ cup salted peanuts, very finely chopped

A Far Eastern spiciness permeates pork kebabs when you use puréed chutney in the marinade. Twirl the grilled kebabs in finely chopped peanuts to lend an authentic Indonesian flavor.

Direct your meatman to bone a pork loin and slice it ¾ inch thick and then into 1-inch squares. This cut will grill quickly to a tender state.

Purée the chutney in a blender until smooth (or finely chop it). Turn into a bowl and add catsup, soy sauce, hot-pepper seasoning, and oil. Add meat squares and let marinate for several hours, turning occasionally. Impale meat on 6 skewers. Barbecue over medium coals about 15 minutes, turning to brown all sides. Immediately roll in finely chopped peanuts, spread out on a small tray or plate, to coat all sides. Makes 6 servings.

East Indian Saté

SKEWER-COOKED

1 tablespoon ground coriander
1 tablespoon salt
½ teaspoon freshly ground pepper
1 cup chopped onion
2 cloves garlic, peeled
½ cup soy sauce
¼ cup lime or lemon juice
½ cup peanut butter
¼ cup brown sugar
½ cup peanut or salad oil
  Dash cayenne or liquid hot-
    pepper seasoning
2 pounds meat (boneless veal leg or
    shoulder, or boned chicken), cut into
    1-inch cubes

This thick tan marinade has a mild peanut flavor that is delicious with veal, pork, or chicken; serve the remaining marinade as a sauce over the cooked meat. Consider alternating the meat with chunks of pineapple that have been dipped in melted butter.

Combine coriander, salt, pepper, onion, garlic, soy sauce, lime or lemon juice, peanut butter, brown sugar, peanut or salad oil, and cayenne or liquid hot-pepper seasoning. Whirl smooth in a blender. Marinate the meat in this mixture for 1 to 2 hours. String on skewers. Grill over hot coals until brown but not dry, about 3 to 4 minutes on each side. Serve with the remaining marinade. Makes 6 to 8 servings.

Indonesian Satés

SKEWER-COOKED

1 large onion, ground
4 cloves garlic, minced or crushed
2 teaspoons pepper
¾ cup lime juice
1 cup soy sauce
½ cup dark molasses
1 cup salad oil
5 pounds boneless lean pork,
    cut in 1 to 1½-inch cubes

Satés, or skewered grilled meats, are sold from little carts at public gatherings in Indonesia as hot dogs are sold at American ball games. This recipe for Indonesian satés uses pork, but chicken, beef, or veal is equally suitable.

Make sauce by combining onion, garlic, pepper, lime juice, soy sauce, molasses, and salad oil. Force this mixture through a sieve or whirl in a blender. Marinate meat in this sauce for 3 to 4 hours. Skewer meat on bamboo sticks, 3 or 4 pieces to each stick. Grill over charcoal until meat is brown and crisp on all sides—15 to 20 minutes. Do not overcook, or the meat will be dry. Heat remaining marinade and serve with the saté. Makes 25 servings.

Italian Sausage with Summer Squash

GRILL-COOKED

Grill Italian garlic sausages (*salsiccia fresche*) over barbecue coals for about 30 minutes, turning to brown all sides. Over the same coals and for the same length of time, grill pattypan or crookneck squash that you have split in half, brushed with butter, and seasoned with salt and pepper; turn occasionally.

👉 *Barbecued Bacon with Pineapple*

GRILL-COOKED

8 slices bacon cut from a slab, each cut
   ½ inch thick
4 slices fresh pineapple, each about ½
   inch thick, peeled (or substitute
   drained canned pineapple slices)
   Melted butter or margarine

Serve this breakfast entrée with scrambled eggs and your favorite muffins. Watch the bacon carefully, turning frequently, and be sure the coals are low; you want to brown the meat slowly for a nice crisp texture, without flare-ups from the drippings.

Arrange bacon on grill about 4 inches above slow coals. Cook about 25 minutes, turning frequently, or until the bacon is crisp and richly browned.

About 15 minutes before bacon is ready, also place on grill the pineapple slices brushed with melted butter or margarine. Cook about 5 minutes on each side or until hot and lightly browned, turning with a spatula. Makes 4 servings.

👉 *Crumb-Coated Pigs' Feet*

GRILL-COOKED

The pigs' feet must be boiled before they are grilled. Cook them, whole or split, in water to cover, with salt, an onion, and an herb bouquet. Simmer until tender—from 3 to 4 hours. Drain, brush well with softened butter, then roll in fine dry bread or cracker crumbs. Grill until nicely browned on all sides. Serve with charcoal-roasted potatoes and sauerkraut heated in a pot at the back of the grill.

BARBECUE BONUS

👉 GRILLED CHINESE PORK APPETIZERS 👈

¼ *cup soy sauce*
2 *tablespoons salad oil*
2 *cloves garlic, mashed*
1 *small dried, hot chile pepper, crushed*
½ *teaspoon sugar*
¼ *teaspoon anise seed*
⅛ *teaspoon cinnamon*
⅛ *teaspoon cloves*
1 *pound lean pork, cut into bite-sized strips or cubes*
1 *small fresh pineapple*
1 *medium-sized green pepper*

Three sweet spices—cinnamon, cloves, and anise—flavor the pork for these unusual hot appetizers. The meat is barbecued with pieces of pineapple and green pepper.

Combine the soy sauce, salad oil, garlic, pepper, sugar, anise, cinnamon, and cloves in a bowl. Add the pork and stir gently to coat each piece with the marinade. Refrigerate meat 1 to 2 hours, stirring occasionally. String pork on skewers with bite-sized pieces of fresh pineapple and green pepper. Grill about 5 inches from the heat for 7 to 10 minutes, turning once. Serve hot.

Lamb

For centuries lamb has been a favorite barbecue meat because it is generally tender and cooks well by this dry heat method.

Cook lamb as you would beef, preferably medium-rare for most tastes; that is, it should be crusty brown outside, delicately pink and juicy within.

For lamb cooked to the medium-rare stage, a properly placed meat thermometer will read about 150°. Medium doneness is about 160°, and more well done meat will have an internal temperature of about 170°.

Many countries do interesting things with lamb, and the recipes in this section reflect this international popularity. The Greeks favor lemon, oregano, and olive oil with lamb. In India or Pakistan the spices are sweeter and hotter—coriander, cumin, cinnamon, chiles. The Turks enjoy mint with lamb, and garlic is a favorite everywhere.

Pages 44 and 45 illustrate varieties of lamb chops suitable for barbecuing and give some useful buying guides.

Basque-Barbecued Lamb

SPIT-ROASTED

¼ cup dry sherry
2 tablespoons olive oil
2 teaspoons mixed herbs (a prepared herb blend can be used)
1 leg of lamb (6 to 7 lbs.), boned
2 slices bacon
  Finely chopped green onion or instant minced onion
  Mixed herbs for lamb
  Basting sauce (recipe follows)

Huge summertime picnics held by Basque communities have spread news of Basque culinary expertise. In this method for barbecuing lamb, seasoned bacon rolls are inserted in the meat to add extra flavor as it cooks. Complete the Basque menu by serving grilled Spanish chorizo sausages, baked beans, mixed green salad, marinated garbanzo beans, and warm sourdough French bread. Dessert could be an orange flan (custard) and coffee.

Prepare a marinade of the sherry, olive oil, and mixed herbs. Marinate the lamb overnight. Drain, saving all the marinade.

Sprinkle each slice of bacon with finely chopped green onion or instant minced onion and mixed herbs; roll up like a jelly roll; then cut each roll crosswise to make 2 smaller rolls. Cut 3 or 4 deep incisions in the thickest parts of the meat and insert a seasoned bacon roll deep into each.

Fold the boned lamb into a compact shape, tucking any ends inside. Skewer the meat together with metal or heavy wooden skewers. Then put the meat on a spit for barbecuing, or on a grill arranged about 1½ feet above the bed of glowing coals. Turn and baste often with the basting sauce (recipe follows). Barbecuing will take about 1½ hours. Makes 8 to 10 servings.

Basting Sauce

To the drained marinade (above) add: ½ cup catsup, ¼ cup wine vinegar, 1 can (6 oz.) tomato paste, 1 teaspoon liquid smoke, ½ teaspoon salt, 1 finely mashed clove garlic (or ⅛ teaspoon garlic powder), and 1 cup dry white wine. Blend the mixture well and use to baste the lamb.

☞ Butterflied Leg of Lamb with Herb Baste

1 cup dry red or white wine
¾ cup regular strength chicken or
    beef broth
2½ tablespoons orange marmalade
2 tablespoons wine vinegar
1 tablespoon minced dried onion
1 tablespoon dried or fresh rosemary
1 tablespoon dried whole marjoram
1 large bay leaf, crumbled
1 teaspoon seasoned salt
¼ teaspoon powdered ginger
1 leg of lamb (5 to 6 lbs.),
    boned and butterflied

If you have a leg of lamb "butterflied" (boned, with the seam left open), you have a fine piece of meat to barbecue flat on the grill. In less than an hour, it cooks to a rich brown outside, with thin portions of the meat well-done and the thick portions slightly pink. There's no bone to deal with in carving, and you can offer well-done and rare slices.

This recipe may seem overloaded with herbs; but the barbecuing process chars them slightly, until they add a distinctive toasty flavor.

Combine in a pan the wine, chicken or beef stock, orange marmalade, and wine vinegar. Stir in onion, rosemary, marjoram, bay leaf, salt, and ginger. Simmer for 20 minutes, stirring occasionally. Brush sauce over entire surface of lamb.

Place meat on grill, fat side up, over medium coals. Cook 50 minutes to an hour, basting frequently with remaining sauce and turning meat occasionally. To carve, start at one end and cut into thin slices across the grain. Makes 6 to 8 servings.

☞ Butterflied Leg of Lamb with Mushrooms

1 leg of lamb (5 to 6 lbs.), boned
8 large mushrooms, each
    about 3 inches in diameter
1 cup olive oil or salad oil
⅔ cup Burgundy
¼ teaspoon thyme
½ teaspoon oregano
1 teaspoon salt
¼ teaspoon pepper
1½ cups finely chopped onion
¼ cup butter
    Salt
    Pepper

Boned and laid out flat on the grill, a butterflied leg of lamb cooks quickly and evenly. Giant mushroom caps, which have been marinated with the lamb, go on the grill for the last 15 minutes.

Slash into the thick portions of the lamb to make it lay as flat and evenly as possible. Carefully break stems from mushrooms and scrape a smooth hollow in the cap. Save stems and scraps. Marinate the lamb and mushroom caps for several hours in a mixture of the olive oil or salad oil, Burgundy, thyme, oregano, salt, and pepper. Finely chop mushroom stems and scraps; combine with the onion. Melt the butter; add mushroom-onion mixture and cook until tender. Season with salt and pepper to taste and set aside.

Lift meat fron marinade and place, fat side down, on a grill 5 to 6 inches over medium-hot coals. Cook for about 45 minutes, turning frequently and basting with marinade.

About 15 minutes before lamb is done, drain mushroom caps and place, hollowed side down, on grill for 5 minutes. Turn onto rounded side and spoon into caps the onion-mushroom mixture; cook about 10 minutes more and baste once or twice with the lamb marinade. Thinly slice lamb across the grain and serve with mushrooms. Makes 8 servings.

👉 Roasted Lamb, Indian Style

SPIT-ROASTED

3 onions, chopped
3 to 6 cloves garlic, minced
1 tablespoon ground cumin
1 green pepper, chopped
2 hot small dried chile peppers
½ teaspoon salt
¼ teaspoon freshly ground pepper
1 leg of lamb (about 6 lbs.), boned
   Melted butter

Exotic seasonings, typical of India, flavor the stuffing and permeate a boneless leg of lamb roast.

Make stuffing by combining the onions, garlic, cumin, green pepper, chile peppers, salt, and pepper. Pound this to a paste in a mortar, and spread in the center of the boned leg of lamb. Roll the meat securely and tie with string. Put on the spit and roast to about 150° internal temperature. Baste occasionally with melted butter. Makes about 6 servings.

👉 Garlic Leg of Lamb with Coffee Baste

SMOKE-COOKED

5 cloves garlic, peeled
1 leg of lamb (5 to 6 lbs.)
   Salt
   Pepper
⅓ cup strong hot coffee
⅓ cup melted butter
1 teaspoon grated lemon peel

Strong hot coffee, lots of garlic, and a two-hour smoking give this roast its special flavor.

Insert garlic cloves in the leg of lamb; rub with salt and pepper. Place over indirect charcoal heat (meat-level temperature about 300°). Cover and roast with smoke about 2 hours or until meat thermometer registers about 150°. Baste during last half of roasting time with a mixture of the coffee, melted butter, and grated lemon peel. Slice and serve while hot. Makes 8 to 10 servings.

BARBECUE BONUS

👉 ENOUGH LAMB FOR A CROWD 👈

For something really different, try this lamb on a tepee. Three poles and fuel enough to keep a fire going for four hours are all you need to barbecue a hind of lamb for twenty-five hungry people. You might serve a hearty soup to start the meal, for the aroma of the meat sizzling on the tepee whets appetites alarmingly.

Sprinkle a hind of lamb (about 22 lbs.) with salt. (The hind includes both legs, large and small loin, and flank.) If necessary, cut through flesh joining legs to flatten the lamb as much as possible. Insert a meat thermometer in a fleshy portion of the leg or loin.

To make the tepee, bind together with heavy twine or wire 3 poles (each approximately 2 inches in diameter and 6 feet long) about 14 inches from the ends. Stand upright tepee fashion.

Loop wire or heavy cord tightly around each leg of the lamb and tie each against a pole 30 inches up from the base. Cavity side should be up. Cut two small gashes through meat near front of the loin on each side of back bone and loop wire through; secure against third pole 30 inches up from base. Spread tepee open to pull lamb taut, and set over a bed of well ignited coals (wood and charcoal). Arrange coals in a triangle, leaving the center area clear. Border with slow burning logs; add fuel as needed. Baste occasionally, if desired, with Burgundy wine. Turn lamb every hour (release each leg and attach to opposite pole). Total cooking time will be about 4 hours or when meat thermometer registers 170° to 180°. Remove to a large tray and carve. Makes approximately 25 servings.

Smoked Leg of Lamb

SMOKE-COOKED

6-pound leg of lamb (bone should not be cracked nor end bone cut off)
2 medium-sized onions, peeled and sliced
1 tablespoon salt
½ teaspoon pepper
½ cup sherry or orange juice
2 tablespoons olive oil
1 teaspoon oregano
½ teaspoon savory

You'll need to begin marinating this meat 8 hours before you plan to cook it. Truss the bone end of the lamb if you plan to cook the meat in a Chinese smoke oven; the meat hangs from this cord.

In a pan large enough to hold the meaty portion of the leg of lamb, combine onions, salt, pepper, sherry or orange juice, olive oil, oregano, and summer savory. Rub mixture evenly over leg of lamb, and let stand at least 8 hours. Insert meat thermometer into thickest portion of the meat, if you wish.

Build barbecue fire about an hour before you plan to begin cooking. Hang the meat from the trussed end in the chimney if you're using a Chinese smoke oven; or, if you're using another covered barbecue, lay the meat on the grill. Cook in medium heat (300° to 350°) about 2¼ hours, or until meat thermometer registers about 150°. Makes about 8 to 10 servings.

Lime-Basted Leg of Lamb

SPIT-ROASTED

1 leg of lamb (about 7 lbs.), shank bone and aitchbone removed, tied

Lime Basting Sauce

1 can (6 oz.) daiquiri mix
½ cup dry white wine
2 tablespoons butter or margarine
½ teaspoon crushed rosemary

Partially boned leg of lamb is easy to balance on a spit and easy to carve and serve. Order a leg of lamb with the shank bone and the aitchbone (pronounced *H-bone*) removed, and the roast tied. One long straight bone will remain near the center of the roast for balancing the meat on the rotisserie.

Guide the spit through the center of the roast parallel with the remaining bone; secure with meat prongs. Start the spit revolving over slowly burning coals or an electric unit.

In a small pan, combine the daiquiri mix, wine, butter or margarine, and rosemary; heat until the butter melts. Baste liberally with the lime sauce as the meat roasts. For best results, use a meat thermometer; cook to about 150° for juicy pink lamb. Time will be about 2 to 2½ hours. Makes about 12 servings.

☛ HOW TO GRILL CAPRETTO ☚

Capretto (Italian for baby goat) is available at some Italian or Spanish meat markets and at some goat dairy farms. Because the supply is limited, you may have to order it two weeks to a month in advance.

The Italians may barbecue a half or whole capretto for large dinners, but for family use, they often barbecue a leg or quarter, or capretto chops.

Barbecued Capretto Leg, Forequarter, or Hindquarter. Make baste by mixing ¼ cup olive oil, juice of ½ lemon, 2 tablespoons white wine, 1½ teaspoons rosemary, ¾ teaspoon salt, ½ teaspoon coarse-ground pepper, a dash of Worcestershire, and 1 minced clove garlic (optional).

Place the quarter or leg of capretto about 8 to 10 inches above coals on grill. Brush with basting sauce. Turning and basting about every 15 minutes, cook until internal temperature reaches 175° (about 50 minutes for forequarter; 1 hour, 15 minutes for hindquarter). If exterior appears to be cooking too fast, raise meat or spread out coals. The forequarter or hind leg makes about 6 servings, the complete hindquarter about 8 servings.

Barbecued Capretto Chops. Brush both sides of capretto chops with a little olive oil and sprinkle with salt and pepper. Place on grill 4 inches from glowing coals and cook for 4 to 5 minutes per side. Chops are small, so plan on about 3 chops for each serving.

☛ *Easy Leg of Lamb*

SPIT-ROASTED

1 short-cut leg of lamb (5 to 6 lbs.)
4 cloves garlic, split
½ teaspoon crumbled dried oregano
1 teaspoon salt
4 tablespoons melted butter
  Juice of 1 lemon

A leg of lamb roasted on the spit is practically self-basting and needs little watching. It is best when still slightly pink in the center and juicy—140° to 150° on a meat thermometer.

Make several cuts in the leg of lamb and insert the garlic and a mixture of the oregano and salt. With any remaining oregano and salt, rub the outside of the meat. Insert the spit almost parallel to the bone and place over medium coals. Mix melted butter and the lemon juice and brush the meat. Basting once or twice, barbecue 1¼ to 1½ hours (140° to 150° on a meat thermometer) for medium rare. Makes 6 to 8 servings.

☛ *Lamb in Onion Juice*

SKEWER-COOKED

2 pounds lean lamb, cut in 1-inch cubes
2 medium-sized onions
½ cup salad oil
1 bay leaf
1 teaspoon salt
½ teaspoon thyme
  Pinch of sage
3 whole black peppers, crushed
1 cup sherry or dry red wine

You can alternate pieces of bacon, onion, green peppers, or even very small tomatoes with these lamb cubes.

Put lamb cubes into an earthen bowl. Run the two onions through the food grinder, using the finest blade. Squeeze the onion pulp through a small muslin sack or cloth onto the meat. Add the oil, bay leaf, salt, thyme, sage, and whole black peppers, working them into the meat. Add the wine and marinate overnight. Then string the meat on skewers and grill to your taste.

☛ Lamb Chops a la Castellane

3 tablespoons butter
3 tablespoons flour
1 cup rich beef stock or bouillon,
    undiluted
¼ cup diced lean ham
1 tablespoon butter
3 tablespoons sherry
2 tablespoons minced green pepper
6 thick slices unpeeled eggplant
    Butter or olive oil
6 loin lamb chops, cut thick
    Parsley sprigs or broiled
        mushroom caps for garnish

Thick-cut small loin lamb chops are served here atop grilled eggplant slices with a flavorful sauce.

To make the sauce, melt the 3 tablespoons butter and stir in the flour. Cook, stirring, until lightly browned; then gradually add beef broth or beef bouillon. Cook until smooth and thick.

In another pan cook the ham in 1 tablespoon butter for a minute or two, then add sherry and green pepper. Add to these ingredients thickened broth.

When the charcoal fire is good and hot, brush the eggplant on both sides with butter or olive oil, and grill until nicely browned (a hinged wire broiler makes turning easy). Keep warm on a serving platter. Broil the lamb chops so that they are pink and juicy inside, crisply brown outside. Reheat the sauce and pour over eggplant slices. Put one chop on each slice of eggplant. Garnish with sprigs of parsley or broiled mushroom caps. Makes 6 servings.

☛ Lamb Leg Chops

4 lamb leg chops or steaks,
    cut ¾ to 1 inch thick
⅔ cup salad oil
⅓ cup lemon juice
1 medium-sized onion, chopped
1 teaspoon salt
1 teaspoon oregano
    Dash pepper
    Parsley sprigs
    Lemon slices
    Onion slices

From one leg of lamb, a family of four can have two dinners: large lamb chops or steaks, then stew or kebabs made from the remaining shank end of the leg.

Marinate leg chops in salad oil, lemon juice, onion, salt, oregano, and pepper at least 4 hours. Drain chops. Grill over hot coals about 6 minutes on each side, or until done. Baste with marinade. Garnish with parsley, lemon and onion slices. Makes 4 to 6 servings, depending on size of chops.

☛ Lamb Rolls with Curry Honey Glaze

6 lamb shoulder rolls, each
    about ¾ pound
    Quartered green pepper pieces,
        parboiled 1 minute in boiling water
    Melted butter or salad oil

Curry Honey Glaze

¼ cup honey
2 tablespoons salad oil
2 tablespoons lemon juice
¼ teaspoon curry powder
½ teaspoon salt
    Dash coarse-ground pepper

Lamb shoulder rolls are tender and juicy; delicious when barbecued. Some markets feature the rolls on their meat counters. If you don't see them at your market, ask your meatman to make them from boneless lamb shoulder chops; they are cut 1 to 1½ inches thick and held with wooden skewers.

Remove wooden skewers from lamb rolls; alternate the rolls on long metal skewers with the parboiled green pepper pieces. Brush the pepper with melted butter or salad oil. Grill over hot coals for 5 to 10 minutes on each side or until meat is done to your liking. During the last 2 minutes of cooking, brush on both sides with curry honey glaze, made by combining the honey, salad oil, lemon juice, curry powder, salt, and pepper. Serve hot. Makes 6 servings.

Kebab Barg

1 leg of lamb (5 lbs.), boned and
    sliced ½ inch thick
1 cup grated onion (or chopped
    and whirled in blender)
3 cups yogurt
1/16 teaspoon powdered
    saffron (optional)
    Salt
    Pepper
    About ½ cup butter
    Chello (recipe below)
10 egg yolks (shells reserved)

A yogurt marinade gives these Iranian lamb kebabs an interesting tart flavor. It is traditionally served with a special rice dish called *chello*, which is white, fluffy, and crusty. Complete the menu with fresh vegetable relishes and Arabian flat bread or hot-buttered flour tortillas.

Trim fat off lamb. Cut in strips 2 inches wide and about 5 inches long. Mix onion with yogurt and saffron, if used. Put lamb in yogurt marinade; refrigerate, covered, for 12 to 48 hours. Thread each piece of meat on two thin skewers, running them lengthwise through long edges of the meat. Sprinkle with salt and pepper, and grill over hot coals for 3 to 4 minutes on each side.

To serve, put about 1 tablespoon butter on each hot serving plate and cover with a mound of chello (recipe follows). Place a half egg shell containing a raw egg yolk on top of each mound and slip meat off skewers; arrange one piece of meat on each side of rice. Each guest will mix the egg yolk with the rice and butter on his plate. Makes 10 servings.

Chello

2 cups long-grained rice
3 quarts water
2 tablespoons salt
¾ cup (1½ cubes) butter, melted
2 tablespoons water

Soak rice in water to cover for 8 hours or overnight; drain. In a 4-quart pan, bring the 3 quarts water and salt to a rapid boil; add the rice and cook 12 minutes. Drain and rinse with warm water. Put ¼ cup of the melted butter in a large pan that has a cover; add 2 tablespoons water. Carefully spoon the rice into bottom of the pan, shaping it to make a high cone. With the handle of a wooden spoon, make a hole from the peak of the cone to the bottom. Pour remaining ½ cup melted butter over the rice, cover, and cook for 15 minutes over medium heat. Lower heat as far as possible, put a folded cloth between the pot and its cover, and cook 5 minutes more. Makes 10 servings.

Lela ka Kabab

2 medium-sized onions, sliced
2 tablespoons ground coriander or
    6 sprigs fresh coriander (Chinese
    parsley) plus 1 tablespoon
    ground coriander
2 teaspoons salt
2 teaspoons ground cumin
1½ teaspoons black pepper
1½ teaspoons ground cloves
1½ teaspoons ground cardamom
1 teaspoon ginger
1 teaspoon cinnamon
1 teaspoon poppy seeds
2 tablespoons *ghee* (see
    explanation at end of recipe) or
    2½ tablespoons melted butter
1 pint (2 cups) yogurt
6 tablespoons lemon juice
12 lamb steaks or round
    bone lamb chops

A spicy brown yogurt sauce serves as the marinade, basting sauce, and final meat sauce for these lamb steaks or chops. As you blend it, the quantity and varied fragrances of the eight spices may seem a little overwhelming, but don't be alarmed; this recipe from northern India turns out superbly seasoned.

Put the onions, coriander, salt, cumin, pepper, cloves, cardamom, ginger, cinnamon, poppy seeds, *ghee* (see below), yogurt, and lemon juice in a blender, and blend until smooth. (Or grind the onions and fresh coriander with a mortar and pestle, adding spices gradually; add to ghee, yogurt, lemon juice.) Place chops in shallow pan, spoon over half of the marinade, and let meat marinate, refrigerated, overnight; or let stand at room temperature 2 hours. Barbecue over glowing coals for about 40 minutes, or to desired doneness. Baste occasionally with sauce. You can heat the leftover marinade and serve it as a sauce over the meat. Makes 12 servings.

(*Ghee*, or purified fresh butter, is made by heating 1 pound butter in a 2 or 3-quart saucepan over very low heat for 1 hour, or until only butter fat remains. Strain through a cheesecloth. The flavor of ghee is quite different from that of butter, and it has a higher smoking point.)

Chelo Kebab

1½ pounds ground lamb
1 large onion, finely chopped
1 egg
½ teaspoon salt
¼ teaspoon pepper
2 tablespoons flour
1½ cups uncooked rice
4 tablespoons butter
    Paprika (optional)
3 tomatoes, halved
    Butter
    Salt
    Pepper

Chelo kebab is Persian for shish kebab. The dish includes ground lamb patties, tomatoes, and rice, so you need only a green salad and dessert to complete the menu.

Mix lamb, onion, egg, salt, pepper, and flour until smooth and creamy. Shape into oblong patties about 5 inches long, 1½ inches wide, and 1 inch thick; put aside.

Cook rice; sprinkle with cold water, shaking gently so kernels won't stick together. Drain 5 minutes. Melt butter in frying pan or shallow casserole (of a material which will stand direct heat) and pile the rice in it in a dome shape; sprinkle with paprika if desired. Place over low heat on grill or range for 10 minutes to dry rice. Meanwhile, cook lamb patties in a hinged wire broiler on barbecue for about 10 minutes on each side. Dot tomato halves with butter; salt and pepper and place on grill for about 8 minutes. Stack cooked lamb patties on rice dome; arrange tomatoes at bottom or on separate plate. Serve hot. Makes 4 to 6 servings.

👉 BASIC LAMB SAUCE 👈

¾ cup sherry
1 slice lemon
1 sprig parsley, minced
2 tablespoons olive oil
1 teaspoon grated onion
1 teaspoon salt
½ teaspoon pepper
1 sprig fresh rosemary, minced, or ½ teaspoon dried
    rosemary
1 sprig fresh oregano, minced, or ½ teaspoon dried
    oregano

This simple sauce adds flavor to any cut of lamb.

Mix ingredients and let stand for several hours to allow flavors to blend.

👉 *Pakistani Kebabs*

SKEWER-COOKED

1½ cups yogurt
1 small onion, chopped
1 clove garlic, crushed
1 teaspoon chopped fresh ginger (or ¼ teaspoon ground ginger)
1 small dried hot chile pepper, crushed
½ teaspoon cumin seed, crushed
½ teaspoon ground nutmeg
¼ teaspoon ground cardamom
¼ teaspoon salt
⅛ teaspoon ground cinnamon
⅛ teaspoon ground cloves
⅛ teaspoon coarsely ground black pepper
2 pounds boneless lean beef sirloin or lamb (shoulder or leg), cut in 1¼-inch cubes, or 5 whole chicken breasts, skinned, boned, and cut in bite-sized pieces

The spice mixture in the marinade for these kebabs is similar to a Pakistani curry. Use beef, lamb, or chicken—or some of each. If you plan to serve a combination of meats, put each kind on an individual skewer.

To make the marinade, combine the yogurt, onion, garlic, ginger, chile pepper, cumin, nutmeg, cardamom, salt, cinnamon, cloves, and black pepper. Stir meat into marinade (keep meats separate if you use several so you can skewer and cook them separately). Cover and refrigerate overnight.

Remove meat from marinade and string on skewers. Barbecue until browned and just tender—about 15 minutes for lamb and beef, 10 minutes for chicken. Makes about 6 servings.

👉 *Arni Souvlakia*

SKEWER-COOKED

3 pounds boneless leg or shoulder of lamb, cut into 1½-inch cubes
    Lemon juice
1 tablespoon salt
1 teaspoon pepper
1 teaspoon oregano
    Olive oil

Here's a skewer entrée idea from Greece. You might alternate the lamb cubes with small tomatoes and green pepper slices. Serve it with a rice pilaf.

Dip each lamb cube in lemon juice. Combine salt with pepper and oregano; sprinkle over the meat cubes. Thread meat on skewers. Broil over charcoal until the meat is brown but still juicy, brushing with olive oil two or three times. Makes 6 servings.

👉 Russian Shashlik

1 whole pomegranate, halved
1 lemon
½ cup chopped onion
¼ cup salad oil
½ teaspoon salt
   Dash pepper
2 pounds boneless
   lean lamb (leg or shoulder meat),
   cut in 1½-inch cubes
2 tablespoons chopped fresh onion
   Lemon slices
   Parsley

Pomegranate juice is the unusual ingredient in the tart, fruit-flavored marinade for these Russian-style lamb kebabs. Use an orange juicer to ream the pomegranate halves. Put the juicer in the sink to protect yourself from the spattering juice; wear an apron and rubber gloves. A complete Russian-American dinner menu featuring these kebabs might also include fried eggplant slices, rice pilaf, breadsticks, salad of sliced tomatoes, onions, and green pepper, sherbet for dessert.

Ream the pomegranate to make about ½ cup juice; then ream the lemon to make about 3 tablespoons juice. Combine with the ½ cup chopped onion, salad oil, salt, and pepper. Pour this marinade over lamb cubes. Stir gently to coat the meat with the marinade. Cover and refrigerate the meat several hours or overnight.

Then drain meat and string on skewers. Broil or barbecue about 5 minutes on each side, turning skewers once. Arrange the lamb on a serving platter and sprinkle with the 2 tablespoons chopped fresh onion. Garnish with lemon slices and parsley, if you wish. Makes 4 to 6 servings.

👉 Lamb Sosaties with Fruit

1½ cups cider vinegar
3 tablespoons apricot or pineapple jam
1½ tablespoons curry powder
1½ tablespoons salt
1½ tablespoons brown sugar, firmly
   packed
¼ teaspoon pepper
4 small dried hot chile peppers,
   crushed (use only 1 or 2 for
   a milder marinade)
2 medium-sized onions, sliced
3 cloves garlic, crushed
6 fresh lemon or orange leaves or
   2 dried bay leaves
4 pounds lean boneless lamb, cut in
   1½-inch cubes
   About 6 cups fruit: pitted apricots,
   pineapple chunks, cantaloupe
   wedges, and spiced crabapples

This method of cooking lamb kebabs, called *sosaties* (pronounced *so-sah-tees*), comes from South Africa, reportedly brought there by Malayan slaves in the seventeenth century. Today the sosaties, thin wooden skewers strung with small cubes of broiled marinated lamb, are popular as an entrée or snack. You might serve this peppery, sweet-sour meat with rice, a mixed green salad, crisp breadsticks, and an ice cream dessert.

In a pan, combine the vinegar, jam, curry powder, salt, brown sugar, pepper, chile peppers, onions, garlic, and lemon, orange, or bay leaves. Bring to a boil to blend the flavors; cool. Pour the marinade over the meat, cover, and refrigerate 8 to 10 hours or overnight, stirring occasionally. Just before you are ready to barbecue the meat, remove the pieces from the marinade and string on skewers. Place meat over medium-hot coals; grill, turning to brown all sides, a total of 15 to 20 minutes.

Strain the marinade, discarding the onions and leaves; bring liquid to a boil and simmer about 5 minutes to concentrate it. Baste the meat occasionally with the marinade. String the fruit on skewers and lay on top of the meat during the last 5 to 10 minutes cooking time. Baste the fruit and the meat with the marinade. The fruit will also help baste the meat and should be on the grill long enough to be thoroughly heated, but not too soft. Makes 8 to 12 servings.

Shish Koftesi

SKEWER-COOKED

2 pounds ground lean lamb or beef
1 cup finely minced onion
3 eggs
1 teaspoon whole thyme
2 teaspoons salt
1 clove garlic, puréed
  Olive oil

Ground meat is used for these Turkish kebabs. It is formed into sausage shapes for threading on the skewers.

Combine ground lamb or beef, onion, eggs, thyme, salt, and garlic; mix well. Chill. Form into sausage-shaped pieces about 3 inches long and 1 inch in diameter; thread lengthwise on skewers, two or three on each skewer. Brush with olive oil and grill over hot coals for 8 to 10 minutes, turning to brown all sides. Makes 6 to 8 servings.

Lamb Breast or Shanks

GRILL-COOKED

4 pounds lamb breast or 4 to
    6 pounds precooked shanks
1 cup orange juice
½ cup lemon juice
2 tablespoons sugar
½ cup chopped, crushed mint leaves
  About ¼ cup salad oil

Either lamb breast or lamb shanks may be barbecued with rewarding success. Lamb breast may be placed directly on the grill, but lamb shanks should be precooked until tender before grilling. To precook shanks, braise them in a small amount of water in a stout, covered pan.

Marinate the lamb breast or precooked shanks in a mixture of the orange juice, lemon juice, and sugar. For the last 2 hours, add the mint leaves to the marinade. Oil the meat well; place on grill over slow fire and cook until thoroughly browned. While cooking, baste with a sauce made of ½ cup of the marinade mixed with ¼ cup salad oil. Heat remainder of the marinade and serve as a sauce with the meat. Makes 4 to 6 servings.

Brochette de Rognons d'Agneau

SKEWER-COOKED

12 lamb kidneys
    Melted butter
    Sauce Bercy for Grilled Meats
      (see page 151)

Remove the fat and skin from the kidneys; split from the inside edge to within ½ inch of the opposite side. Open up and remove the white membrane from inside each kidney. Thread on skewers, using a big stitch to hold kidneys open. Brush with melted butter and grill over hot coals, basting with butter, for 3 to 4 minutes on each side. Be careful not to overcook them or they will be tough. Serve with Sauce Bercy for Grilled Meats (see page 151 of chapter on Sauces and Marinades). Makes 4 to 6 servings.

Game

In order to enjoy wild game, a hunter must first have a successful hunting trip. Then, in the flush of his success, he can turn chef and barbecue the roasts, steaks, and chops for a special occasion.

Today it's also possible to do big-game hunting right in the supermarket. Occasionally you may find a store selling buffalo meat—generally a brief, special sale in the fall. Buffalo cuts are similar to beef in tenderness and can be cooked in much the same way.

Recipes in this section are for those special occasions when you might have venison, buffalo, or bear cuts suitable for barbecuing. These meats are less marbled with fat than is beef; if young, tender, and properly aged, it doesn't need marinating. However, a marinade is recommended for older animals, and it adds flavor to any cut. When barbecued, game meat requires quick cooking and frequent basting with melted butter or a seasoned butter baste.

☞ *Grilled Venison Steak*

GRILL-COOKED

Have steaks cut thick—never less than 1 inch, preferably 1½ inches. Rub with garlic, if you wish; brush with olive oil or butter, and grill over hot coals 8 to 14 minutes, depending on the thickness of the steak and rareness desired. Connoisseurs prefer venison rare.

☞ *Ripple-Skewered Venison Steak Sandwiches*

SKEWER-COOKED

1¾ to 2-pound good quality venison
    steak (about 1½ inches thick)
1 cup rosé or dry white wine (or 1
    cup regular strength beef broth)
2 tablespoons lemon juice
1 tablespoon honey
1 teaspoon seasoned salt
    Few drops liquid hot-
      pepper seasoning
½ cup catsup
6 French rolls or frankfurter buns
    Chopped green onion

For best flavor and texture, serve the prime cuts of venison rare or medium-rare.

Cut steak across the grain into diagonal strips about ½ inch wide. Combine the wine. lemon juice, honey, seasoned salt, and hot-pepper seasoning. Pour over meat, and marinate several hours or overnight. Drain meat well, saving marinade. Thread steak strips onto skewers, ripple fashion; grill, close to the barbecue coals until rare or medium-rare. In the meantime, add the catsup to the remaining drained marinade; heat to boiling. Heat or toast 6 split and buttered French rolls or buns. Slip venison strips from skewers into rolls. Spoon hot sauce over meat and sprinkle generously with chopped green onion. Makes 6 servings.

THE CLASSIC BARBECUE ACCOMPANIMENTS

The pièce de résistance of your barbecue will, of course, be the meat that you lift piping hot from the grill, the spit, or the coals. The side dishes that you serve with this flavorsome main course should not in any way detract from it; yet they should be sufficient to satisfy the hearty appetites that go with outdoor dining. The classic favorites are surprisingly simple:

■ A cool crisp salad, deftly seasoned and skillfully tossed.

■ Hot-buttered French bread, with or without garlic.

■ Relishes for flavor contrast—all kinds of pickles and olives, green onions, radishes, celery, carrots, tomatoes, green pepper, raw cauliflower, cucumbers.

■ A wine of your choosing.

■ Gallons of coffee or tea, iced or hot.

■ For dessert, a tempting cheese tray, chilled ripe fruit (melon, papaya, pineapple, strawberries), ice cream, berry pie, or a big cake.

Venison Steak with Trio of Butters

GRILL-COOKED

Trim fat from good quality venison steaks or chops; brush with oil. Grill over charcoal until rare or medium-rare. Remove to hot platter; sprinkle lightly with seasoned salt and coarse black pepper. Serve with a selection of three seasoned butters, to be spooned onto steak.

Green Chile Butter

To make this seasoned butter, simply blend 1 tablespoon finely chopped canned green chile into ½ cup softened butter.

Sesame-Cheese Butter

Scatter 1 teaspoon sesame seeds on baking sheet; lightly brown in 400° oven. Blend toasted sesame seeds and 2 tablespoons crumbled Roquefort or shredded Cheddar cheese into ½ cup softened butter.

Vegetable Butter

Blend 2 tablespoons chopped onion and ¼ cup peeled and finely grated carrot into ½ cup softened butter.

Venison Roast with Cinnamon Apples

1 venison roast (about 5 lbs.),
    fat trimmed off
¼ pound salt pork
2 or 3 cloves garlic
½ cup sage honey
⅔ cup soy sauce
1 cup orange juice
⅔ cup catsup
1 cup wine vinegar
1 teaspoon salt
1 teaspoon dry mustard
1 teaspoon paprika
½ teaspoon liquid hot-pepper seasoning
    Cinnamon apples (recipe follows)
    Spiced peaches (optional)

This venison roast, to be cooked on your barbecue rotisserie, should be of even diameter and tied, if necessary. It's basted with a spicy barbecue sauce. You can prepare the cinnamon apple garnish while the meat roasts.

Wipe roast with a damp cloth or paper towel. Slice salt pork into thin strips, peel and sliver garlic cloves. Make slits in the roast and insert the salt pork and garlic slivers.

To make basting sauce, combine in a small pan the honey, soy sauce, orange juice, catsup, vinegar, salt, mustard, paprika, and liquid hot-pepper seasoning.

Insert a meat thermometer in the thickest part of the meat, but without touching the bone. Place the roast on the spit of your barbecue rotisserie. Brush the outside with the basting sauce. Roast over medium-hot coals until the meat thermometer registers 145° (rare) to 175° (well done). Baste occasionally with the sauce.

When the meat is cooked, remove it to a large platter and garnish with the cinnamon apples and spiced peach halves, if desired. Makes 8 servings.

Cinnamon Apples

1 package (4 oz.) hot
    cinnamon candies
1 cup water
12 small apples, peeled, but not cored

Combine cinnamon candies with water in a saucepan; simmer 10 minutes or until medium-thick syrup forms, stirring occasionally. Poach apples in the syrup until tender and rosy red, about 30 minutes. Drain on waxed paper and use to garnish the roast venison.

Saddle of Bear with Juniper

Bear meat can be cooked in the same ways as beef—steaks, roasts, pot roasts, stews, and hamburgers. But there are two limitations to this rule. One is that bear meat usually needs larding because it isn't marbled with fat like top-grade beef. The other—and it is important—is that although bear meat is delicious when cooked rare, there is danger of trichinosis if it is eaten this way. However, if the meat is frozen and held at −10° F. for 30 days or longer, the danger is eliminated. The marinades suggested for venison are equally good used with bear; but the flavor of the meat is so delicious that connoisseurs prefer it cooked without high seasoning or marinating.

If the bear is young, this is a prized dish: Roast the saddle (the double loin) over charcoal, as you would lamb, basting with 2 cups red wine to which you have added 1 sliced large onion and 2 teaspoons crushed juniper berries. Cook to the extent you like, but remember that if served rare, it must have been frozen first. Serve with Madeira sauce (recipe follows).

Madeira Sauce

Cook together ½ cup cubed ham, ½ cup chopped onions, ¼ cup sliced celery, ¼ cup sliced carrots, and 1 large chopped, peeled tomato in 2 tablespoons butter until vegetables are soft. Stir in 2 tablespoons flour; cook 2 minutes more. Add 2 cups beef broth, 1 bay leaf, 1 parsley sprig, and dash thyme. Simmer for 1 hour; strain. Add ¼ cup sherry; chill, and then skim off fat. This recipe makes about 2½ cups.

Buffalo in Tomato-Wine Sauce

2½ pounds buffalo stew meat
1 large onion, thinly sliced and separated into rings
⅓ cup olive oil or salad oil
1 cup Burgundy
1 cup regular strength beef broth
1 cup tomato purée
1 bay leaf
1 teaspoon salt
1 teaspoon monosodium glutamate
⅛ teaspoon pepper
Buttered noodles

Here is a way to use boneless buffalo stew meat. Searing the meat first over a barbecue fire gives it a pleasantly smoky flavor that enhances the tomato sauce. If you cook this stew entirely on the barbecue, use a heavy cast iron pan.

Sear buffalo on oiled barbecue grill over glowing coals, turning to brown on all sides. Remove, cool slightly, and cut into 1-inch cubes (if necessary). In pan, sauté onion in heated oil until soft; add meat. Blend in wine; cook quickly until wine is reduced by half. Stir in broth, tomato purée, bay leaf, salt, monosodium glutamate, and pepper. Cover and simmer slowly (over the charcoal or on your range) for about 1 hour, or until meat is very tender. Remove bay leaf. Serve over noodles. Makes 4 to 6 servings.

Buffalo Steak with Wild Rice Dressing

1 cup uncooked wild rice
2 cups water
1 teaspoon salt
1 pound ground buffalo, crumbled
½ cup finely chopped onion
½ pound mushrooms, sliced
2 tablespoons salad oil
3 cups (about 6 slices) cubed
    French bread, crusts removed
1 cup hot regular strength beef broth
¼ teaspoon rubbed sage
    Dash pepper
6 buffalo T-bone, club, or rib steaks
    Salt
    Herb butter, optional (recipe follows)

The steaks you barbecue for this elegant combination should be seared quickly on each side to seal in the plentiful juices. The wild rice dressing, which incorporates ground buffalo meat, can also be used to stuff game birds or to accompany other full-flavored meats.

Wash rice, cover with water, and add ½ teaspoon of the salt; bring to a boil, cover, lower heat, and cook for about 30 minutes or until tender. Drain well.

Meanwhile, brown ground buffalo, onion, and mushrooms in oil, stirring frequently. Place bread in bowl, cover with broth, and let stand until soft. Stir in rice, meat mixture, remaining ½ teaspoon salt, sage, and pepper. Place in a greased 2-quart casserole, cover, and bake in a moderate oven (350°) for 1 hour.

About 15 minutes before serving, quickly barbecue steaks to stage desired. Salt on both sides. Place on a hot platter and top, if you wish, with slices of herb butter; serve with dressing. Makes 6 servings.

Herb Butter

¾ cup (⅜ lb.) soft butter
½ cup finely chopped parsley
½ teaspoon lemon juice
¼ teaspoon salt
¼ teaspoon Worcestershire
⅛ teaspoon garlic powder
    Dash pepper
    Ice water

Blend soft butter with parsley, lemon juice, salt, Worcestershire, garlic powder, and pepper. Mold into a 16-inch roll on a sheet of moistened plastic film; wrap film tightly around roll, and chill in ice water until firm. Slice into ½-inch discs and then place atop hot steaks.

HALVED DUCKLINGS *get final browning over direct fire after being cooked in foil with an orange-celery stuffing.* *For the recipe—Orange Barbecued Duckling—turn to page 122.*

BARBECUE RECIPES
CHICKEN, TURKEY, DUCK

Tender, mild-flavored poultry is so versatile on the barbecue that it's a close second to beef in popularity. To be perfectly cooked, poultry should be lightly browned outside, tender and juicy within. A meat thermometer inserted into the thickest part of a turkey breast will register 175° when turkey is done. For smaller birds, a leg joint will move easily when done and the fleshy part of the drumstick will feel soft.

For grill cooking, choose small birds(such as Cornish game hens) split down the back and opened flat; broiler-fryer chickens cut in halves, quarters, or pieces; halved or quartered ducklings; or turkey pieces, such as breasts, drumsticks, wings.

Goose and duck (particularly domestic varieties) tend to be quite a bit fatter than other poultry. When barbecuing either, puncture the skin often with a fork to release fat. (You can save the drippings for sauce or gravy by placing a shallow drip pan made of foil under the cooking bird.) The outside will be pleasantly crusted and the inside moist

👉 Barbecued Breast of Chicken

8 very large chicken breasts
    (almost ½ lb. *each*), split
About ¾ cup melted butter
About 1½ cups flour
Salt
Pepper
About ¼ cup melted butter

This special method of cooking chicken breasts results in tender meat that's juicy and delicious. Success depends on cooking it quickly over hot coals; timing is important.

Rinse and dry chicken breasts thoroughly. Dip pieces, one at a time, into about ¾ cup melted butter, then shake in a paper bag with flour, seasoned with salt and pepper, to coat thoroughly. Place pieces on a greased grill 6 to 12 inches above hot coals (grill temperature should be about 375°). Cook 10 to 12 minutes on each side. Baste during cooking with about ¼ cup melted butter. Serve immediately. Makes 8 servings.

👉 Spread Eagle Chicken

An unusual way to grill a whole chicken is to cut through the length of its back and open the bird out flat.

Allow a 2½-pound broiler-fryer for each 2 or 3 servings. Have your meatman cut through the length of the back of each chicken. Open each chicken out flat, breaking the breastbone so chicken stays flat. Sprinkle each with salt and pepper. Grill over medium-hot coals about 6 inches from heat source for about 45 minutes or until meat is tender when pierced with the tip of a sharp knife; turn occasionally and baste frequently with melted butter. Serve hot or cold. Cut in halves or pieces to serve.

👉 Herbed Chicken

1 cup sherry
½ cup salad oil
1 large onion, grated, or 1 tablespoon
    minced dried onions
1 tablespoon Worcestershire
1 teaspoon soy sauce
1 teaspoon lemon juice
1 teaspoon powdered garlic
1 teaspoon whole thyme
1 teaspoon whole oregano
1 teaspoon whole rosemary
1 teaspoon whole marjoram
⅛ teaspoon monosodium glutamate
2 broiler-fryer chickens (about 2½
    lbs. *each*), cut into quarters or
    serving-sized pieces

This barbecue baste for chicken is mild, with a hint of Japanese teriyaki flavor.

Several hours before barbecuing, mix together thoroughly the sherry, salad oil, onion, Worcestershire, soy sauce, lemon juice, garlic, thyme, oregano, rosemary, marjoram, and monosodium glutamate. About 1 hour before barbecuing, pour sauce over chicken pieces. Grill chicken over low coals about 40 minutes or until tender. Turn frequently and brush with remaining sauce. Makes 8 servings.

If using halves or quarters, break the hip, knee, and wing joints to keep the bird flat during grilling. Shape the wings akimbo style, bringing the wing tips onto the cut side. Rinse the chicken; pat dry.

Brush the chicken pieces with melted fat or basting sauce. Place the chicken on a greased grill, skin side up, about 6 to 12 inches above coals giving medium heat.

Cook slowly until tender, turning with tongs and basting frequently. Total time will be about 40 minutes. When done, drumstick meat is soft.

Cook chicken breasts quickly over hotter coals (grill temperature should be about 375°). They will be tender after 10 to 12 minutes on each side.

Baste frequently.

👉 *Lemon-Basted Chicken with Peaches*

GRILL-COOKED

2 small broiler-fryer chickens
   (about 2 to 2½ lbs. *each*),
   cut in half lengthwise
⅓ cup lemon juice
2 tablespoons honey
1 teaspoon salt
6 tablespoons melted butter
4 large freestone peaches or nectarines
   Honey (optional)

Brush the fruit immediately after peeling with the lemon baste to prevent it from darkening. Grill the fruit just long enough to heat it through; two large spoons make the pieces easier to turn without mashing.

Place chickens, cut side up, in a single layer in a pan. Mix together lemon juice, honey, and salt. Pour evenly over chicken; chill, covered, for about an hour. Lift chicken from marinade, draining off juices. Pour marinade into melted butter. Brush chicken with this mixture and place, cut side down, on a grill about 6 inches above medium-hot coals. Allow about 45 minutes cooking time, turning occasionally and brushing with marinade.

Meanwhile, peel, cut in half and pit the peaches or nectarines. Coat with the chicken basting mixture. About 10 minutes before the chicken is done, place fruit, flat side down, on the grill and let heat for 3 or 4 minutes. Turn (use 2 large spoons) onto rounded side and cook about 5 minutes more, brushing with the baste. Serve fruit with chicken. (You can drizzle a little honey over the fruit just before serving if it is not especially sweet.) Makes 4 servings.

Pakistani Barbecued Chicken

GRILL-COOKED

Use whole chicken legs and thighs for this quick-cooking chicken entrée—and have the rest of your dinner almost ready before barbecuing the chicken.

For 6 servings, buy 6 whole legs and thighs. With your fingers and a sharp knife, remove skin from each piece and discard. Sprinkle chicken evenly with 1 teaspoon salt, 1½ teaspoons chile powder, and 3 tablespoons lemon juice. Let stand about 30 minutes.

Barbecue until just tender, yet still moist, about 20 minutes. Baste occasionally with ¼ cup melted butter or margarine and turn pieces after about 10 minutes.

Barbecued Chicken, Spanish Style

GRILL-COOKED

1 large broiler-fryer chicken (3 to 3½ lbs.), quartered
½ cup (¼ lb.) butter or margarine
1 clove garlic, minced or mashed
¾ teaspoon salt
¾ teaspoon savory
½ teaspoon paprika
⅛ teaspoon cinnamon
⅛ teaspoon crushed tarragon
Rice with sausage (recipe follows)

Combining barbecued chicken quarters with a colorful rice mixture, this dish is a simple adaptation of the Spanish *arroz con pollo*.

Wash chicken quarters in cool water; pat dry with paper towels. Melt butter with garlic, salt, savory, paprika, cinnamon, and tarragon. Place chicken quarters on barbecue grill over slowly burning coals; brush frequently with butter mixture, turning occasionally, until chicken is tender and well browned, 40 to 50 minutes. Reserve any remaining butter mixture. Serve chicken atop hot rice-sausage mixture in warm individual casseroles or on a shallow platter. Makes 4 servings.

Rice with Sausage

2 Italian-style pork sausages (2½ to 3 oz. each) cut into ¼-inch slices
2 medium-sized onions, finely chopped
3 cups cooked rice
1 cup frozen peas, thawed
1 tomato, peeled, seeded, and coarsely chopped

Brown pork sausage slices in a frying pan over medium heat. Add onions, and cook until soft and golden. Stir in rice, peas, and tomato. Cover and simmer until thoroughly heated, about 10 minutes; gently blend in any butter mixture reserved after basting the chicken.

☞ Spicy Yogurt Chicken

2 broiler-fryer chickens (2 to
  3 lbs. *each*)
1 pint (2 cups) plain yogurt
1 clove garlic, crushed
1 teaspoon ground ginger
1 teaspoon chile powder
1 teaspoon cardamom
½ teaspoon ground cloves
½ teaspoon ground cinnamon
2 teaspoons salt
4 bay leaves, ground or crushed

This unusual marinade and baste for chicken was inspired by the way meats are seasoned in East Indian countries. Use it for grilled chicken quarters or spit-roasted whole chickens.

To grill the chickens, cut in quarters and twist wings enough so each wing tip is lock around the back side of its quarter. For spit roasting, truss whole birds; tie or skewer wing tips over breasts, fasten neck skin to backs with a skewer, and tie drumsticks to tails. Combine yogurt with all seasonings. Put chickens in bowl or baking dish; cover with yogurt mixture. Marinate chickens at least 4 hours, or overnight. Remove from marinade and place on greased grill, skin side up. Cook slowly until tender, turning and basting with marinade; or put whole birds on spit and baste as they turn and roast. Cook until meat is tender when pierced. Makes 8 servings.

☞ Ranch-Style Chicken

½ cup white apple vinegar
⅓ cup salad oil
1½ teaspoons Worcestershire
½ teaspoon minced onion
1 clove garlic, minced
3 teaspoons salt
1 teaspoon paprika
1½ teaspoons tomato paste
6 to 8 drops liquid hot-
  pepper seasoning
¼ teaspoon dry mustard
3 broiler-fryer chickens, cut up
  Melted butter

If possible, make the basting sauce for this chicken at least twenty-four hours ahead to blend flavors.

Make the basting sauce by combining the vinegar, salad oil, Worcestershire, onion, garlic, salt, paprika, tomato paste, liquid hot-pepper seasoning, and dry mustard. Brush chicken pieces with melted butter and place over hot coals for about 5 minutes to sear; then turn. Brush chicken with sauce and turn every 3 to 5 minutes, basting with sauce at each turn. Time required is about 35 minutes. Makes 6 servings.

☞ Smoked Chicken with Brandy Baste

Salt
Pepper
2 broiler-fryer chickens, split
½ cup melted butter
¼ cup lemon juice
¼ cup brandy
¼ cup brown sugar
1 cup fresh (or drained canned)
  dark sweet cherries
12 ripe fresh apricot halves

Chicken, cherries, and apricots are brushed with brandy baste and smoked for this dinner entrée.

Salt and pepper chickens. Set on grill over direct heat; cover grill and cook about 40 minutes, basting occasionally with mixture of the butter, lemon juice, brandy, and brown sugar. In a shallow pan fashioned of foil, place cherries; in another pan, put apricot halves, cut side up. Brush fruits with basting sauce. Cook and smoke over direct heat during last 10 minutes that chickens cook. Serve fruit alongside chicken. Makes 4 servings.

👉 HOW TO SPIT ROAST CHICKEN 👈

Use a barbecue rotisserie to roast whole or split broiler-fryer or roasting chickens (stuffed or unstuffed). You can spit roast at one time as many chickens as the length of the spit allows.

Rub the cavity or cut side of the chicken lightly with salt. Spoon in stuffing and close cavity by placing skewers across body opening; lace shut with cord if necessary.

For a whole bird, tie or skewer the wing tips over the breast; fasten the neck skin to the back with a skewer. Push the spit through the bird from the tail end of the bird toward the front so that the point of the spit emerges between the branches of the wishbone. Anchor the chicken to the spit with crossed drumsticks and tail tied together. To spit roast halves, pierce them with the spit through the thigh meat, then the breast meat; anchor. Be sure the spit prongs are firmly in place and that the bird is balanced on the spit.

Brush the chicken with fat or oil. No further basting is necessary. If you wish, baste the chicken with a seasoned basting sauce several times during the last 20 to 30 minutes of cooking.

Place the chicken over glowing coals; spit-level temperature should be about 400°. Time required will be approximately the same as for oven roasting. When done, the breast meat near the wing joint will be fork-tender; the drumstick meat will be soft.

👉 *Smoke-Glazed Chicken*

SMOKE-COOKED

1 fresh broiler-fryer chicken (2 to 3 lbs.)
2 slices hickory-smoked bacon

Cook this chicken in a smoke oven, or in a regular barbecue with any sort of hood over the top to trap the smoke but keep it moving ever so slowly through the "chimney." The important thing is to get the chicken well browned and thoroughly cooked.

Remove the giblets, rinse and dry chicken, and place in a smoke oven. Set a pan of hot coals about 8 inches below the fryer. Lay the 2 strips of good quality hickory-smoked bacon on top of the fryer. To make smoke, occasionally lay on the coals some small pieces of green spicy wood, preferably green apple wood, but green oak or grape is also good.

As the bacon melts, it absorbs smoke from the green wood and forms a glaze on the fryer. As soon as the chicken is rich brown on one side, turn it over and change the bacon again to the top side. About 1¼ hours in a light smoke, with the oven almost closed, produces a flavor quite distinct. (Salt and spices have purposely been omitted because very little of either is needed.) Makes 2 to 4 servings.

Orange-Baked Chicken

COAL-COOKED

1 broiler-fryer chicken (2 to
    3 lbs.), cut up
  Salt
  Pepper
4 tablespoons frozen concentrated
    orange juice, thawed
4 tablespoons butter

Wrap this chicken in foil and place the packets right on the hot coals to cook; then cover with more coals. You might also cook skewered vegetables and bake potatoes in the coals.

Divide chicken pieces into 4 servings. Sprinkle each serving with salt and pepper, and place it on a piece of heavy duty foil. Pour 1 tablespoon concentrated orange juice over each serving; dot each with 1 tablespoon butter. Wrap foil around each serving of chicken, sealing edges tightly. Bake in hot coals about 1 hour, or until tender. Makes 4 servings.

Indonesian Chicken Appetizers

SKEWER-COOKED

2 whole chicken breasts
1 package (8 oz.) broken
    walnuts (2 cups)
⅔ cup lime juice
2 tablespoons regular strength
    chicken broth
2 green onions, cut up
2 small cloves garlic, mashed
½ teaspoon salt
1 cup yogurt or commercial sour cream

This chicken appetizer is an adaptation of a classic Indonesian entrée. You can do all of the advance preparations early in the day and refrigerate the meat until it's time for you or your guests to cook the appetizers.

Cut the uncooked chicken from the bones into bite-sized pieces and set aside. Combine the nuts, lime juice, chicken stock, onions, garlic, and salt in an electric blender and whirl until the nuts are quite fine. Mix ½ cup of this nut mixture with the yogurt or sour cream to serve as a dip with the chicken; chill thoroughly.

  Gently coat the pieces of chicken with the remaining nut mixture and refrigerate for 2 to 3 hours. Then string the coated chicken pieces on skewers and refrigerate until you are ready to cook the meat. Grill the chicken about 5 inches from the source of heat for 5 to 7 minutes, turning once. Serve with the yogurt or the sour cream mixture.

Pakistani Kebabs

The spice mixture in the marinade for these kebabs is similar to a Pakistani curry. Use beef, lamb, or chicken—or some of each. If you plan to serve a combination of meats, put each kind on a separate skewer.

Purchase 2 pounds boneless lean beef sirloin or lamb (shoulder or leg) cut in 1¼-inch cubes, or 5 whole chicken breasts, skinned, boned, and cut in bite-sized pieces.

For the marinade, combine 1½ cups yogurt with 1 small chopped onion; 1 clove crushed garlic; 1 teaspoon chopped fresh ginger (or ¼ teaspoon ground ginger); 1 small dried hot chile pepper, crushed; ½ teaspoon cumin seed, crushed; ½ teaspoon nutmeg; ¼ teaspoon *each* ground cardamom and salt; and ⅛ teaspoon *each* ground cinnamon, ground cloves, and coarsely ground black pepper. Stir meat into marinade (keep meats separate if you use several so you can skewer and cook them separately). Cover and refrigerate overnight.

Remove from marinade and string meat on skewers. Barbecue until browned and just tender—about 15 minutes for lamb and beef, 10 minutes for chicken. Makes about 6 servings.

BASIC CHICKEN BASTES

The mild flavor of chicken adapts well to many different marinades, bastes, and sauces. Here are basting sauces designed to complement barbecued chicken. Each mixture can be brushed on the chicken before barbecuing (unless other directions are given); brush chicken frequently with the baste while cooking and spoon any remaining baste over the cooked chicken just before serving. Each is enough for 1 broiler-fryer chicken.

Lemon-Herb Butter Baste. To ½ cup (¼ lb.) butter, add 1 tablespoon lemon juice, ¼ teaspoon dried fines herbes, and ¼ teaspoon dried whole chervil.

Brown Sugar-Tarragon Vinegar Baste. Combine in a pan 1 cup firmly packed brown sugar, ½ cup tarragon vinegar, and 2 tablespoons butter; bring to a boil just to blend flavors.

Herb Baste. Melt together ¼ cup butter, dash dried whole savory, dash dried whole rosemary, and dash dried whole thyme.

Golden Glaze Baste. Combine ¼ cup melted butter, 3 tablespoons lemon juice, ½ teaspoon paprika, and ¼ teaspoon liquid hot-pepper seasoning.

Teriyaki Baste. Combine and heat together 1 cup soy sauce, ½ cup sugar, ¼ cup salad oil, 2 teaspoons grated fresh ginger, 1 clove crushed garlic (optional), and 1 teaspoon monosodium glutamate. Baste chicken during last 30 minutes of cooking.

French Dressing Baste. Baste chicken during last 30 minutes of cooking with oil-and-vinegar salad dressing.

Mustard-Honey Baste. Mix ½ cup honey, ¼ cup prepared mustard, 2 tablespoons lemon juice, and 1 teaspoon salt. Baste chicken during last 10 to 15 minutes cooking time.

Spiced Currant Baste. Combine in a pan 1 jar (10 to 12 oz.) currant jelly, 2 tablespoons lemon juice, 1 tablespoon Worcestershire, 1 teaspoon ground allspice, dash salt, dash pepper; bring to a boil to blend flavors. Baste chicken during last 10 to 15 minutes cooking time.

Chicken Liver Kebabs

18 chicken livers
  Salt and pepper
 6 slices bacon
  Mushrooms
  Olive oil
  Fresh bread crumbs
  Butter, melted
  Lemon juice
  Parsley

If you like chicken livers, here's an easy and delicious way to skewer-cook them.

Wash chicken livers, and dry well with clean cloth. Sprinkle with salt and pepper. Cut each liver in half. Broil bacon slices, one minute to each side, and cut each slice into 6 pieces.

Take skewers, run one through center of liver slice, a piece of bacon, a mushroom, until all skewers are filled. Roll in olive oil, dip in fresh bread crumbs, and grill over hot coals.

Arrange skewers on a hot dish, and over them pour melted butter to which lemon juice and chopped parsley have been added. Makes 6 servings.

Buttery Cornish Hens

 4 frozen Rock Cornish game hens
    (12 oz. to 1 lb. *each*), thawed
  Salt and pepper
 · Herb butter (recipe follows)
 2 tablespoons lemon juice
 ¼ cup warm, strained apricot jam
  Watercress sprigs and fresh
    apricot halves, for garnish

Herb butter, used both inside and outside, blends with a glistening apricot glaze to flavor these juicy Cornish hens. They should be cooked on a barbecue that can be covered; the surface of the grill should be large enough for heat to circulate around the pan holding the hens.

Wash Cornish hens, pat dry, inside and out, with paper towels. Sprinkle skin and cavities lightly with salt and pepper. Place about 1 tablespoon of the herb butter in large cavity of each; fasten cavities with wooden picks or small metal skewers. Tie legs together.

Melt remaining herb butter with lemon juice. Place hens, breasts up, on a double thickness of heavy foil; turn up a 1-inch rim on all 4 sides to form a shallow pan. Place on grill over glowing coals. Cover barbecue, adjust drafts to keep fire burning slowly, and cook, basting occasionally with herb butter, for 45 minutes to 1 hour or until tender and golden brown.

When almost done, brush hens evenly with warm apricot jam; cover again and continue cooking until nicely glazed. Serve on wooden board or platter, garnished with watercress and apricots. Makes 4 servings.

Herb Butter

To make herb butter, blend ½ cup (¼ lb.) soft butter or margarine with 2 tablespoons chopped chives (fresh or freeze-dried) and ¼ teaspoon rosemary, crushed.

HOW TO BARBECUE CORNISH GAME HENS

Spit Roasting. Season the cavity of each bird with salt and pepper. Skewer shut the neck and abdominal openings.

Run the spit diagonally through the breastbone to the backbone just above the tail and secure with the holding prongs. Space the birds about an inch apart.

Place the spit 6 inches above (or below) the heat source. Baste frequently with melted butter, about ¼ cup for 2 birds.

Roast until leg joint moves easily, about 45 minutes.

Grilling. Cut the birds in half along the backbone and center of breast (scissors work well here), or just split along the backbone and lay out flat. Tuck the wing tips behind the shoulders.

Season with salt and pepper and brush with melted butter (seasoned if you wish), about 2 tablespoons for each bird.

Turkey Parts in Blue Cheese Sauce

SMOKE-COOKED

Either turkey legs and thighs or turkey breasts are juicy and tender when cooked in a foil pan on a covered barbecue. A thick blue cheese sauce coats the meat and absorbs a mild smoke flavor.

Buy a split turkey breast (half breast of about a 14-lb. turkey), or a pair of turkey legs and thighs, or buy a whole turkey and have it cut up and freeze the parts you don't barbecue. Shape a pan of double-thick heavy foil to just fit around the turkey parts, securing the corners to prevent sauce from leaking out (or use a foil cake pan). Cover the bottom of the pan with some of the blue cheese sauce. Arrange turkey in the pan, then spread the rest of the sauce over the top to coat the meat completely. Set pan in a hooded barbecue. Cover barbecue and cook slowly for about 1 hour and 45 minutes, or until tender. No basting is needed. Serve with some of the juices collected in the foil pan. Makes about 4 servings.

Blue Cheese Sauce

1 cup (½ pt.) cottage cheese
2 ounces blue cheese
¼ cup chopped parsley
¼ cup butter or margarine
½ teaspoon salt
1 small clove garlic, crushed

Combine in an electric blender the cottage cheese, blue cheese, parsley, butter or margarine, salt, and garlic. Whirl until smooth. You can do this ahead; refrigerate until needed.

Brush the inside of the bird with basting sauce or sprinkle lightly with salt. It is best to cook the stuffing separately.

Start the barbecue fire early to have briquets burning evenly for a low, steady heat. Arrange the well ignited briquets at the back of the firebox.

Place a drip pan in front of the coals. You can make your own disposable drip pan by folding a double thickness of 18-inch heavy foil into a pan shape.

Insert the spit rod into the center of the neck skin; run it through the body cavity parallel to the backbone. Bring the rod out just above the tail. Insert the spit fork into the breast and the other fork into the tail. Tighten the screws with pliers.

Tie twine around the turkey to hold the wings close to the body. Tie the tail and legs together in the back of the spit so that the thighs are not pressed against the body and the dark meat will cook faster.

Check the turkey for balance by rotating the spit between the palms of the hands. A counterweight attached to the spit will help to keep the bird balanced and reduce wear on the motor.

Insert the thermometer into the thickest portion of the thigh, being careful that it does not touch a bone.

Attach the spit and brush the turkey with melted butter or salad oil. Start the motor as directed by the barbecue manufacturer.

Baste occasionally, adding drippings from the pan to the basting mixture while barbecuing. If you use a barbecue sauce, brush it on the bird only during the last 30 to 40 minutes of cooking.

Turkey is done when thermometer in the thigh registers 185°. Time required will be approximately the same as for oven roasting.

A boned turkey roll or a turkey breast, which has been boned and tied as a roast, can be barbecued on a spit or in a covered smoke cooker. Thaw the frozen roll first by letting it stand at room temperature overnight.

To cook on a spit, place over medium coals and cook about 37 minutes per pound. To cook in a smoke cooker, place meat on grill over low coals (without smoke chips); put cover on cooker and make draft openings small to keep temperature consistently low. Allow about 35 minutes per pound. It is best to use a roasting thermometer; insert it in the thickest part of the roast before barbecuing and cook until it reaches a temperature of 170° to 175°.

🕊 *Teriyaki Turkey Roll*

SMOKE-COOKED

1 cup soy sauce
1 cup sherry
½ cup honey
6 cloves garlic, peeled and halved
¼ cup grated fresh ginger
1 turkey roll (about 3 lbs.)

This turkey roll is marinated in a teriyaki sauce and roasted in a covered barbecue. The meat takes on a shiny dark surface and a rich smoke-teriyaki flavor. Plan to start marinating the turkey roll twenty-four hours before you smoke-cook it.

Combine the soy sauce, sherry, honey, garlic, and fresh ginger. Pour this marinade over the turkey roll; cover and marinate for 24 hours, turning the meat 3 or 4 times.

Start the fire 30 minutes to an hour before you start cooking. Follow directions given by the manufacturer of your barbecue for starting the fire and maintaining low even heat. Insert a meat thermometer into the center of the turkey roll and place in the center of the grill. Close the lid of the barbecue. Baste the meat with the marinade 2 or 3 times while cooking. You may want to use a grill thermometer if your barbecue doesn't have one; keep the heat regulated between 300° and 350°. Cook for about 2 hours, or until meat thermometer registers about 185°. Makes 6 servings.

Chile-Barbecued Turkey Drumsticks

Chile marinade (recipe follows)
4 turkey drumsticks (4½ to 5 lbs.)
½ cup commercial sour cream

You barbecue these turkey drumsticks (either fresh, or frozen and thawed) with a chile-flavored baste. Add sour cream later to form a tangy sauce. Use either a covered or uncovered barbecue; uncovered, the cooking time will be longer.

Pour chile marinade over turkey drumsticks in a shallow bowl. Cover and chill for about 1 hour, turning once. Drain; reserve marinade; heat in a small pan.

Place drumsticks on grill over slowly burning coals; cover loosely with a tent of heavy foil, or use barbecue cover, and cook, turning and basting occasionally with warm chile marinade, until turkey is tender and well browned, about 2 hours (if you use a covered barbecue, you can expect cooking time to be less, about 1½ hours). Adjust grill height or drafts on barbecue to prevent turkey from browning too quickly. Near end of the cooking period, insert a meat thermometer into the thickest part of one of the drumsticks; continue cooking until temperature reaches 185°.

When turkey is nearly done, beat ¼ cup of the remaining chile marinade gradually into sour cream until blended. Heat sour cream mixture slowly just until heated through (do not boil). Serve sauce separately to spoon over turkey. Makes 4 servings.

Chile Marinade

1 cup salad oil
½ cup dry red wine
2 tablespoons brown sugar
2 teaspoons chile powder
¾ teaspoon seasoned salt
¾ teaspoon whole oregano
¼ teaspoon garlic powder
¼ teaspoon seasoned pepper

Combine salad oil, red wine, brown sugar, chile powder, salt, oregano, garlic powder and pepper; shake together in jar or whirl in blender to combine.

Smoky Turkey with Fruit Dressing

1 hen turkey (12 lbs.)
½ cup soy sauce
¼ cup honey
¼ cup sherry
1 tablespoon grated fresh ginger root
3 cloves garlic

Fruit Stuffing

4 tart apples, quartered (unpeeled)
½ cup water
¼ cup brown sugar
1 cup cooked, pitted dried prunes
1½ cups cooked, mixed dried fruits
      (apricots, pears, peaches)
¼ teaspoon ground cinnamon
¼ teaspoon ground nutmeg
¼ teaspoon ground mace
½ cup dry sherry

For an unusual way to prepare turkey, marinate it, stuff it with a fruit dressing, and then smoke it.

Marinate the turkey overnight in a mixture of the soy, honey, sherry, ginger, and garlic.

To make the stuffing, simmer apples in water and brown sugar until barely tender. Add prunes, mixed fruits, cinnamon, nutmeg, mace, and sherry. Stuff turkey lightly, and skewer openings closed. Truss with string, and make a double loop at the drumstick end so that you can hang the bird from a hook.

Build a small fire in a smoke oven, using charcoal and fruitwood, and place bird on hook in chimney. Smoke-cook at a temperature between 300° and 350° until the meat thermometer registers 180°, or approximately 5 to 5½ hours for a 12-pound bird. (Figure about 25 per cent longer than for oven roasting at 325°.)

HOW TO SMOKE ROAST TURKEY

Turkey is one of the meats most enhanced by smoke flavor, and smoking gives you an exceptionally well-flavored and beautifully browned turkey. Should you decide to vary a holiday menu by serving smoked turkey, it will free the kitchen and oven for all the other cooking that must be done on the big day.

You will need a barbecue with a cover, but if your barbecue is of the brazier type, construct a foil dome to cover it as directed in the chapter on smoke cooking. Such a dome will accommodate the largest turkey you can buy. A drip pan is needed, and this can also be made of foil.

Arrange 20 briquets on each side of the drip pan (if you pre-soaked briquets to start the fire, place five of them on the bottom of each charcoal pile).

Start the two charcoal piles at the same time, 30 to 45 minutes before you plan to start the turkey (the briquets should burn down to an even gray color).

Prepare and stuff the turkey exactly as you would for oven roasting. Cooking time will be about the same as for oven roasting, but because the heat is more difficult to control, it is especially helpful to use a meat thermometer for judging how fast the turkey is cooking and

when it is done. Set the turkey on the grill with a strip of foil about 5 inches wide directly under its back and with the turkey centered over drip pan.

Place cover on barbecue; if using a foil hood, open two small draft holes on opposite sides of the hood by unfolding seams to about 1 inch above the base ring—this will be your means of regulating the heat of the oven as your turkey roasts. Open the drafts wider to raise the heat, close them more to slow the heat. At the end of each hour, add six or eight briquets to each side.

You'll also find it worthwhile to add wood chips or green wood to your fire to create smoke for flavor. Use any of the prepared wood chips, shavings, or sawdust (usually available wherever briquets are sold). Soak them in water at least 30 minutes before using. Or you can use green woods such as hickory, oak, or apple. Don't use soft woods that give off resinous smoke, such as pine.

After you have a bed of glowing charcoal, simply top it with a thin layer of the green wood or handfuls of the soaked dry wood. For subtle smoke flavor, add it 1 to 2 hours before the turkey is done; for more pronounced flavor, use it during the entire roasting time.

👉 *Duckling with Orange Baste*

SPIT-ROASTED

1 duckling (4 to 5 lbs.)
½ cup orange juice
¼ cup soy sauce
1 teaspoon honey
½ teaspoon monosodium glutamate
⅛ teaspoon pepper

This orange baste enhances the flavor of duckling whether it's barbecued or oven-roasted.

Truss duckling compactly and spit it from just in front of the tail (through the bone), diagonally to a point near the apex of the wishbone (again through the bone). Spit-roast the duckling 1½ to 2 hours over a medium to low barbecue fire. Baste frequently with orange sauce:

To make sauce, combine orange juice, soy sauce, honey, monosodium glutamate, and pepper. Heat on the side of the grill and brush it warm on the bird. Using poultry shears, cut duckling into quarters to serve. Makes 4 servings.

👉 *Duckling with Raisin Sauce*

SMOKE-COOKED

4½ to 5-pound duckling
2 stalks celery, coarsely sliced (include tops)
3 sprigs parsley
½ lemon, thinly sliced
4 teaspoons flour
¼ teaspoon pepper
2 tablespoons soy sauce
2 cups dry white wine (or 1 cup *each* wine and chicken broth)
1 bay leaf
¾ cup golden raisins

This elegant barbecued duck with a wine and golden raisin sauce will serve 2 or 3 people. Brown the duck first to remove most of the fat; then wrap it in foil to finish cooking.

Place a foil pan about the same size as the duckling on firebed of a barbecue that has a cover; arrange charcoal around pan, ignite, and let burn until coals are glowing. Wash duckling in cool water; dry with paper towels. Place celery, parsley, and lemon in large cavity; close cavity with wooden picks or small metal skewers, and tie legs together.

Place duckling, breast up, on grill over foil drip pan; cover barbecue, adjust drafts to keep fire burning slowly, and cook for about 1½ hours or until duckling is well browned. Remove duckling, and discard drip pan and fat; spread coals into center.

Center duckling on a double thickness of heavy foil large enough to completely enclose it; turn sides up slightly while you add the remaining ingredients.

Blend flour, pepper, and soy sauce; stir in wine. Pour wine mixture over duckling. Top with bay leaf and raisins. Enclose duckling in foil, sealing top and ends.

Return foil-wrapped duckling to barbecue, adding more charcoal if needed. Cover barbecue again, and continue cooking over slowly burning coals for 1 hour longer. To serve, unwrap carefully and place duckling on a warm platter or serving board; remove celery, parsley, and lemon from cavity and discard. Pour raisin sauce from foil and serve separately to spoon over duckling. Makes 2 or 3 servings.

👉 *Orange-Barbecued Duckling*

A veteran outdoor chef devised this method of cooking duck outdoors; the recipe is a combination of cooking in foil and browning over the fire.

Orange-Celery Stuffing

For each duckling, select 1 large, thin-skinned orange. Slice off and discard both ends of the orange; with a thin sharp knife, cut orange in thin slices. Set aside about half the slices to use on outside of duckling. Chop the rest of the orange and put into a bowl. Slice and add 3 large stalks celery, 1 small onion, thinly sliced, and ¼ teaspoon thyme. Mix well. Makes enough for 1 large domestic duck.

To Cook the Duckling

Remove giblets. (If you wish, cook giblets and add the cooking stock and giblets to the gravy.) Wash duckling and dry well. Sprinkle about 1 teaspoon salt and ⅛ teaspoon pepper inside cavities. Fill body cavity with orange stuffing (if any is left over, put into a saucepan to use later). Fold neck skin back, but do not truss bird with pins or skewers that might puncture the foil. Arrange the orange slices all over the outside skin.

Have ready a double-thick sheet of heavy foil; if necessary, put two pieces together by folding edges over twice (drugstore fold). Wrap the bird and seal the foil tightly—it is important to contain all the cooking juices. Put on grill over a fairly hot fire. Turn over every 10 minutes; cook about 1 hour to 1 hour 20 minutes.

Remove foil package to a utility pan and cool slightly. Unwrap, saving all the juices. Discard foil and orange on outside of duckling. Spoon stuffing into the saucepan. With poultry scissors, cut duckling in half and put back onto the grill. Cook, turning as needed, until the skin is crisp and brown and the duckling fully tender. Cook the celery mixture a few minutes more, if needed; season to taste with butter and salt and pepper, and serve with the duck. Each duckling makes about 2 servings.

Orange Gravy

Pour the drippings collected in the utility pan into a small pan; skim off most of the fat. Add giblet stock or canned chicken broth to make about 1½ cups. Blend 2 tablespoons instant type all-purpose flour with 2 tablespoons sherry or water; stir into drippings. Add chopped cooked giblets, if you wish. Cook, stirring until thickened. Salt and pepper to taste.

👉 HOW TO BARBECUE WILD DUCK 👈

Spit Roasting. Pluck and clean wild duck as soon as possible after the "shoot." Plucking is usually preferred to skinning because the skin adds much to flavor and appearance. A blowtorch will help you to remove the last stubborn feathers.

Wild duck is not usually stuffed; however, a slice of onion, a rib of celery, and a piece of apple may be put into the cavity. If you prefer, use instead a sprig of parsley and 2 or 3 juniper berries. Skewer body cavities closed.

Balance the duck on a spit and rub with butter. Roast over hot charcoal for 12 to 25 minutes, depending on how well done you wish the meat. Duck on the rare side will be tenderer, juicier, and more flavorful.

If a crisp skin is desired, pour a little heated brandy over each duck when it is done and allow to flame, or stop the spit and let the fat drip into the fire and flare. Add salt and pepper.

Grilling. Split each duck with carving shears and remove the backbone. Brush with butter and broil over hot coals, skin side up. After 8 minutes, turn and continue cooking until done to your liking. Salt and pepper to taste.

👉 *Broiled Mallard Duck*

GRILL-COOKED

1 mallard duckling (2 to 3½ lbs.)
1 cup prepared French dressing
1 teaspoon dry mustard
2 teaspoons Worcestershire
2 teaspoons grated orange peel
1 teaspoon grated lemon peel

Split down the back and then pressed out flat, this duckling is cooked in a hinged wire broiler.

Split duck down backbone with poultry shears. Place, breast side down, on meat cutting board and break down breast bones by pressing with another board or by pounding gently with a meat tenderizing mallet.

Mix together the French dressing, mustard, Worcestershire, orange and lemon peel and use mixture to baste the duck liberally. Place duckling in a hinged wire broiler and grill over hot coals until done to taste (7 to 10 minutes each side), basting it at least once more while cooking. Divide duck at breastbone into two portions and serve. Makes 2 servings.

👉 *Kamo No Koma-Giri*

1 duckling (4 to 5 lbs.)
3 tablespoons soy sauce
1 tablespoon sake or sherry

These elegant ground duckling meatballs—delicious either as a main dish or as hors d'oeuvres—may seem like a lot of trouble, but the result is worth it. You can alternate the balls on skewers with wedges of unpeeled apple dipped in melted butter.

Grind the meat from the uncooked duckling; it will yield about 1½ pounds ground meat. Mix the ground duckling with soy sauce and sake or sherry until thoroughly blended. Chill about 1 hour, or until mixture is stiff enough to handle. Form into balls about 1 inch in diameter and thread on thin wooden or metal skewers. Flatten balls slightly, then grill over hot coals until brown on both sides. (Brown the balls well on one side before you turn them over, so they won't fall off the skewers.) Makes 4 servings as a main dish, 8 to 10 as hors d'oeuvres.

👉 *Crisp-Roasted Goose*

SPIT-ROASTED

Buy a small (6 to 9 lbs.) goose. If the goose has been frozen, be sure it is completely thawed, and dried thoroughly. Rub the inside with salt and a cut half of lemon.

Spit the goose, securing it firmly. Roast over medium coals for 1¾ to 2½ hours, or until it is fork tender and the skin is crisp (about 2¼ hours is long enough for a 6 to 7-pound goose).

👉 *Pheasant Barbecue*

GRILL-COOKED

Serve charcoal broiled pheasant with an orange and watercress salad.

Split young, hung birds in half, brush on both sides with melted butter, and sprinkle with salt and pepper. Grill over hot coals, starting with skin side up. Brush occasionally with butter, and turn after 10 minutes. Continue broiling and basting for another 10 to 25 minutes, depending on size of the bird. To avoid dryness, do not overcook pheasant.

Pheasant with Cashew Stuffing

1 young pheasant (2½ to 3 lbs.), hung
1 cup coarsely chopped cashew nuts
1 cup chicken broth
4 slices bacon, cooked and chopped
2 tablespoons butter
½ teaspoon salt
   Dash pepper
3 slices bacon

If the pheasant is frozen and was not hung beforehand, you can do this after thawing, as it will make a big difference in the meat's tenderness. "Hanging" the pheasant simply means letting it age (well wrapped) at room temperature for two days, or in the refrigerator for four days.

Carefully wipe out the inside of the pheasant with a damp cloth. Stuff with this dressing: Simmer cashew nuts in chicken broth until tender and liquid is absorbed. Mix in the 4 slices of cooked and chopped bacon, the butter, salt, and pepper. Stuff pheasant, truss, and tie 3 slices of bacon over the breast. Impale with spit and roast over medium-hot coals for 50 to 60 minutes, depending on size of the bird. Makes 2 servings.

Surprised Squab

4 squabs (or Rock Cornish game hens)
3 tablespoons soy sauce
¼ teaspoon monosodium glutamate
1 tablespoon brown sugar
3 tablespoons Scotch whisky
   Salt and pepper to taste
1 medium-sized onion, chopped
4 squab gizzards, sliced
3 tablespoons butter
2 cups diced white bread
3 medium-sized cooked shrimp
   or 6 dried Chinese shrimp,
   broken in small pieces
6 water chestnuts, sliced
1 cup milk
1 teaspoon salt
¼ teaspoon pepper
   Salad oil

This recipe utilizes traditional Chinese ingredients to develop a dish that is unusual and tantalizing, but not too exotic for most tastes. Serve it on the patio, and your guests can feel more free about wresting the succulent meat from this bird's multitude of tiny bones.

Marinate the squabs in a mixture of the soy sauce, monosodium glutamate, brown sugar, whisky, salt and pepper for about 1 hour. Brush the inside and outside of each bird with this mixture several times during the hour.

  Fry the onion and gizzards in 1 tablespoon of the butter until brown. Add the remaining 2 tablespoons of melted butter and mix with the diced bread, shrimps, water chestnuts, milk, salt, and pepper. Spoon this stuffing inside each bird, and skewer skin to cover the openings. Skewer together each pair of legs or tie with light wire. Brush skin with oil and hang in a moderate (300° to 400°) Chinese smoke oven for about 1 hour and 15 minutes. Brush the skin with salad oil once again during the cooking process. Serve one juicy squab per person.

FANCY SERPENTINE DESIGN is used to skewer shrimp for Japanese recipe, Onigari Yaki (page 136). The shellfish are brushed with soy-wine sauce, making them glazed and juicy when done.

BARBECUE RECIPES
FISH AND SHELLFISH

Fish that are moderately fat and full-flavored are the best to barbecue, for the smoky flavor accents their own flavor. Salmon, trout, albacore, barracuda, mackerel, rockfish, sablefish (black cod), sturgeon, swordfish, and striped bass are all excellent for barbecuing.

Serving-sized steaks, fillets, or small whole fish are easiest to handle if held inside a hinged wire broiler, then placed over the barbecue fire. Thicker steaks or fillets may be placed directly on a greased grill. Some

whole fish also barbecue well; however, they need special care. See recipes for specific directions.

All fish need frequent basting while on the barbecue. Use melted butter, plus a little lemon juice.

Since fish cooks so quickly on the barbecue, you need to watch it carefully in order not to overcook it. Fish is done when it flakes easily upon testing with a fork. Shellfish requires very little cooking and is done when it becomes less translucent and more opaque.

Boned Mackerel in Crumb Crust

GRILL-COOKED

½ cup dry bread crumbs
½ cup grated Parmesan cheese
2 cloves garlic, crushed
¼ teaspoon salt
  Dash pepper
⅓ cup salad oil
⅓ cup lemon juice
1 tablespoon chopped parsley
½ teaspoon whole dried basil
4 mackerels (about 1 lb. each),
  split and boned

The most popular mackerel, the Pacific mackerel (often called blue or American mackerel) is a member of the tuna family. Its dark meat is moderately high in fat content and pronounced in flavor. Its easiest to barbecue if you have it split and boned at the market.

Mix dry crumbs with Parmesan cheese, 1 clove of the garlic, the salt, and pepper. Also have ready a basting sauce made by combining salad oil and lemon juice with the remaining 1 clove garlic, chopped parsley, and basil. Dip each fish fillet in the basting sauce, then in crumb mixture. Set over slow coals on a greased grill. Cook slowly, turning once and basting often, until fish flakes (about 15 minutes). Makes 4 servings.

Striped Bass with Tomato Sauce

GRILL-COOKED

One fish delicacy that's reserved for the sportfisherman, a striped bass is lean, white, and mild in flavor. For this recipe, fillets are basted with your favorite tomato barbecue sauce.

Fillet and skin a striped bass weighing 7 to 8 pounds. Chill fillets for 30 minutes. Place in a single layer in a hinged wire broiler about 6 inches from heat and cook over hot coals, turning occasionally and basting frequently with barbecue sauce. Cook just until flesh flakes easily when tested with a fork, about 20 minutes total cooking time. Serve with remaining sauce. Makes 8 to 10 servings.

Fish with Fennel

GRILL-COOKED

Next time you grill fish outdoors, try this method so popular in Provence, France.

Use any whole, firm-fleshed fish. Clean, remove head if you wish, and make a few diagonal incisions in both sides. Brush with olive oil and sprinkle with salt and pepper. Lay a few branches of fennel (anise) across the fish on both sides, and fasten in a greased wire hinged broiler. (If you don't have fennel, use thyme, bay leaves, or dill, preferably branches, though the crushed herbs may be sprinkled on.) Grill the fish on both sides, sprinkling a few times with a little more oil. When it's cooked, arrange it on a flameproof platter, sprinkle with brandy, and flame. Serve with lemon wedges and Remoulade Sauce (see page 152).

Moderately fat and full-flavored fish, such as salmon, trout, and albacore, are best for the barbecue because the smoke enhances their flavor; smoke might overpower delicately flavored fish.

Serving-Sized Steaks, Fillets, and Small Whole Fish. Fairly thick fish steaks or fillets may be placed directly on the greased grill of your barbecue, but smaller fish pieces are easier to handle if held inside a hinged wire broiler.

Cut fish into serving-sized steaks or fillets; they should be at least ½ inch thick. Clean small, whole fish and remove heads, if you wish. Wipe with a damp cloth.

Place fish over moderately hot coals. Baste with melted butter, with equal parts melted butter and lemon juice, or your favorite baste for fish.

Grill, turning once, and basting often until fish is browned and flakes when tested with a fork; time will be about 8 to 16 minutes, depending on thickness. Salt and pepper to taste. Serve at once.

Whole Fish, Five to Seven Pounds. Whole fish, such as barracuda, sablefish (black cod or butterfish), and salmon, may be barbecued easily. Trim fins off cleaned fish. If you wish to leave head and tail on, wrap them with oiled waxed paper next to skin; hold them in place with heavy foil. Season fish cavity with salt, pepper, herbs, and lemon slices, if you wish.

Slip fish inside folded strip of expanded aluminum, (a wire mesh available at hardware stores), with tail in the fold. Lace side of metal strip together with wire; keep it loose, for fish will expand as it cooks.

Place fish on grill and brush lightly with salad oil. Place a foil-covered piece of wood under head and tail to protect them from heat. Cover with barbecue hood or a large sheet of heavy foil; cook slowly, turning as needed. Insert thermometer through back opening into thickest part when you turn fish. Add hickory chips or hardwood to the fire for extra smoke. Fish is done when it flakes when tested with a fork, or reaches about 120° on meat thermometer (120° isn't marked on most meat thermometers, but can be estimated).

Remove fish from grill. Cut wires and fold back top layer of metal strip. Grasp fish and metal strip, pull toward you, and lift over on to serving board. Remove foil and top skin, and serve.

Large Fish Fillets. Fillets of albacore, giant sea bass, small halibut, lingcod, rockfish, sablefish, salmon, and white seabass (or totuava) all do well on the barbecue. Have fish cut into fillets (weighing 3 to 5 pounds), leaving skin on. Cut pieces of heavy foil about the same size as the fillets and place against skin side of each fillet; lay on grill, skin sides down. Cover barbecue with lid or blanket of heavy foil and cook over slow coals until fish flakes when tested with a fork. Baste occasionally with equal parts of melted butter and lemon juice or your favorite baste for fish. (A 3 to 4-pound fillet will take about 25 minutes to cook approximately 1 foot above moderate coals.)

When fish is done, lift each foil-lined fillet to a serving plate or plank. To serve, cut across fillets and just to the skin; lift each serving away from skin. Serve with additional lemon-butter baste or your favorite sauce for fish.

Butterflied Trout

Boned, butterflied trout marinate in Italian-style dressing, and then are barbecued; serve them with nut butter.

Bone 4 medium-sized dressed trout as directed below; place in shallow pan and pour about 1½ cups Italian-style oil and vinegar dressing over fish; allow to stand, covered, in refrigerator about 30 minutes. Remove fish from marinade; place, skin side down, on barbecue grill. Cook about 10 minutes, or until flesh of trout is white and moist. If you wish, brush occasionally with marinade. Meanwhile, melt ½ cup (¼ lb.) butter or margarine, and add ½ cup chopped salted macadamia nuts; keep warm. Remove trout to heated platter; serve with nut butter. Makes 4 servings.

How to Bone Trout

To bone dressed, uncooked trout and keep the head and tail in place, open the body cavity; insert a sharp knife at the head end under the backbone and cut between ribs and flesh, releasing the bones from the fish back (take care not to cut through the back of the fish). Repeat to free the other side of the backbone and rib cage. Ease backbone free, leaving back flesh of trout intact. Using kitchen scissors, snip backbone at head and tail; lift out bony skeleton and discard. Cut off and discard fins. Fish is now ready for barbecuing open.

Barbecued Lean White Fish

You can barbecue thick boneless pieces of any firm-fleshed, lean white fish using this method. Some examples are: halibut, rockfish, lingcod, giant sea bass (black sea bass), white seabass, and totuava.

Cut 4-pound fillet of firm, white fish into pieces about 1 inch wide, 2 inches long, and 1 inch thick. Combine ½ cup soy sauce, 1 cup dry white wine, 2 tablespoons lemon juice, 2 cloves garlic (crushed), 1 teaspoon powdered ginger, and ½ cup salad oil. Pour over fish pieces and marinate 4 hours. Pour off marinade and reserve. Sprinkle fish pieces generously with about 2 tablespoons fresh rosemary and about 6 tablespoons fresh chopped parsley. Skewer carefully or slip inside a hinged wire broiler and place on the grill over low coals. Cook until fish flakes when tested with a fork, about 10 to 15 minutes, basting occasionally with part of the marinade.

In the meantime, sauté 1 pound sliced fresh mushrooms in ⅓ cup butter; add remaining marinade, heat through, and pour over broiled fish. Makes 8 servings.

Salmon with Lemon Rice Stuffing

If you don't have a covered barbecue, wrap the salmon in foil and turn it from side to side as it cooks.

Lemon Rice Stuffing

Heat ⅓ cup butter or margarine in a frying pan. Add 1 cup sliced celery, 1 small onion (chopped), and 1 to 2 cups sliced fresh mushrooms (optional); sauté about 5 minutes. Add ¼ teaspoon monosodium glutamate, ¼ teaspoon thyme, 1½ teaspoons salt, ⅛ teaspoon pepper, 2 teaspoons grated lemon peel, ¼ cup lemon juice; and 1⅓ cups water. Bring to a boil. Mix in 1¾ cups packaged precooked rice and cover; remove from heat; let stand 5 minutes. Makes enough for an 8-pound fish.

To Cook the Salmon

Fill the cavity of a 3 to 8-pound salmon with the lemon rice stuffing. Sew the opening closed with a heavy thread (any stuffing that doesn't fit into the fish can be wrapped in foil and heated on the grill while the fish cooks). If your barbecue has a hood, shape a piece of heavy foil to fit around bottom of fish; grease the foil. Cut very thin slices from a small, thin-skinned grapefruit; place slices against skin on both sides of fish; then set fish on greased foil. Put on grill over low heat; cover grill. Baste with a little melted butter several times while fish cooks. If your grill doesn't have a hood, wrap the grapefruit-covered fish in double-thick foil. Set it over slowly burning coals (or set the grill as high as possible above coals), and turn about every 10 minutes. Time required is usually about 1 hour. A 4-pound salmon makes about 8 servings.

Smoked Fresh Salmon Fillet

The rich meat of salmon is especially delicious smoked, and you can smoke a fresh fillet on your barbecue grill in two hours.

Place a 1-pound piece of fresh salmon fillet on a sheet of heavy foil cut to fit the fillet; place on grill over charcoal arranged for indirect heat (high above the coals). Keep temperature low (not over 275°), cover the grill, and smoke (adding wood as needed) for 2 hours. Salt to taste. Use for hors d'oeuvres, sandwiches, or entrées. Makes 20 generous canapés of salmon on buttered bread, or 4 entrées.

☛ *Baluk Shish Kebab*

2½ pounds salmon, halibut, or
    swordfish, cut in 1-inch
    cubes (leave skin on one side
    of each cube)
Salt
Pepper
White wine
Bay leaves
Olive oil

These Armenian skewered fish cubes should be tender and juicy, so be careful not to overcook them. You can alternate the fish pieces with small canned or parboiled onions if you wish.

Sprinkle fish cubes with salt and pepper and cover with white wine. Refrigerate for 3 hours, then drain and thread on skewers with half a bay leaf next to each piece of fish. (Be sure to put skewer through the skin on each fish cube.) Brush with olive oil; grill over hot coals 3 to 4 minutes on each side or until the flesh loses its translucent look. Do not overcook. Makes 6 to 8 servings.

☛ *Fish Smoked in Paper*

Fish cooked this way is moist and has a mild smoky flavor; if you have any left over, it's delicious served cold. This is a good way to prepare and carry fish to a picnic site, as the paper will keep the fish cold for several hours. The rest of the picnic menu might be: small pumpernickel bread and butter sandwiches, husk-roasted corn, white wine or lemonade, watermelon, and coffee.

You can use salmon, flounder, or rockfish, allowing about 1 pound per person. For 8 to 10 people, plan on 3 fish of about 3 pounds each, or 2 fish of 4 to 4½ pounds each. You'll need long tongs for turning the fish while cooking, and water to quench any flames.

Clean the fish, removing heads and tails; rub with salt (about 1 teaspoon per pound of fish) and sprinkle with pepper. Stuff the cavity of each fish with equal parts chopped parsley and finely chopped onion. Wrap each fish well in buttered waxed paper, then in several layers of newspaper so there is a 1-inch thickness of paper (you'll need about 8 double sheets of newspaper for a 3-pound fish). To make the packet easier to handle, tie with string.

Dip the packets in water to moisten the outer layer of paper, and place on hot coals (not in flames). Let the newspaper smoulder but not flame (quench flames with water). Using long tongs, turn packets over 4 or 5 times in the first half hour and moisten the charred paper. When packets have smouldered down to the waxed paper layer (it takes about 1¼ hours for a fish of about 3 pounds to cook), use tongs to remove from hot coals onto a tray or cooky sheet. Remove charred newspaper and waxed paper from one side of each fish and turn over onto serving platter; then remove the paper from the other side of each fish. Serve with melted butter and lemon slices.

Fish Steaks with Bran

SMOKE-COOKED

If you like the special flavors that cooking with smoke adds to foods, try this suggestion for fish steaks or fish fillets.

Sprinkle the fish on both sides with salt and pepper, and spread generously with butter. Put in a hinged wire broiler. Have ready a good charcoal fire, and sprinkle it with 2 cups whole bran that you've mixed with 3 tablespoons brown sugar. Put fish over the fire, and cover with the barbecue hood (or make a hood of heavy foil). Grill fish for 3 or 4 minutes, then turn and cook on other side, replacing the hood. (Length of cooking time depends upon the thickness of the fish. Test by flaking with a fork.) If the smoke dies down before the fish is cooked, add more sweetened bran.

Orange-Soy Swordfish

GRILL-COOKED

½ cup soy sauce
¼ cup catsup
¼ cup chopped parsley
½ cup orange juice
2 cloves garlic, mashed
2 tablespoons lemon juice
1 teaspoon pepper
1½ to 2 pounds swordfish,
    cut 1 inch thick

The firm, white, boneless meat of swordfish holds together well and is easy to manage on the barbecue. To prevent breakage when turning, use kitchen tongs.

Combine in a bowl the soy sauce, catsup, parsley, orange juice, garlic, lemon juice, and pepper. Mix well. Marinate swordfish in this mixture for 1 hour. Grill about 4 inches above hot coals for about 8 minutes. Turn fish and grill 7 minutes on other side. Brush with marinade frequently during cooking. Makes 4 servings.

Slow-Smoked Garlic Swordfish

SMOKE-COOKED

1½ lemons, very thinly sliced
1 large swordfish steak (about
    1½ lbs.), cut 1 inch thick
1 large clove garlic, minced or mashed
⅓ cup butter
    Salt
    Pepper

From June or July (depending upon the weather) until about the end of October, you can buy fresh swordfish. The rest of the year, frozen swordfish is available in most markets.

Place lemon slices over bottom of shallow pan fashioned of heavy foil. Lay swordfish steak on lemon. Pour garlic butter (made by heating garlic in butter) over steak. Sprinkle with salt and pepper to taste. Place on grill over indirect very low heat (not over 275°). Cover grill and smoke for 2 hours. Baste with juices in pan. Makes 4 servings.

☛ *Swordfish Piraeus*

¼ cup salad oil or olive oil
½ cup dry white wine
2 tablespoons lemon juice
1 teaspoon salt
1 teaspoon dried oregano, crumbled
¼ teaspoon garlic salt
1 tablespoon instant minced onion
3 swordfish steaks (about
    2 pounds), cut ¾ inch thick
1 large green pepper
12 bay leaves
12 cherry tomatoes
6 mushroom caps (about 1½
    inches in diameter)
1 lemon, cut in wedges
    Oregano

Offer traditional Greek seasonings—lemon wedges and a bowl of dried oregano—to sprinkle over these fish kebabs at the table. It's important to marinate the swordfish overnight so the seasonings have a chance to permeate.

For marinade, mix together in a bowl the oil, wine, lemon juice, salt, oregano, garlic salt, and onion. Cut fish steaks into 1¼-inch squares, place in the marinade, cover and chill overnight, turning several times. Cut pepper in half, remove seeds, and cut in 1¼-inch squares.

Compose 6 skewers in the following pattern: alternate 1 piece swordfish, 1 square of pepper, swordfish, bay leaf, tomato, swordfish, bay leaf, tomato, swordfish, pepper, swordfish, and end with a mushroom cap.

Barbecue skewers over medium coals for 10 minutes, turning to brown both sides and basting several times with the marinade. Accompany with lemon wedges and a small dish of oregano. Makes 6 servings.

BARBECUE BONUS

THREE GRILLED SHRIMP APPETIZERS

While the meat is roasting, keep the hungry horde happy with one or more of these shrimp appetizers.

Shrimp and Anchovy Appetizers. Shell jumbo shrimp and split each deeply down the back, removing the sand vein. Insert a fillet of anchovy in each slit; wind with a half-slice of bacon (split bacon lengthwise) and fasten with a pick. Broil over charcoal until the bacon is crisp. Don't overcook if you want these at their best; they should be hot and juicy, never dry.

Butterflied Shrimp Appetizer. Remove shells, tails, and veins from 1 pound jumbo or medium shrimp. Slit each shrimp down back side, cutting almost all the way through so it will lay flat (take care not to cut entirely in half). Dip shrimp in 1 egg, slightly beaten with ¼ teaspoon salt and ¼ teaspoon pepper; then dip in fine dry bread crumbs to coat each side (you'll need about ½ cup of crumbs).

Thread each shrimp on a single, long, thin bamboo skewer. Insert point of skewer at tail of shrimp and impale its full length so that the point of the skewer just shows at the head end of the shrimp. Refrigerate until ready to cook. Cook over hot coals; baste occasionally with a mixture of ½ cup melted butter and ¼ cup lime or lemon juice. Serve with lime wedges to squeeze over shrimp. Makes about 16 large or 25 medium appetizers.

Spicy Shrimp Appetizers. Wash, shell, and devein about 2 pounds medium-sized shrimp or prawns (or use about 1½ pounds frozen deveined large shrimp—they need not be thawed). In a bowl or glass jar, blend 1 teaspoon chile powder with 1 tablespoon vinegar, ¼ teaspoon pepper, 1 clove minced or mashed garlic, 1 teaspoon salt, 1 teaspoon basil, and 1 tablespoon finely chopped fresh mint. Stir in ¾ cup salad oil and shake or mix until well blended. Pour over the shrimp; cover the dish and marinate in the refrigerator for at least 4 hours, or overnight. Thread the shrimp on skewers and grill for 6 to 10 minutes (depending on size), turning once and basting liberally with the marinade. Makes 50 appetizers.

Spiny Pacific (or rock) lobsters are easiest to handle if they are first boiled, then cleaned and split for barbecuing; care must be taken only to reheat the meat, not further cook it.

Live Northeastern lobsters may be killed, cleaned, split, then barbecued; this method is not for the squeamish, but it results in the most succulent and tender barbecued lobster.

To Boil Live Lobsters. In a large pan, bring to boiling enough water to generously cover the lobsters; add about 1 tablespoon salt for each quart water. Grasp lobster from behind large front claws or front legs (you may wish to wear gloves when handling spiny lobsters to protect your hands from the sharp spines). Plunge lobsters headfirst into the boiling water; bring water back to simmering; then cover and simmer about 7 minutes for a 1-pound lobster, or about 10 minutes for 2-pound ones. Remove and plunge into cold water; rinse and drain.

To Clean Cooked Lobster. With a sharp knife, split lobster end to end through the shell. Remove the small sac (stomach), which lies just behind the head, and pull out the intestinal vein, which runs down to the end of the tail. Don't discard the coral colored roe (if any) or the yellow liver. (Beat the roe of one lobster with ¼ to ½ cup butter and serve in place of melted butter). Twist off and discard spiny lobster legs. Crack claws of Northern lobsters. If you wish to remove all the meat

from a spiny lobster at once, grasp tail and body and bend the shell backward at the joint until it breaks.

To Barbecue Cooked Lobster. Spread each half of the split, cleaned lobster with melted butter or whipped seasoned butter; wrap each half in foil and place, shell side down, on a grill over medium heat just until lobster is heated through; this will take about 15 minutes.

To Barbecue Uncooked Northern Lobster. First kill the lobster instantly by holding it on its back and inserting the tip of a sharp knife between the tail section and the body shell, cutting to sever the spinal cord. Split the lobster lengthwise and remove the stomach and intestinal vein as described above.

Place split lobster on a greased grill, meat side down. Barbecue about 4 inches from coals for about 5 minutes. Turn and brush meat generously with melted butter or whipped seasoned butter. Barbecue 5 to 7 minutes longer or until meat is cooked, basting often. Serve with melted butter, lemon butter, or a flavored mayonnaise.

To Barbecue Frozen Lobster Tails. Frozen lobster tails are all of the spiny lobster type; they are usually frozen uncooked and may or may not be in the shell. It is important that they be completely thawed before barbecuing. Barbecue lobster tails as directed above for uncooked Northern lobster.

👉 *Barracuda Steaks*

GRILL-COOKED

The flavor and texture of barracuda meat is something like dark-meat tuna. Relatively strong in flavor, it takes well to robust seasonings and is an excellent fish to barbecue. Have the whole fish dressed at the market; it is easy to cut steaks or pieces from it at home.

Prepare either a lemon, garlic, or teriyaki baste for this fish (see chapter on Sauces and Marinades). Cut barracuda steaks or fillets about ¾ inch thick. Brush well on both sides with the baste (or marinate in a shallow pan about 10 minutes). Set steaks or fillets on the grill on top of a piece of heavy foil (with holes punched in it), or hold the fish pieces in a hinged wire broiler over the fire. Cook over medium-hot coals, turning and basting as needed, for 8 to 10 minutes, or until the fish flakes easily.

👉 Soy-Grilled Albacore Steaks

GRILL-COOKED

4 to 6 albacore steaks
⅓ cup soy sauce
⅓ cup salad oil
2 cloves garlic, minced or mashed
2 teaspoons meat seasoning sauce
2 teaspoons Worcestershire

Firm, meaty slices of fresh albacore are an excellent choice for barbecuing. If your fish dealer doesn't carry the white fleshed tuna regularly in the summer, ask him to order one for you.

Ask your dealer to clean and dress the albacore and cut it into steaks about 1 inch thick. At home, cut the dark meat and bone from each steak, leaving skin intact. Press pieces together (don't be concerned if meat seems soft—it firms quickly over heat) and secure with several picks.

Combine the soy sauce, oil, garlic, meat sauce, and Worcestershire, and pour over prepared steaks. Marinate for 20 to 30 minutes, remove from marinade, and place on a greased grill over medium-hot coals for 10 to 15 minutes, turning once and brushing often with marinade. Makes 4 to 6 servings.

👉 Whole Abalone with Almond Butter

GRILL-COOKED

If you wish to enjoy the full delicate flavor of abalone and save yourself the steps of slicing whole abalone into steaks and pounding each one, try this method of barbecuing whole pounded abalone quickly over hot coals.

Shuck 3 large abalone, rinse in cold water, and trim lacelike dark portions from edges of each foot. Trim ¼ inch off each sole (the side of the foot that attaches to the rock). You should have about 2 pounds trimmed abalone. Let stand until muscles relax. Slice about ¼ inch off rounded top of each abalone; pound evenly with smooth side of wooden mallet until limp.

Melt ½ cup (¼ lb.) butter or margarine with 1 tablespoon lemon juice over low heat. Barbecue abalone quickly about 5 inches from hot coals; brush frequently with butter mixture. Turn once, allow 2 to 3 minutes on each side. Add ½ cup toasted sliced almonds to remaining butter in pan. To serve, cut abalone in thin slices; spoon some of the almond butter over each serving. Makes 4 servings.

👉 Shellfish Kebabs

⅓ cup soy sauce
1 medium-sized white onion, chopped
2 tablespoons grated fresh ginger
2 cloves garlic, finely chopped
2 teaspoons dry mustard
1 teaspoon prepared horseradish
½ teaspoon curry powder
2 pounds large shrimp
1 pint medium-sized oysters
½ pound very lean bacon
4 to 6 tomatoes
12 to 16 pearl onions
2 green peppers

Serve this as an entrée with fried rice, or as hors d'oeuvres with any remaining marinade kept hot in a chafing dish for dunking purposes.

Prepare marinade by combining soy sauce, white onion, ginger, garlic, mustard, horseradish, and curry powder. (The marinade can be mixed the night before, allowed to stand overnight in the refrigerator, then brought out about 6 hours before broiling to allow it to come to room temperature.)
Shell and devein shrimp, then marinate at least 2 hours.
Puff oysters slightly in hot water and cook bacon to the limp stage. Then wrap oysters in half slices of bacon, using toothpicks to hold. Cut tomatoes into quarters, leave onions whole, and cut peppers into bite-sized chunks. Impale all ingredients on skewers and grill over a medium-hot charcoal fire for 3 to 5 minutes, or until done to taste, basting frequently with heated marinade during the cooking. Makes 6 to 8 servings as an entrée, at least twice that many for hors d'oeuvres.

👉 Onigari Yaki

½ cup Mirin (Japanese wine) or sherry
1 cup soy sauce
1 tablespoon sugar
About 3 pounds shrimp

In this recipe you skewer shrimp to make a fancy serpentine design as shown on page 126. Brush with the soy-wine sauce while barbecuing.

In a small saucepan, combine Mirin or sherry, soy sauce, and sugar; bring to a boil. Thread 6 medium-sized shrimp or prawns on each of 6 skewers, alternating heads and tails as follows: Thread the head of one shrimp, with the tail curling over top of skewer; then thread the head of another shrimp with tail curling up from bottom of skewer. Thread the tail of the first shrimp, the head of a third shrimp, then the tail of second shrimp, and so on. Shrimp will be alternately uncurled and downcurled. Cook over hot coals, brushing constantly with sauce until shrimp are shiny and glazed. Makes 6 servings.

MUSHROOMS EN BROCHETTE, *flamed with Cognac, make a dramatic accompaniment for barbecued steak, or almost any meat. For directions on grilling the skewered mushrooms before flaming, see page 141.*

BARBECUE RECIPES
FRUITS AND VEGETABLES

When you barbecue an entrée for dinner, take advantage of the barbecue fire for cooking other foods on the menu. Many fruits and vegetables have a natural affinity for the smoky barbecue flavor and can be cooked directly on the grill. Others may be wrapped in foil and heated on the grill or near the coals, steaming in their own juices or in added butter or liquid.

If you skewer fruit or vegetables to cook along with meat, it's usually best not to put them on the same skewers; fruit and vegetables generally take a shorter cooking time than meat. If you're just heating fruit, place the skewered fruit right on top of the meat during the last few minutes cooking time. This lets the escaping juices baste the meat.

Frequent basting is necessary when cooking fruits and vegetables over the barbecue fire.

Skewer combinations featuring fruits and vegetables are suggested on pages 20 and 21.

Ginger-Buttered Fruit Kebabs

Children can handle this last-minute job of grilling fruit kebabs. Transfer some hot coals from the barbecue to a small hibachi if space is short on the barbecue.

For each fruit kebab, cut a thick half-slice of orange with peel, a red apple wedge, a thick diagonal slice of banana, and a fresh pineapple chunk (or use canned pineapple chunks). Thread small bamboo skewers each with the 4 fruits; grill 5 to 10 minutes or until lightly browned, basting frequently with ginger butter (recipe follows). Allow 1 fruit kebab for each serving. Serve warm.

Ginger Butter

In a small pan, melt ½ cup (¼ lb.) butter; stir in 2 tablespoons sugar and 1 teaspoon ground ginger. Makes enough baste for 12 to 18 kebabs.

IDEAS FOR GRILLING FRUITS AND VEGETABLES

■ Cut unpeeled apples in thick slices and dip in butter. Grill on both sides, sprinkling with cinnamon and sugar toward the end of the cooking.

■ Remove pits from dates and stuff with Cheddar cheese; wrap in bacon and grill for an appetizer.

■ Wrap fresh figs in bacon and grill them until bacon is crisp.

■ Cut unpeeled oranges in thick slices; dip in melted butter and dust lightly with flour. Heat on both sides.

■ Peel bananas and cut in half. Wrap with bacon and grill on both sides. Or use unpeeled bananas and make a slit about 3 inches long in the skin of each one. Force 1 tablespoon of honey into each opening and let stand for ½ hour. Place on grill and cook for about 8 minutes, turning frequently.

■ Cut a fresh pineapple into 8 lengthwise spears. Place in baking pan and drip honey—about a tablespoon to a section—over the fruit. Let stand for ½ hour and then grill. Or, use sliced pineapple, either canned or fresh, and brush with melted butter before broiling on both sides.

■ Cut grapefruit in halves and remove seeds. Loosen segments from the skin and section membranes. Cover with brown or granulated sugar. Dot tops with butter; pour about a tablespoon of sherry or rum over each half. Place on grill and cook until fruit is thoroughly heated.

■ Use fresh or canned peaches. If fresh, they should be peeled and halved. Brush with butter and grill, cut side down, until brown; then turn and fill cavities with butter and brown sugar, and continue grilling until brown on the bottom. If desired, put a little sherry or rum in the cavities and serve them as a dessert with cold sour cream or ice cream.

■ Use cooked artichoke bottoms; marinate them in French dressing before grilling.

■ Cook unpeeled carrots just until tender; peel and dip in butter; then heat on grill.

■ Cut green peppers in quarters; remove seeds and dip in olive oil before grilling.

☞ Soy-Pineapple Apple Slices

GRILL-COOKED

The same sauce used for basting these apple slices can be used to baste chicken.

Core apples and cut into slices about ⅜ inch thick. Place on barbecue grill and broil until tender (about 5 minutes on each side), basting with mixture of ¾ cup soy sauce, ¾ cup unsweetened pineapple juice, and 3 tablespoons sugar.

☞ Pineapple-Banana-Bacon Grill

SKEWER-COOKED

About 12 strips thickly sliced bacon
1 small pineapple, cubed
3 large bananas, sliced 1-inch thick

Bacon flavor permeates the chunks of fruit as you grill the fruit on skewers.

Use wooden skewers for these. For each skewer, weave 1 strip bacon around 3 cubes of fresh pineapple and 2 banana slices. Keep foods chilled until time to cook. Grill over hot coals until bacon is cooked (about 2 minutes), turning as needed. Makes 6 servings.

☞ Mixed Vegetable Grill

SKEWER-COOKED

Prepare the vegetables early in the day and let them marinate until you are ready to cook them; then skewer vegetables and cook over hot coals.

Plan to serve approximately 1 cup vegetables per person—or enough to fill a medium-length skewer. A good selection includes: frozen artichoke hearts (thawed), cucumber chunks or slices, eggplant cubes, small whole mushrooms, pieces of green pepper, and cherry tomatoes.

Cut vegetables in bite-sized pieces; marinate for several hours in your favorite French dressing, or in a mixture of 1 cup salad oil, 1/3 cup lemon juice, ¼ teaspoon salt, dash pepper, and dash sugar. Just before cooking, remove vegetables from marinade and string on skewers. Place skewers over coals; cook 3 to 5 minutes, turning once. Baste vegetables with some of the marinade while they are cooking.

👉 Zucchini-Tomato Kebabs

2 medium-sized zucchini
About 2 cups salted water
½ teaspoon oregano
Cherry tomatoes
Melted butter
2 tablespoons Parmesan cheese
Salt
Pepper

Thread skewers with the vegetables either just before grilling or several hours in advance (refrigerate).

Parboil zucchini for 4 to 5 minutes in salted water seasoned with oregano. Remove and cut each crosswise into 4 sections. Thread alternately with cherry tomatoes on 2 small skewers. Baste with melted butter and cook about 8 inches above hot coals for about 10 minutes, turning and basting frequently. Just before removing from grill, sprinkle each kebab with 1 tablespoon Parmesan cheese and a dash of salt and pepper. Serve immediately. Makes 2 servings.

👉 Tangy Eggplant Wedges

½ cup olive oil or salad oil
2 tablespoons white wine vinegar
1 clove garlic, mashed
2 teaspoons salt
¼ teaspoon oregano
1 medium-sized eggplant, washed, stem removed (do not peel)

If you're barbecuing lamb or beef, you can cook eggplant at the same time to serve with the meat.

Mix and shake together olive or salad oil, vinegar, garlic, salt, and oregano. Let stand for 1 hour or more to blend flavors. Shake well just before using. Cut eggplant lengthwise into 8 equal-sized wedges. Brush with oil mixture on all sides and place on grill over hot coals. Cook until tender, turning once. Brush frequently with remaining oil mixture. Makes 4 servings.

👉 Roasted Stuffed Eggplant

6 large eggplants, halved lengthwise
6 large onions, chopped
1 cup minced parsley
1 cup (½ lb.) butter or margarine
Salt
Pepper
Juice of 2 or 3 lemons

When barbecuing for a crowd of hungry people, stuff eggplants and roast them in the coals beneath the meat.

Scoop out centers of eggplants, leaving about ½-inch walls. Dice centers, combine with onions and parsley. Simmer this mixture in butter or margarine until vegetables are tender. Season to taste with salt and pepper and lemon juice. Spoon mixture into eggplant shells and put shells back together. Seal each in 2 layers of heavy foil. Roast on hot coals for 30 minutes, or until vegetable feels soft. Turn occasionally; do not pierce foil. Cut in quarters. Makes 24 servings.

If your barbecue equipment has multiple spits, such as those used for shish kebabs, you can roast an entire meal on the spit. Whole fruits and vegetables will cook to tenderness right alongside the meat.

Fruits and vegetables take longer to cook by this method than by roasting in the coals, but the slow steady turning causes them to cook more evenly. Whole green peppers, acorn squash, zucchini, potatoes, onions, yams, apples, and eggplant can all be prepared in this manner. If you choose fruits and vegetables of uniform size, they will finish cooking at the same time.

Before starting to cook them, brush vegetables with olive oil. The baste or marinade which you use on the meat can also be used to baste the fruit and vegetables. Remove them from the fire when they stop turning with the spit (interior is cooked at this point).

A similar method of spit roasting is to cut up the fruits or vegetables and, if you wish, alternate them with pieces of meat. Good candidates are chunks of unpeeled eggplant, slices of onion and green pepper, quartered green tomatoes, banana chunks, pieces of pineapple, and papaya wedges.

Mushroom Caps in Butter

GRILL-COOKED

Select large mushrooms; allow 2 or 3 for each serving. Cut stems flush with caps. Dip in melted butter (seasoned with tarragon, chives, or dill, if desired) and place in a hinged wire broiler, cap sides up. Cook, cap sides up, over hot coals; do not spill juices that accumulate in the mushrooms. Season with salt and pepper. Serve as an appetizer or with any meat, shellfish, or poultry.

Mushrooms en Brochette, Flambé

SKEWER-COOKED

2 pounds medium-sized,
    uniform mushrooms, cleaned
    (remove stems and save for
    another purpose)
Melted butter
Olive oil or salad oil
Salt
Pepper
¼ cup cognac, warmed

To dramatize a steak, serve it with mushrooms grilled on skewers and flamed.

Using sharply pointed skewers, carefully impale mushroom caps on 6 skewers. Brush them all over with a mixture of half melted butter and half olive oil or salad oil; sprinkle with salt and pepper. Grill over charcoal turning to brown on all sides, and basting once or twice with the olive oil and butter mixture. Cooking time is about 10 minutes. Arrange mushrooms on a hot flameproof dish and pour over them the warmed cognac; light. When flames die down, serve with steak. Makes 6 servings.

👉 *Buttered Tomatoes*

Cut firm tomatoes in halves, brush with butter, sprinkle with salt and pepper, and grill, cut side down. When brown, turn, brush with more butter, and continue cooking until barely tender. Buttered toast crumbs may be sprinkled on the cut side after turning.

👉 *Onion Packets*

COAL-COOKED

Onions, seasoned and wrapped in foil, can be cooked right in the hot barbecue coals.

For each serving, peel 2 small white onions and make a cross in the stem end. Place on a small sheet of heavy foil, dot with butter, and season with salt and pepper. Wrap securely. To cook, place directly in the barbecue coals for 30 minutes.

👉 IDEAS FOR GRILLING FOIL-WRAPPED FRUITS AND VEGETABLES 👈

Compared to the other methods of charcoal cookery, this one makes serving and eating easy, though the foods do not have the smoky flavor of those exposed directly to the charcoal.

Fruits. Here are suggestions for fruits which may be heated in a foil wrapping on the barbecue; serve them with grilled meats or as a dessert for a barbecued meal:
■ Apples. Peel and slice; season with butter and sugar, then with cinnamon, coriander, or mace. Wrap in foil and grill until fork tender.
■ Bananas. Peel and slice or quarter; season with sugar and butter; wrap in foil and grill.
■ Oranges. Peel and divide into segments. Season with butter, sugar, and cinnamon or rosemary. Wrap and grill.
■ Peaches. Peel and cut in slices. Season with butter and brown sugar. Wrap and grill.

■ Pears. Peel and slice; season with butter, sugar, and ginger, or add slivered candied ginger. Wrap and grill.
■ Pineapple. Use pineapple chunks. Season with butter and sugar. Wrap and grill.

Vegetables. Some vegetables to wrap in foil and cook on the grill are as follows: shredded peeled beets, sliced carrots, corn cut from the cob, sliced peeled eggplant, sliced mushrooms, sliced onions (or whole small white onions with a cross slashed in stem end), sliced green peppers, sliced or diced white or sweet potatoes, shelled peas, and sliced squash.

Season vegetables with salt and pepper and plenty of butter before wrapping. If desired, vegetables may also be cooked in combinations, such as onions and potatoes, corn and green peppers, peas and mushrooms.

Foil-Barbecued Potatoes

Foil-potatoes cook quickly on the barbecue when you start with the vegetable partially cooked.

Use leftover cooked whole potatoes, or precook fresh potatoes until almost tender. Peel and cut each into 4 sections. Place thin onion slices between potato sections and reassemble potatoes. Place each potato on a square of heavy duty foil, the center of which is spread with 1 tablespoon butter or margarine. Wrap foil tightly to enclose potato and hold sections together. Barbecue for 20 to 30 minutes, or until onion is tender.

Charcoal-Roasted Corn on the Cob

There are many ways to cook corn on the cob over a charcoal fire, and these are just a few of the variations:

1) Use unhusked ears. Lay back husks and remove silk. Return husks to former positions and wire them into place (with any fine wire) at center and near tip of cob, covering the kernels as well as possible. Roast on the grill 15 or 20 minutes, turning 3 or 4 times so that all surfaces are exposed to the heat. Snip the wires with wire cutter; husk the ears (gloves are necessary) and serve.

2) Open husk at one end; let about 2 tablespoons of barbecue sauce run inside the ear. Smooth husk back in place; tie and cook as above.

3) Pull husks back, remove silk, brush corn generously with garlic butter. Replace husks and place ears on grill. Dip a clean burlap sack in warm water, wring it out slightly, and place it over the ears so that they will steam. Let the ears grill 10 minutes on one side. Remove burlap, turn ears, re-cover with burlap, sprinkle it with more water. Grill 5 or 10 minutes longer.

4) Strip ears down to last 3 or 4 husks and place in ice water 30 minutes or longer. Drain well and grill for only 15 or 20 minutes.

5) Husk corn, wrap in bacon, and grill until bacon is crisp and the exposed corn brown.

6) Husk and remove silk from each ear of corn. Place each ear on a sheet of heavy foil. Mix together ½ cup melted butter and 3 tablespoons soy sauce; pour about 1 tablespoon of the mixture over each of 12 ears of corn. Wrap securely, using a freezer-style wrap. To cook, place in the barbecue coals for 15 minutes, turning several times.

HOW TO COOK FRUITS AND VEGETABLES IN COALS

To cook fruits or vegetables right in the coals, first wrap them securely in a double layer of foil; then place in or around the ashes. Turn once or twice during the cooking. Test for doneness by piercing through the foil with a long-pronged fork.

Apples. Core apples and fill holes with sugar and a piece of butter; you can also add cinnamon or nutmeg, if you wish. Wrap in foil and cook for 30 minutes, or until fork tender.

Bananas. Wrap unpeeled bananas in foil and roast like apples; or peel the bananas, dip in melted butter, and sprinkle with sugar before wrapping.

Beets. Wrap whole unpeeled beets in foil and roast until tender. Serve with butter and lemon wedges. Let guests peel and season their own beets, or if you prefer, you can peel the beets before roasting.

Potatoes. Wrap unpeeled potatoes in foil and roast until fork tender, or if you like a hard, blackened skin (and many do), roast potatoes without wrapping. Cook until fork tender and turn during cooking. They will take from 30 to 60 minutes. Serve with plenty of butter or with sour cream and chives. Sweet potatoes or yams may be cooked the same way.

Eggplant. Wrap a whole eggplant in foil and roast it over the coals. When fork tender, the skin will peel off easily.

Onions. Wrap whole peeled or unpeeled onions in foil and roast until fork tender. Serve with butter.

Parboiled Vegetables en Skewer

SKEWER-COOKED

These skewers simplify the vegetable accompaniment for barbecued meat; you can use the same basting sauce for the vegetables as for the meat.

Parboil zucchini (cut in 1-inch lengths), mushrooms, and small white onions for 3 minutes in boiling water and string on skewers. Grill over coals for 5 minutes. Brush with melted butter or the baste being used on barbecued meat.

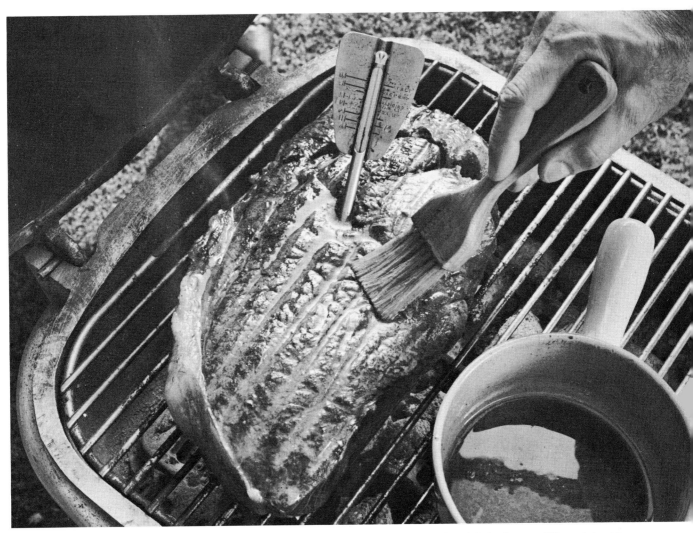

SAVORY BASTE *for thick, top round steak is made using marinade from a jar of artichoke hearts. The mixture is first used to marinate the meat, then brushed on it as it cooks. Recipe on page 64.*

BARBECUE RECIPES

SAUCES AND MARINADES

Barbecuing adds new dimensions to meats, since flavor from the smoke penetrates and accents the natural meat flavors. Remember this when you choose a complementary marinade, baste, or sauce for steaks, chops, or roasts.

Marinating meat accomplishes several purposes: the acid in a marinade (such as vinegar, wine, citrus juice) acts as a tenderizer; fat (salad oil or melted butter) adds moistness to very lean meats; seasonings impart interesting flavors.

A baste—often leftover marinade—is brushed onto meat while cooking. Bastes should contain either melted butter, margarine, or salad oil to lubricate the surface of the meat and keep it from drying. A baste generally has seasonings for flavoring. (Basic chicken bastes are given on page 115 of the poultry chapter.)

The word sauce is often used interchangeably with marinade and baste, but can specifically mean a dressing for cooked meat. It might be the marinade heated and spooned over the barbecued meat.

👉 All-Purpose Barbecue Sauce

¼ cup salad oil
¼ cup bourbon or sherry
2 tablespoons soy sauce
1 teaspoon Worcestershire
1 teaspoon garlic powder
Freshly ground black pepper to taste

This subtle barbecue sauce adds good flavor to meat, fish, or chicken.

Combine salad oil, bourbon or sherry, soy sauce, Worcestershire, garlic powder, and pepper. Pour over meat and marinate in refrigerator (turning occasionally). Marinate roasts 24 to 48 hours; steaks, 4 hours; salmon or chicken, 2 hours. Also use as a basting sauce.

👉 Soy-Ginger Marinade and Baste

2 tablespoons salad oil
⅓ cup soy sauce
2 tablespoons honey or firmly packed brown sugar
1 tablespoon red wine vinegar
1 teaspoon freshly grated ginger
1 clove garlic, crushed

This teriyaki-type marinade adds flavor to beef, chicken, spareribs, and fish.

Combine salad oil, soy sauce, honey or brown sugar, vinegar, ginger, and garlic. For beef, marinate 8 hours in this mixture for delicate flavor, overnight for more pronounced flavor. For chicken or spareribs, marinate 4 to 8 hours. For fish (such as shrimp, swordfish steaks, giant sea bass steaks), marinate 2 to 4 hours. Use the sauce also to brush on meat while grilling.

👉 Soy-Lemon Marinade for Beef

½ cup soy sauce
½ cup lemon juice
½ cup salad oil
1 bay leaf
½ teaspoon seasoned pepper
1 clove garlic, crushed

A six-pound roast can be marinated up to three days in this marinade, using a heavy plastic bag for the marinating process.

Combine soy sauce, lemon juice, salad oil, bay leaf, pepper, and garlic. Put meat and marinade in a heavy plastic bag. Tie bag securely; place in a bowl. Refrigerate overnight or up to 3 days, turning frequently. Drain meat before roasting. Baste meat with marinade, if you wish. Makes enough marinade for a 6-pound roast.

👉 Mustard-Soy Marinade

1 tablespoon dry mustard
1 cup water
2 cups soy sauce
3 cloves garlic (about the size of the end of your thumb)
6 tablespoons brown sugar
4 tablespoons sherry or bourbon

In addition to exceptional penetration of its own flavors, this marinade has some tenderizing effect on steak. Try it, too, for spareribs, pork or lamb chops, shortribs.

Mix mustard gradually with 1 cup water to form a paste, then add soy. Add thinly sliced or crushed garlic, sugar, and sherry or bourbon. The entire sauce should be kept at room temperature. The meat should be marinated in this sauce at room temperature from 1 to 2 hours, depending on how thoroughly you wish to have this sauce permeate the meat. Makes about 5 cups marinade.

👉 IDEAS FOR FLAVORED BUTTERS 👈

A cooking shortcut that may appeal to you, especially if you're the kind of cook who likes to "season to taste," is this: Spend a little time in the kitchen flavoring some butter. Then when you've a meal to prepare quickly, you can add a distinctive touch by melting some flavored butter on plain broiled steak, fish fillets, even hamburger patties or poached eggs.

You can use flavored butter to season vegetables, to spread on French bread or little tea sandwiches, or in many other ways. Butter is an effective medium for carrying such seasonings as onion, mustard, and herbs—flavors that aren't easily added to quickly cooked dishes.

Flavored butters are not intended for long-time storage; for best flavor, plan to use them within a week or two. Butter and margarine can be used interchangeably in most of the recipes that follow (or you can use part of each).

Fines Herbes Butter. Combine ½ cup (¼ lb.) butter or margarine, 1 tablespoon minced parsley (fresh or freeze-dried), 1 tablespoon chopped chives (fresh or freeze-dried), ½ teaspoon tarragon, ½ teaspoon chervil, ¼ teaspoon salt, and dash of pepper; beat until fluffy. Cover and refrigerate.

Suggested use: Try on fillet of sole, hamburger patties, poached eggs, sautéed liver, and green vegetables. Spread on appetizer sandwiches or French bread.

Garlic Butter. Combine ½ cup (¼ lb.) butter or margarine, 2 to 3 cloves garlic (minced or mashed), and 2 tablespoons minced parsley (fresh or freeze-dried); beat until fluffy. Cover and refrigerate.

Suggested use: Melt this on hot, broiled salmon or swordfish, or on broiled lamb chops or beef steaks; season boiled new potatoes, or heat on French bread slices.

Basil Butter. Combine ½ cup (¼ lb.) butter or margarine, ½ cup lightly packed, chopped fresh basil leaves (or 2 tablespoons dried basil), 2 tablespoons minced parsley, 1 tablespoon lemon juice, and ¼ cup grated Parmesan cheese in blender and whirl until smooth (or crush basil and parsley with mortar and pestle, and beat together with other ingredients). Cover and refrigerate.

Suggested use: Season minestrone and other vegetable soups; spread on tomato slices before broiling; season baked potatoes, zucchini, eggplant, green beans, and peas; melt on sautéed fish.

Red Onion Butter. Sauté 1 medium-sized red onion (finely chopped) in 2 tablespoons butter until soft, about 5 minutes; add 2 tablespoons dry red wine and cook until all liquid is evaporated. Cool thoroughly. Then combine the onion mixture, ½ cup (¼ lb.) butter, and ¼ teaspoon salt; whirl in the blender or beat until fluffy. Cover and refrigerate.

Suggested use: Use to butter fresh corn or almost any vegetable. Season beef steak, ground beef, veal, or lamb chops. Heat on French bread slices.

Shallot Butter. Sauté 3 fresh shallots (peeled and minced) in 2 tablespoons butter until soft, about 5 minutes; add 2 tablespoons dry sherry and cook until all the liquid is evaporated. Cool thoroughly, then combine with ½ cup (¼ lb.) butter and ¼ teaspoon salt. Beat until fluffy. Cover and refrigerate.

Suggested use: Serve on sautéed sole or other fish or on lamb, beef, or veal cuts; melt and use to baste chicken pieces when you roast or barbecue them; season baked potatoes or other vegetables.

Maître d'Hôtel Butter. Combine ½ cup (¼ lb.) butter or margarine, 2 teaspoons lemon juice, 2 teaspoons minced parsley, ¼ teaspoon salt, ¼ teaspoon whole thyme, and ⅛ teaspoon pepper; beat until fluffy. Cover and refrigerate.

Suggested use: Use to season sautéed fish or clam chowder; melt and use as baste on chicken while grilling or roasting; season vegetables, especially carrots, onions, and peas.

Mustard Butter. Prepare Maître d'Hôtel Butter as directed above, omitting thyme. Beat in 2 tablespoons Dijon-style mustard.

Suggested use: Spread on bread for meat or cheese sandwiches; season asparagus, zucchini, or carrots; serve on broiled hamburgers, sautéed liver, or fish.

Dill Butter. Press 2 hard-cooked egg yolks through a wire strainer; combine with ½ cup (¼ lb.) butter or margarine, 4½ teaspoons dill weed, ½ teaspoon salt, and ⅛ teaspoon white or black pepper; beat until fluffy. Cover and refrigerate.

Suggested use: Season shrimp, salmon, or other fish, or poached eggs. Try it on vegetables, such as new potatoes, carrots, green beans, or peas.

Blue Cheese Butter. Crumble 4 ounces blue cheese into ½ cup (¼ lb.) butter or margarine; add 2 tablespoons heavy cream and ¼ teaspoon paprika; beat until blended and fluffy. Cover and refrigerate.

Suggested use: This is good melted on hamburgers or beef steak, or on salmon or swordfish. Or spread it on appetizer sandwiches. You can also use it to season hot baked potato or cauliflower.

SPECIAL MEXICAN SAUCES FOR BEEF

These three Mexican sauces are found in many delicious Mexican dishes. Each is also very good served with barbecued beef.

Red Chile Sauce. Place 6 ounces (about 10 to 12) whole dried chiles pasillas or California chiles (or 3 ounces of each) on a baking sheet. Bake in a hot oven (400°) for 3 or 4 minutes. Remove from oven, let cool to touch, then remove and discard stems, seeds, and any pink pithy material inside the chiles. Rinse in cool water, drain briefly, then cover chiles with 3 cups hot water; let stand 1 hour.

Place chiles in an electric blender and add just enough of the water to blend; whirl until smooth (or rub chiles through a wire strainer, or mash to a paste in a mortar and pestle). Add remaining water, ¼ cup tomato sauce or tomato paste, 1 small clove garlic, ¼ cup salad oil, 1½ teaspoons salt, 1 teaspoon oregano, and ¼ teaspoon ground cumin. Simmer sauce gently for 10 minutes, stirring occasionally. You can freeze this sauce. Makes 3½ cups. (Thin sauce to any desired consistency with meat or poultry broth.)

Fresh Tomato and Green Chile Sauce. Peel and finely chop 6 medium-sized tomatoes. Mix with ½ cup (or more) thinly sliced or diced canned green chiles, ⅓ cup minced onion, 1 teaspoon salt, and as many minced chiles jalapeños (or other hot chiles) as please your taste (about 1 jalapeño to each cup of sauce will make it noticeably hot). Makes 3 cups.

Guacamole. Mash 2 large peeled and pitted ripe avocados with a fork until fairly smooth. Blend in 1 small mashed or minced garlic clove, 2 or 3 tablespoons lemon or lime juice (or to taste), ¼ teaspoon ground coriander (optional), dash of cayenne, and salt to taste. For a touch of heat, add 2 or 3 chopped canned green chiles. Makes about 1⅔ cups.

☛ *Fresh Tomato Barbecue Sauce*

1 medium-sized onion, chopped
3 stalks celery, chopped
3 tablespoons butter or margarine
2 cups meaty tomatoes, peeled, seeds and pulp removed, diced
¼ cup salad oil
¼ cup cider vinegar
¼ cup lemon juice
6 tablespoons brown sugar
2 tablespoons prepared mustard
2 tablespoons Worcestershire
1 tablespoon salt
1 tablespoon pepper

Barbecue sauces made with fresh tomatoes are exceptionally good. If you have an abundant supply of home-grown tomatoes, a sauce is a good way to use a large quantity quickly. This sauce freezes well and is a complement to beef, pork, poultry, and more strongly flavored fish.

Sauté onions and celery in butter over medium heat until translucent. Add tomatoes and cook over medium-low heat for 5 minutes. Add salad oil, vinegar, lemon juice, sugar, mustard, Worcestershire, salt, and pepper; cook for 10 minutes, stirring sauce occasionally. Makes 3 cups.

☛ *Sweet-Sour Tomato Barbecue Sauce*

1 medium-sized onion, sliced
1 green pepper, seeded and sliced
2 tablespoons butter or salad oil
1 can (1 lb., 12 oz.) whole tomatoes
¼ cup brown sugar, firmly packed
2 tablespoons white wine vinegar
1 small can (8¾ oz.) pineapple tidbits
½ teaspoon salt
½ teaspoon Worcestershire
    Dash pepper
    Dash liquid hot-pepper seasoning
1 whole lemon, sliced

With sweet-sour overtones, this rich tomato sauce is good with barbecued ribs (beef or pork), beef steaks, or chicken. Use it as a baste; then heat and serve it with the cooked meat.

Sauté onion and pepper in butter just until tender. Add undrained tomatoes, brown sugar, vinegar, pineapple and syrup, salt, Worcestershire, pepper, and liquid hot-pepper seasoning. Simmer, uncovered, about 15 minutes. Add lemon slices and simmer sauce about 5 minutes more or until liquid is reduced and slightly thickened.

☛ Three-Way Tomato Relish

4 pounds medium-sized ripe
    tomatoes (about 12)
3 large onions, peeled and chopped
2 cups white vinegar
2 cups chopped celery
¾ cup sugar
¼ cup prepared horseradish
2 teaspoons salt
2 teaspoons dry mustard
½ teaspoon paprika
2 cloves garlic, minced or mashed
1 teaspoon whole dried basil
2 teaspoons whole mixed
    pickling spices
2 green peppers, seeded and chopped
3 small dried hot chile peppers, crushed

This tomato relish is made with three different degrees of spiciness. Each pint gets a little hotter, and you can flavor beef, pork, fowl, and strong-flavored fish with whichever version you choose. The relish keeps in the refrigerator for up to a month, or may be cooled slightly and frozen.

Peel tomatoes and chop coarsely. Place chopped tomatoes in a large deep pan (at least 5 quarts) with onions, vinegar, celery, sugar, horseradish, salt, mustard, paprika, garlic, and basil, along with the pickling spices (tied in a square of cheesecloth). Bring tomato mixture to a boil, reduce heat, and boil slowly, uncovered, for 1 hour, stirring occasionally. Add green pepper and continue cooking for 1½ hours longer, stirring frequently. Remove seasoning packet and discard it. Ladle ⅓ of the sauce into a clean 1-pint jar. To remaining sauce, add 2 of the dried hot chiles and continue cooking for 15 minutes more; ladle ½ of this mixture into another clean 1-pint jar. Add remaining chile to sauce still in the pan and cook the mixture for 15 minutes before placing in a third jar. Serve at room temperature. Makes 3 pints of sauce.

☛ Fresh Red Chile Salsa

This easy version of Mexican red chile sauce is made with fresh tomatoes. Fish with assertive flavors, as well as beef, pork, and poultry benefit by this sauce.

Peel 4 firm medium-sized red tomatoes and chop fine. Mix with 1 can (4 oz.) drained, chopped green chile peppers, 1 medium-sized, finely chopped onion, ¼ teaspoon salt, and a dash pepper. Stir in 2 tablespoons cider vinegar and a dash liquid hot-pepper seasoning. Let stand for 1 to 2 hours before serving to allow flavors to blend well. Makes 4 to 5 cups.

☛ Kebab Sauce

1 can (10½ oz.) condensed tomato soup
  Water
  Oil or shortening
1 teaspoon dry mustard
1 teaspoon sugar (firmly packed
    brown, or granulated)
1 teaspoon salt
2 teaspoons chile powder
3 to 4 tablespoons wine or vinegar
  Worcestershire
  Paprika   Pepper
1 onion, finely chopped
1 large clove garlic, finely chopped
  Pinch rosemary
1 tablespoon liquid smoke

You can make this sauce in quantity and store it in the refrigerator for use on beef, pork, poultry, and fish with pronounced flavors.

Pour soup into a pan; fill can about three-fourths full of water, and add enough shortening or oil to bring water to top of the can; pour into saucepan. Add mustard, sugar, salt, chile powder, wine or vinegar, Worcestershire, paprika, pepper to taste, chopped onion, chopped garlic, rosemary, and liquid smoke.

    Heat to boiling and cook for about 5 minutes, or until all ingredients are well blended. Makes about 2¾ cups of sauce.

Tomato-Ginger Baste with Variations

1½ cups catsup
 ¼ cup soy sauce
 ⅓ cup brown sugar, firmly packed
 1 teaspoon salt
 1 teaspoon dry mustard
 1 clove garlic, crushed
2½ teaspoons ground ginger

Brush this tomato-ginger baste (or the cranberry or apricot variation) on chicken, pork chops, spareribs, or hamburgers.

Combine catsup, soy sauce, brown sugar, salt, mustard, garlic, and ginger, mixing well. Cover and let stand 2 hours to blend flavors, or refrigerate until ready to use. Brush on meat during the last 10 minutes of cooking. (It will burn easily, so watch it carefully.)

Cranberry-Ginger Baste

Omit catsup and add 1 small can (7 oz.) jellied cranberry sauce and ¼ cup more brown sugar.

Smoky Apricot Baste

Omit catsup and soy sauce and add 1 cup puréed canned apricots, ¼ teaspoon liquid smoke flavoring, and 3 tablespoons lemon juice.

Western Sauce

 1 can (1 lb.) tomatoes
 2 cups water
 1 can (6 oz.) tomato paste
 2 dried chile peppers
 ½ cup tomato catsup
 2 tablespoons sugar
 2 teaspoons Worcestershire
 2 teaspoons chile powder
    Juice of 2 lemons
 ¼ cup wine vinegar
2½ teaspoons salt
 ¼ teaspoon cayenne
 ¼ teaspoon liquid hot-
       pepper seasoning
 2 teaspoons freshly
       ground black pepper
 1 large onion, chopped
 1 clove garlic, chopped
 2 bay leaves
 ½ pound butter
 2 teaspoons dry mustard

This sauce can be kept for several weeks in the refrigerator. Spread it on beef; or you can try it on pork, poultry, and even fish, if they're stronger-flavored ones.

Combine all ingredients and let simmer over low flame in covered pan for about 30 minutes. Strain through coarse sieve. Cool; pour into refrigerator containers and refrigerate until needed.

👉 Bercy Butter for Grilled Meats

For grilled meats, butter is flavored with the ingredients usually found in the creamy Bercy Sauce. It's delicious on barbecued lamb or beef.

Cook 1 tablespoon minced shallots or green onions in ½ cup dry white wine until wine is reduced by half. Cool and add 6 tablespoons butter creamed with 1 tablespoon minced parsley. Add salt and freshly ground black pepper to taste.

👉 Sauce Bercy for Grilled Meats

In a saucepan, cook 1 tablespoon minced shallots or green onions in 2 tablespoons butter until soft. Add 1 cup dry white wine; simmer until liquid is reduced by half. Mix together ¼ cup (⅛ lb.) butter and 2 teaspoons flour; add to the liquid in pan. Cook, stirring, until thickened. Stir in 1 tablespoon minced parsley and salt and pepper to taste.

👉 Cheddar-Sherry Sauce

¼ pound process Cheddar cheese
½ cup sherry
1 teaspoon dry mustard
½ teaspoon seasoned salt
¼ teaspoon paprika
   Salt to taste

Serve cheddar-sherry sauce hot over steaks, lamb chops, or any other meats.

Melt cheese in double boiler and add sherry, a little at a time, stirring constantly. When well blended, add mustard, seasoned salt, paprika, and salt to taste, stirring thoroughly. Serve hot.

👉 Shallot Sauce

The French consider the shallot (a small onion-like bulb) to be a choice flavoring ingredient in many dishes. It's the important flavor in this quickly-made sauce to serve with barbecued beef steak.

For each steak, melt 1½ teaspoons butter in a frying pan. Add 1½ tablespoons chopped shallots and sauté until shallots are soft, but not browned. Add 2 tablespoons dry red wine and reduce the liquid over high heat until most of the liquid is gone. Serve at once over piping hot meat. Makes enough sauce for 1 steak.

For all of these fish sauces, you will find suggestions of the fish each best complements. The sauces may be served at once or refrigerated.

Hollandaise Sauces

For these two sauces you make Hollandaise in a blender, then add either chopped cucumber or shrimp. Serve warm or rewarm them over hot water.

Sauce Hollandaise with Cucumber (salmon, halibut, trout, albacore). Combine in the blender 3 egg yolks (at room temperature) and 1½ tablespoons lemon juice. Melt ¾ cup butter or margarine and heat until it bubbles—don't brown. Add 1 tablespoon hot water to the egg, turn blender on high speed, and immediately pour in hot butter in a steady stream (takes about 5 seconds). Add 1 teaspoon prepared mustard and ½ teaspoon salt and whirl until blended, about 30 seconds. Turn into a bowl and stir in 1 tablespoon each chopped parsley and chives. Peel 1 cucumber, cut in half, scrape out large seeds, chop, and stir into sauce. Makes about 2 cups.

Sauce Hollandaise with Shrimp (salmon, sole, halibut, sea bass, rockfish). Prepare as for Sauce Hollandaise, above, except omit salt; turn into a bowl, omit cucumber, and stir in 1 can (about 5 oz.) shrimp, which have been rinsed and drained.

Tomato Sauce

The word Portugaise is often used to designate a tomato sauce. A short cut is employed to make this sauce, using canned stewed tomatoes. Its robust flavor is best suited to fish that have assertive flavors themselves.

Portugaise Sauce (halibut, rockfish, sea bass, swordfish, albacore). Sauté 1 medium-sized onion (chopped) in ¼ cup butter or margarine until soft. Add 1 crushed clove garlic, ½ teaspoon thyme, ¼ teaspoon crushed rosemary, and 1 can (1 lb.) stewed tomatoes (break up tomatoes with spoon). Simmer, uncovered, stirring occasionally, until reduced to about half—takes about 15 minutes. Add salt and pepper to taste.

Mayonnaise Sauces

Mayonnaise is the base of a number of cold fish sauces. Use them on sautéed, broiled, or barbecued fish—served cold on the sizzling hot fish—or on chilled, poached fish.

Here is an easy way to make mayonnaise sauces with a wire whip and round-bottomed bowl or your electric mixer. (If you happen to add oil too fast, causing the mayonnaise to separate, start again with 1 egg yolk in a clean bowl and slowly beat in curdled mixture.)

Herb Mayonnaise Sauce (for any fish). Put into the bowl 2 egg yolks, ½ teaspoon *each* dry mustard, salt, thyme, and tarragon, dash cayenne, 2 tablespoons chopped parsley, 1 tablespoon chopped chives, and 2 tablespoons lemon juice; beat until blended. Measure 1 cup salad oil (may be all or part olive oil); slowly add the oil (about 1 tablespoon at a time), beating constantly. As the mixture begins to get thick, you can beat in the oil more rapidly—in a slow stream. Beat in about 1 tablespoon hot water to make a good sauce consistency. Makes about 1½ cups.

Brown Butter Almond Sauce (any fish, but best with salmon, halibut, trout). Heat 1 cup (½ lb.) butter until it melts and turns a golden brown; cool to lukewarm. Following Herb Mayonnaise recipe above, add mustard and cayenne to egg yolks, but omit the salt, herbs, parsley, and chives, and reduce lemon to 1 tablespoon. Instead of salad oil, beat the browned butter into egg mixture exactly as directed for the mayonnaise, above. Beat in 1 tablespoon dry sherry with the hot water. Then stir in ½ cup toasted, slivered almonds. If this becomes too stiff, beat in a little more hot water.

Rémoulade Sauce (sole, rockfish, sea bass, halibut, trout). Prepare the Herb Mayonnaise, above, omitting salt, thyme, and chives; add 1 teaspoon anchovy paste and ½ teaspoon chervil to the egg mixture. After all oil has been added (omit water), stir in ¼ cup finely chopped dill pickle, 1 tablespoon chopped capers, and 2 hard-cooked eggs, chopped.

☛ *Herb Wine Marinade*

1 cup dry white wine
¼ cup lemon juice
2 tablespoons wine vinegar
2 cloves garlic, crushed
1 teaspoon salt
1 teaspoon dried whole
   tarragon or rosemary
2 tablespoons melted butter
   or salad oil

Here's a marinade for chicken with two variations: one that can be used for lamb, and another for beef or pork.

In a saucepan, combine the wine, lemon juice, vinegar, garlic, salt, tarragon or rosemary, and butter or salad oil; heat just to simmering; remove from heat. Cover and let stand for 1 hour to allow flavors to blend. Pour sauce over broiler-fryer chicken halves or quarters, and let marinate 1 to 4 hours, depending on how thoroughly you wish the flavors to penetrate. Use the remaining sauce to baste the chicken while barbecuing.

Honey-Wine Marinade for Lamb

Omit lemon juice and tarragon or rosemary in recipe above, and add ⅓ cup honey and 1 teaspoon fresh or dried chopped mint. Pour sauce over lamb chops, steaks, shanks, or breast, and let marinate 1 to 4 hours depending on how thoroughly you wish the flavor to penetrate. Use the remaining sauce to baste the lamb while barbecuing.

Red Wine Marinade for Beef or Pork

Use dry red wine in place of the white wine in basic recipe above; omit the lemon juice and tarragon or rosemary. Add 1 teaspoon dried whole oregano or basil. Pour sauce over steak, spareribs, or pork chops, and let marinate 2 to 6 hours, depending on how thoroughly you wish the flavors to penetrate.

☛ *Bercy Sauce for Barbecued Fish*

This sauce is good with most fish—baked, broiled, or barbecued.

Melt 3 tablespoons butter in a pan; add 2 teaspoons minced shallots or green onions and cook until translucent. Stir in 2 tablespoons flour, and cook 1 minute. Then stir in 1 cup fish stock (or substitute ½ cup chicken stock, ½ cup dry white wine). Season to taste with salt and pepper, and at the last, stir in 1 teaspoon minced parsley. Makes about 1¼ cups.

Basic Lemon Butter Baste

½ cup (¼ lb.) butter, melted
¼ cup lemon juice
½ teaspoon salt

Use this basic mixture for chicken halves or quarters, or on any kind of fish that you wish to barbecue. Variations are given to use with turkey, lamb, and hamburgers.

Combine the butter, lemon juice, and salt. Brush the baste onto the meat several times during the entire cooking time.

Herb Butter Baste for Chicken or Turkey

Add ¼ teaspoon rosemary and ¼ teaspoon thyme to the melted butter before adding the lemon juice and salt.

Parsley Orange Baste for Lamb

Add 2 tablespoons grated orange peel, 2 tablespoons finely chopped parsley, and 2 tablespoons honey to the butter before adding lemon juice and salt.

Savory Baste for Hamburgers

Add 2 teaspoons brown bottled gravy sauce and ¼ teaspoon pepper to the basic recipe.

Sauce Potpourri

1 clove garlic, minced
1 small onion, minced
¾ teaspoon dry mustard
1 tablespoon grated fresh horseradish
1 tablespoon mixed minced herbs
   (thyme, marjoram, parsley)
2 tablespoons vinegar
3 cups water
¾ teaspoon salt
1 tablespoon bottled meat
   sauce or Worcestershire
⅔ cup butter
½ cup catsup
½ teaspoon liquid hot-pepper seasoning
2 teaspoons sugar
¾ teaspoon chile powder
¼ teaspoon freshly ground black pepper

Use sauce potpourri to baste meat or fish while cooking, or dip slices or chunks of hot cooked meat into the heated sauce before serving.

Combine all ingredients and cook slowly for 45 minutes. Makes 3 cups sauce.

Horseradish Mayonnaise

This cool creamy sauce is quite delicious with barbecued salmon.

Combine in the blender ¼ cup lemon juice, ¾ teaspoon salt, ½ teaspoon sugar, and 1 egg; whirl at high speed. With motor running, remove blender top and add 1 cup salad oil in slow, steady stream; continue whirling about 2 minutes. Stir in 3 tablespoons prepared horseradish. Fold in 1 cup commercial sour cream or 1 cup heavy cream, whipped. Serve immediately, or chill before serving. Makes 2½ cups.

Golden Papaya Baste

1 can (9 oz.) undrained sliced papaya, puréed (or use mashed fresh fruit with 3 tablespoons sugar)
2 tablespoons white wine vinegar
2 tablespoons sherry or fruit juice
2 tablespoons salad oil or melted butter
1 tablespoon honey
½ teaspoon salt
¼ teaspoon powdered ginger or curry powder

The golden color of papaya coats chicken (or pork) with its own color. In places where the baste caramelizes, the papaya flavor becomes even richer.

Combine papaya, vinegar, sherry or fruit juice, salad oil, honey, salt, ginger or curry powder. Bring to a boil; simmer 10 to 15 minutes. Makes about 1¼ cups.

Purple Plum Baste

1 can (1 lb.) purple plums with syrup (or cooked fresh plums), puréed
¼ cup lemon juice or vinegar
2 tablespoons chopped onions
2 tablespoons brown sugar, firmly packed
2 tablespoons salad oil or melted butter
½ teaspoon salt

Use either fresh plums or canned purple plums for this baste for chicken or pork. If you use canned plums, simply pit and purée. If you use fresh plums, cook 8 to 10 plums with ½ cup water and ⅓ cup sugar until tender, then purée.

Combine plum purée, lemon juice or vinegar, onions, sugar, salad oil, and salt. Bring to a boil; simmer 10 to 15 minutes. Makes about 2 cups sauce.

👉 *Savory Raisin Baste*

½ cup raisins (or cooked
    prunes, pitted)
¼ cup chopped onion
1 small clove garlic, minced or mashed
½ cup catsup
½ cup regular strength beef
    broth or dry white wine
3 tablespoons salad oil
2 tablespoons wine vinegar
1 tablespoon brown sugar,
    firmly packed
1 teaspoon prepared mustard
1 teaspoon liquid smoke
½ teaspoon salt
⅛ teaspoon dill weed

This full-flavored, moderately thick baste becomes a crusty glaze on the meat, fruity and slightly sweet-sour in flavor. It's especially good on rare beef steak.

Purée raisins (or chop very fine). Combine with onion, garlic, catsup, broth or wine, salad oil, vinegar, sugar, mustard, liquid smoke, salt, and dill. Simmer 10 to 15 minutes. Makes about 1¾ cups.

👉 *Smoky Peach or Apricot Baste*

1 can (about 9 oz.) peaches or apricots,
    undrained (or use about ½ cup
    peeled and sliced ripe fresh fruit
    mashed with 3 tablespoons sugar)
¼ cup catsup
3 tablespoons lemon juice
2 tablespoons salad oil or melted butter
½ teaspoon liquid smoke
½ teaspoon salt
⅛ teaspoon grated lemon peel

If you use peaches for this baste, try a dash of allspice to bring out the peach flavor. Try the baste first on lamb, but you may also like it on pork or chicken.

Purée fruits. Combine with catsup, lemon juice, salad oil, liquid smoke, salt, and lemon peel. Bring to a boil; simmer 10 to 15 minutes. Makes about 1½ cups.

👉 *Sweet-Sour Pineapple Baste*

1 can (8½ oz.) crushed
    pineapple, undrained
¾ cup regular strength chicken
    broth or dry white dinner wine
3 tablespoons white wine vinegar
2 tablespoons salad oil
1 tablespoon soy sauce
1 tablespoon chopped onion
1 tablespoon brown sugar,
    firmly packed
1 teaspoon lemon juice
½ teaspoon garlic salt

Brush this over swordfish as it grills over the barbecue coals, or try it on other fish, chicken, or spareribs to add moistness and richness.

Combine pineapple, chicken broth or wine, vinegar, salad oil, soy sauce, onion, sugar, lemon juice, and garlic salt. Bring to a boil and simmer 10 to 15 minutes. Makes about 1⅔ cups.

INDEX

A

Appetizers
Bacon and Bread Poles, 62; Beef Jerky, 59; Beef-Oyster, 56; Cheese, Grilled, 75; Chicken, Indonesian, 114; Dates with Cheese, 138; Duckling Meatballs, 124; Frank and Cheese Roll-Ups, 62; Ham-Broiled Holiday Cherries, 62; Hawaiian Bamboo-Beef, 69; Mushroom Caps in Butter, 141; Pork, Grilled Chinese, 91; Salmon, Smoked Fresh Fillet, 130; Shrimp, 133; Skewered, 9

B

Bacon, see Pork
Bastes, see also Marinades, Sauces; Basic Chicken, 115; Basic Lemon Butter, 154; Cranberry-Ginger, 150; definition, 145; Golden Papaya, 155; Herb Butter for Chicken or Turkey, 154; Purple Plum, 155; Savory, for Hamburgers, 154; Savory Raisin, 156; Smoky Apricot, 150; Smoky Peach or Apricot, 156; Soy-Ginger, 146; Sweet-Sour Pineapple, 156; Tomato-Ginger, 150
Beef
Brains, see Variety Meats; Frankfurters: and Cheese Roll-ups, 62; how to barbecue, 77. Hamburgers: and Cheese Stacks, 73; Cheeseburgers with Guacamole, 73; Chef's, 70; Crunchy Onion-Beef, 73; Hamburger Steak in the Round, 71; Mushroom-Filled Hamburger Cups, 72; Soy-Dipped, 72; Stretched, 71. Heart, see Variety Meats; Jerky, 59; Kebabs: Indonesian Satés, 90; Pakistani, 115. Kidneys, see Variety Meats; Liver, see Variety Meats; Meat loaf: Individual Meat and Spinach Loaves, 74; Pizza-Flavored, 74. Pit-cooked, for a crowd, 46; Rib Bones, Barbecued, 68; Shanks, Herbed, with Summer Squash, 67; Shortribs: Argentine, 30; Korean, 69; Marinated, 68
Beef Roasts
Boneless cross-rib, Lazy Holiday Roast, 66; buying guide, 42-43; Chuck: Chef's, 66; Savory, 67. rolled rib, 28; rump, 28; sirloin, 28; Spencer, 28; Spit-roasting time, 28; Standing Rib Roast, 13, 28; tenderloin or fillet roast, 42
Beef Steaks
Blade bone chuck steak, 41; buying guide, 40-41; Chuck: Garlic Steak in a Crust, 66; With Anchovy Butter, 65. Club, Pepper Steak, 54; cooking on the coals, 52; Cube, Pizza-Style, 54; Eye of Round, Grilled, 63; Filet Mignon Aubergine, 51; Fillet: Oyster-Topped Beef, 49; Whole with Blue-Cheese Log, 50. Flank: Cumin Steak Strips and Cheese, 61; Tender Teriyaki Steak Strips, 61; With Roquefort Butter, 61. Grilling time, 22; Japanese-Style, 55; Market Steaks, Oyster-Stuffed, 53; New York, Pepper Steak, 54; Porter-house: cooked on a plank, 51; With Béarnaise, 49. Rib eye: Honolulu Steak, 53; With Seasoned Butters, 52. Seven-bone chuck, 41; Sirloin: à la Mirabeau, 55; Ginger Beef Teriyaki, 54; Hawaiian Bamboo-Beef Appetizers, 69; Skewered Beef-Oyster Appetizers, 56; Tip, Smoked, 57. Skirt: Argentine style, 30; Beef Skirts-Kebab, 59; Teriyaki, 60; With Burgundy Sauce, 60. Tenderloin: Hanging, 60; Steak Casanova, 52. Top round: Barbecue Strognoff, 63; Family Barbecue, 64; Giant Beef-Lobster Kebabs, 58; Jalisco, 62; Sweetbreads and Steak Brochette, 79; With Artichoke Hearts, 64, 145. Top sirloin: Giant Beef-Lobster Kebabs, 58; Rosemary Barbecued, 55; Steak Kebabs, 58; Steak Sandwiches with Mushroom Sauce, 57. Western Barbecue, 56
Butters, flavored
Basil, 147; Blue Cheese, 147; Dill, 147; Fines Herbes, 147; for venison: Green Chile, 104; Sesame-Cheese, 104; Vegetable, 104. Garlic, 147; Ginger, for Fruit Kebabs, 138; Herb: baste, 76; For Buffalo Steak, 107; For Cornish Game Hens, 116. Lemon-Anchovy Butter Ring, 65; Maître d'Hôtel, 147; Mustard, 147; Red Onion, 147; Rib Eye Steaks with, 52; Roquefort Butter, Steak with, 61; Shallot, 147

C

Center-cut cross rib steak, 40, 41
Cheese
Beef Stacks, 73; Blue: Butter, 147; Sauce for Turkey, 117. -burgers with Guacamole, 73; Cheddar: Grilled with Dates, 138; -Sherry Sauce, 151. Cumin Steak Strips, 61; Frank Roll-Ups, 62; Jack, Grilled Appetizer, 75
Chicken, see also Poultry
Breasts, 30; Halves or Quarters, 13; Kebabs: East Indian Saté, 90; Indonesian Satés, 90. Livers, 20; Skirt Steaks with Burgundy Sauce, 60
Chile Sauces: Fresh Red Salsa, 149; Fresh Tomato and Green Chile, 148; Kebab, 149; Red, 148; Three-Way Tomato Relish, 149; Western, 150
Chuck fillet or Scotch tender, 43
Club roast, 42
Club steak, 40
Coal cooking: Recipes, 30, 34, 51, 52, 62, 94, 114, 131, 140, 142, 144; Roasted Stuffed Eggplant, 140; Steak, 52; Vegetables, 144
Corn on the cob, 21; charcoal-roasting, 143
Cross rib, shoulder clod, and English cut roasts, 43

E

Eggplant: for skewer cooking, 20, 21; Lamb Chops à la Castellane, 97; With Filet Mignon Aubergine, 51

Electric barbecues, 8, 10, 11
Equipment, 7-13
Eye of round roast, 42, 43

F

Fire
Fuels, 15; how to light: chimney starters, 16; electric starters, 16; kindling, 15; other methods, 16; special packs and egg cartons, 15. Lining firebed, 14; rake, 11
Firemanship, 16; grilling, 22; special aromas, 17; spit roasting 28
Firepit cooking: Beans, 46; Beef, 46; cooking time, 38; covering pit, 38; kind of wood, 37; preparing meat, 38; recipes, 35-37, 46; Salmon, 35-37; size of pit, 36-37; techniques, 35-38; timing fire, 37-38
Fish
Albacore, 20, 21; large fillets, 128; Soy-Grilled Steaks, 135. Anchovy, 20, 21; and Shrimp Appetizers, 133; Chuck Steak with Anchovy Butter, 65; Sirloin à la Mirabeau, 55. Barracuda: Steaks, 134; Whole, 128. Bercy Sauce for, 153; boning trout, 129; Fillets, 13; Flounder, Fish Smoked in Paper, 131; for skewer cooking, 20-21; grilling time, 22; Halibut, 128, 129; Kebabs, Baluk Shish, 131; Lingcod, 128, 129; Mackerel, Boned, in Crumb Crust, 127; Rockfish, 128, 129; Sablefish, 128; Salmon, 24: Baluk Shish Kebab, 131; Large Fillets, 128; Smoked Fresh Fillet, 130; Smoked in Paper, 131; With Lemon Rice Stuffing, 130. Sea bass: Barbecued Lean White, 129; Large Fillets, 128; spit-roasting time, 28. Striped Bass, With Tomato Sauce, 127; Swordfish: Orange-Soy, 132; Piraeus, 132; Slow-Smoked Garlic, 132. Tips on barbecuing: fillets, 128; small whole fish, 128; steaks, 128. Totuava, Barbecued Lean White, 129; Trout, 128: Butterflied, 129; how to bone, 129
Flank steak, 41
Flatiron or triangle roast, 43
Foil cooking: Chicken, Orange-Baked, 114; fruits and vegetables, 143, 144; Duckling with Raisin Sauce, 121; Orange Barbecued Duckling, 108, 122
Frankfurters, see Beef
Fruit
Apple, 20, 21: Cinnamon, with Venison Roast, 105; Coal-cooked, 144; Foil-wrapped, 142; fruit dressing for turkey, 120; Ginger-Buttered Fruit Kebabs, 138; Soy-Pineapple Slices, 139; Spit roasting, 141. Apricot, 20: Glaze for Cornish game hens, 116; Smoked Chicken with Brandy Baste, 112; Smoky Baste, 156. Banana, 20, 21: Coal-cooked, 144; Foil-wrapped, 142; Ginger-Buttered Fruit Kebabs, 138; Pineapple-Banana-Bacon Grill, 139; Spit roasting, 141. Cherries, Smoked Chicken with Brandy Baste, 112; Dates, 138; Dressing for turkey, 120; Figs,

Fruit (continued)

138; For skewer cooking, 20-21;
Ginger-Buttered Kebabs, 138;
Grapefruit, 138; Lamb Sosaties
with, 101; *Orange:* -Baked
Chicken, 114; Baste for duckling,
121; Foil-wrapped, 142; Ginger-
Buttered Fruit Kebabs, 138.
Papaya, Spit roasting, 141;
Peaches: Chicken with, 110;
Grilling idea, 138. *Pineapple:* and
Apple Slices, Soy-, 139;
-Banana-Bacon Grill, 139; Foil-
wrapped, 142; Ginger-Buttered
Fruit Kebabs, 138; Spit roasting,
141. Raisin, Sauce for Duckling,
121; skewer combinations, 20-
21; tips on barbecuing, 137
Fuels, 15

G

Game
    Bear: Saddle, With Juniper, 106;
    trichinosis, 106. *Buffalo:* Ground,
    With Wild Rice Dressing, 107;
    Steak, With Wild Rice Dressing,
    107; Stew, In Tomato-Wine
    Sauce, 106. Buying guide, 103;
    how to cook, 103; *Venison:* With
    Cinnamon Apples, 105; Grilled,
    103; Ripple-Skewered Sand-
    wiches, 103; With Trio of
    Butters, 104
Garlic: Butter, 147; Leg of Lamb
    with Coffee Baste, 94; Slow-
    Smoked Swordfish, 132; With
    corn on the cob, 143
Gas barbecue, 10, 11
Goat, Capretto, how to grill, 96
Goose, *see* Poultry
Grill-cooked recipes, 13, 20-21, 30,
    48, 75, 77-81, 83-85, 88-91, 93,
    96-104, 106-107, 109-112, 114-
    117, 122-124, 127-129, 131-
    136, 138-144
Grill Cooking
    Chicken, 110; Cornish game
    hens, 117; salmon for a crowd,
    24; shish kebab combinations,
    20-21; skewer-cooking, 19-21;
    foods, 20; Special techniques,
    18-20; Time and temperature
    chart, 22-23

H

Ham: *see also* Pork; 20, 21, 22, 28
Hamburgers, *see* Beef
Hanging tenderloin, 41
Hibachi, 8
Hickory chips, 10, 17, 24; bar-
    becuing fish, 128; Hickory-
    Smoked Ham for a Crowd, 87;
    smoke roasting turkey, 120
Hollandaise sauce: With Cucumber,
    152; With Shrimp, 152

J

Jerky, beef, 59
Juniper, Saddle of Bear, 106

K

Kamado, 9-10
Kebabs, *see* Beef, Chicken, Grill
    Cooking, Lamb, Pork
Knackwurst, 20, 21
Kumquats, 20

L

Lamb
    Baby lamb (kid), 28; Brains, *see*
    Variety Meats; Breast, 102;
    buying guide, 43-45; *Chops,* 30,
    44-45: à la Castellane, 97; Lamb
    Leg, 97; Kela ka Kabab, 99; or
    steaks, 22. *Ground:* Chelo Kebab,
    99; Shish Koftesi, 102. Hind, for
    a crowd, 94; how to cook, 92;
    Kebabs: Arni Souvlakia, 100;

Brochette de Rognons d'Agneau,
    102; Chelo Kebab, 99; Indian
    Seekh Kabob, 100; Kebab Barg,
    98; Lamb in Onion Juice, 96;
    Pakistani, 115; Rolls with Curry
    Honey Glaze, 97; Russian
    Shashlik, 101; Shish Koftesi,
    102. Sosaties with Fruit, 101.
    Leg: Basque-Barbecued, 92;
    Butterflied, with Herb Baste, 93;
    Butterflied, with Mushrooms, 93;
    Easy, 96; Garlic, with Coffee
    Baste, 94; grilled, 13; Lime-
    Basted, 95; Roasted, Indian
    Style, 94; Smoked, 95. Loin, 28;
    Rack (ribs),28; Rolls with Curry
    Honey Glaze, 97; Saddle, 28;
    Sauce, Basic, 100; Shanks, 102;
    Shoulder, 28; Steaks, Lela ka
    Kabab, 99
Lemon: Basic Lemon Butter Baste,
    154; -Basted Chicken with
    Peaches, 110; Marinade for Beef,
    Soy-, 146; -Rice Stuffing for
    Salmon, 130
Lobster, 20, 22: *see also* Shellfish;
    Giant Beef-Lobster Kebabs, 58
Luncheon Meat, 21; Barbecued
    Bologna, 75; Spit-Roasted Meat
    Logs, 76

M

Marinades, *see also* Bastes, Sauces;
    Apple-Soy for Pork, 82; Chile,
    for Turkey, 119; *Herb Wine:* for
    beef or Pork, 153; for Chicken,
    153; for lamb,153. Mustard-Soy,
    146; purpose, 145; Red Wine,
    57; Soy-Ginger, 146; Soy-
    Lemon for Beef, 146; Teriyaki, 63
Market Steak, 40
Meat Loaf: Chef's Ground Beef, 70;
    Individual Meat and Spinach
    Loaves, 74; Pizza Flavored, 74
Meatballs, 20, 21
Meats, *see* Beef, Beef Roasts, Beef
    Steaks, Game, Ham, Lamb, Pork,
    Sausage, Steak, Variety Meats,
    Veal
Metal Brush, 10, 12
Mexican Braseros, 8
Mushrooms, 20, 21, 49: Barbecued
    Beef Stroganoff, 63; Barbecued
    Lean White Fish with, 129;
    Butterflied Leg of Lamb with, 93;
    Caps in Butter, 141; Chicken
    Liver Kebabs, 116; en Brochette
    Flambé, 137, 141; -Filled Ham-
    burger Cups, 72; Porterhouse
    with Béarnaise, 49; Skewered
    Beef-Oyster Appetizers, 56; Skirt
    Steaks with Burgundy Sauce, 60;
    Steak Sandwiches with Mush-
    room Sauce, 57; Sweetbreads
    and Steak Brochette, 79; Sword-
    fish Piraeus, 133; Tournedos
    Héloise, 48; Wild Rice Dressing
    for Buffalo Steak, 107

N

New York strip roast, 42
Nuts: Almonds, Whole Abalone
    with Almond Butter, 135;
    Cashews, Stuffing for Pheasant,
    125; Macadamia, Butterflied
    Trout, 129; Walnuts, Indonesian
    Chicken Appetizers, 114

O

Olives, 20, 21
Onions, 20, 21: -Beef Burgers,
    Butter, Red, 147; Crunchy, 73;
    Lamb in Onion Juice, 96;
    Shellfish Kebabs, 136
Oranges, 20; Beefsteak Jalisco, 62;
    -Celery Stuffing for Duckling,
    122; Gravy with Duckling, 122;
    -Soy Swordfish, 132

Oysters, 20; Shellfish Kebabs, 136;
    Skewered Beef-Appetizers, 56;
    -Stuffed Market Steaks, 53;
    -Topped Beef Fillet, 49

P

Pâté de foie gras: Tenderloin Steak
    Casanova, 52; Tournedos
    Héloise, 48
Pheasant, *see* Poultry
Pineapple, 20, 21; Barbecued
    Bacon, 91; Grilled Chinese Pork
    Appetizers, 91; Skewered Veal
    Barbecue, 70; Spareribs, 88;
    Sweet-Sour Baste, 156; Sweet-
    Sour Tomato Barbecue Sauce,
    148
Pit-cooked recipes, 35-37, 46; *see
    also* Firepit cooking
Pork
    Appetizers, Grilled Chinese, 91;
    Bacon: and Bread Poles, Toasted,
    62; Barbecued with Pineapple,
    91; Basque-Barbecued Lamb,
    92; Canadian Bacon, Spit-
    Roasted Meat Logs, 76; Chicken
    Liver Kebabs, 116; Foie de Veau
    en Brochette, 77; Grilled with
    dates, 138; Grilled with Figs,
    138; Liver 'n Bacon Grill, 79;
    Pheasant with Cashew stuffing,
    125; Pineapple-Banana-Bacon
    Grill, 139; Shellfish Kebabs, 136;
    Smoked-Glazed Chicken, 113;
    With Corn on the Cob, 143.
    buying guide, 45; Butt, Vene-
    zuelan Barbecued, 83; Chops or
    Steaks, 22, 82; Ground, Indivi-
    dual Meat and Spinach Loaves,
    74; *Ham:* -Broiled Holiday
    Cherries, 62; grilling time, 22;
    Hickory-Smoked, for a Crowd,
    87; Honey-Glazed, 86; Smoky
    Steaks, 85; Spicy Steak, 84;
    Spit-Roasted Meat Logs, 76;
    spit-roasting time, 28; Steak with
    Cantaloupe, 84. How to Cook,
    82; *Kebabs:* East Indian Saté, 90;
    Indonesian Satés, 90; Satés Bali,
    89. Kidneys, *see* Variety Meats;
    Leg, Rolled, Hawaiian-Style, 82;
    Loin: with Prunes, 83; Roast, on
    Melon Ring, 84. Pigs' Feet,
    Crumb-Coated, 91; Roasts, 82;
    Salt: Venison Roast with Cinna-
    mon Apples, 105; Whole Liver,
    78. *Sausages:* how to barbecue,
    77; Italian, with Summer Squash,
    90; Rice, Spanish Style, 111.
    Spareribs, 22, 28, 82; Chinese,
    87; Garlic, 87; Ginger-
    Barbecued, 88; Pineapple, 88;
    Smoked, in Barbecue Sauce, 89.
    Suckling pig, 28; How to spit
    roast, 85
Portable barbecues, 8
Portable grill, 13
Porterhouse steak, 40
Poultry
    Chicken: Appetizers, Indonesian,
    114; basic bastes for, 115;
    Breasts, 30, 109: Barbecued,
    109; Pakistani Kebabs, 115.
    Grilling time, 22; Herbed, 109;
    how to grill, 110; how to spit
    roast, 113; Kebabs, Liver, 116;
    Kebabs, Pakistani, 115; Lemon-
    Basted, 110; Liver Kebabs, 116;
    Orange-Baked, 114; Pakistani
    Barbecued, 111; Ranch-Style,
    112; Smoke-Glazed, 113;
    Smoked, with Brandy Baste,
    112; Spanish Style, 111; Spicy
    Yogurt, 112; spit-roasting time,
    28; Spread Eagle, 109; With
    Peaches, 110. *Cornish Game
    Hens,* 22, 28: Buttery, 116;
    Herb Butter, 116; how to bar-
    becue, 117. *Duck:* Broiled
    Mallard, 123; how to barbecue,
    108; Kamo no Koma-Giri, 124;

Poultry (continued)
Meatballs, 124; Orange Barbecued, 108, 122; With Orange
Baste, 121; With Raisin Sauce,
121. *Goose,* 28: cooking tips,
108; Crisp-Roasted, 124; how
to cook, 108. *Pheasant:* Barbecue, 124; With Cashew stuffing,
125. Rock Cornish Game Hen,
Surprised Squab, 125; Squab,
22, 28; *Turkey,* 22, 28: Chile-
Barbecued Drumsticks, 119;
Parts in Blue Cheese Sauce, 117;
Roll, how to barbecue, 118;
Smoke cooking, 118; Spit
roasting, 118; Smoke Roasting,
120; Smoky, with Fruit Dressing,
120; Teriyaki Roll, 118

Q

Quantity barbecuing, 30: Argentine
asado, 30; cooking underground,
46; Lamb for a Crowd, 94;
portable grill, 13; *Salmon:*
Broiled in Foil, 24; Indian style,
34

R

Rib eye, market roast or Spencer
roll, 42
Rib eye steak, 40
Rice: Chello, 98; Chelo Kebab, 99;
Lemon Rice Stuffing for Salmon,
130; Wild Dressing for Buffalo
steak, 107; With Sausage, for
Chicken, Spanish style, 111
Rolled rib roast, 42

S

Salmon, 24; *see also* Fish; cooking
underground, 35-37
Sandwiches
Beef, Cumin Steak Strips and
Cheese, 61; Fish, Smoked Fresh
Salmon Fillet, 130; Hamburgers,
see Beef; Steak, with Mushroom
Sauce, 57; Venison Steak,
Ripple-Skewered, 103
Sauces, *see also* Bastes, Marinades;
All-Purpose Barbecue, 146;
Basic Fish: Hollandaise, 152;
With Cucumber, 152; With
Shrimp, 152. *Mayonnaise:*
Brown Butter Almond, 152;
Herb, 152; Remoulade, 152.
Three-Way Tomato Relish, 149;
Tomato, 152; Portugaise, 152.
Basic Lamb, 100; Béarnaise, 49;
Bercy for Barbecued Fish, 153;
Bercy for Grilled Meats, 151;
Blue Cheese, for Turkey, 117;
Cheddar-Sherry, 151; Chimi-
churri, 30; Definition, 145;
Fresh Red Chile Salsa, 149;
Fresh Tomato Barbecue, 148;
Horseradish Mayonnaise, 155;
Kebab, 149; Madeira, for Saddle
of Bear with Juniper, 106;
Potpourri, 154; Raisin, for
duckling, 121; Shallot, 151;
Simple Madeira, 48; Special
Mexican, for Beef, 148; Sweet-
Sour Tomato Barbecue, 148;
Tomato Béarnaise, 58; Tomato-
Soy, 74; Western, 150
Sausage, 20, 21; *see also* Beef, Pork
Blood, 20; Bratwurst, 20;
Chinese, 20; *how to barbecue:*
Blood, 77; Cocktail, 77; Frank-
furters, 77; German garlic
(knackwurst), 77; Italian garlic
(salsiccia), 77; Italian simmering
(coteghino), 77; Smoked Polish
(kielbasa or kolbassy), 77; Swiss
(bratwurst), 77. Rice with, 111
Seven-bone chuck steak, 41
Shellfish
Abalone, With Almond Butter,

135; *Lobster:* barbecuing, 134;
boiling, 134; cleaning, 134;
frozen tails, 134; Northern, 134;
Northeastern, 134; Spiny Pacific,
134. *Shrimp Appetizers:* Butter-
flied, 133; Spicy, 133; With
Anchovy, 133. *Kebabs:* Onigari
Kaki, 136; With Oysters, 136
Shish-Kebab, *see* Beef Steaks,
Chicken, Lamb, Shellfish,
Skewers
Shortribs, 30; Korean style, 39, 47,
69
Shoulder clod (cross rib) roasts, 46
Shrimp, 20, 21; Sauce Hollandaise
with, 152; *see also* Shellfish
Sirloin tip steak, 41
Skewer, 11, 12: -Cooked Recipes;
Beef-Oyster Appetizers, 56;
Cooking, 19-21: Foods for, 20;
shish kebab combinations, 20-
21; special techniques, 19-20.
Holders, 8
Skirt Steak, 30, 41
Smoke cooking, 31-33; adding
special wood flavors, 32;
advantages, 32; Chinese smoke
oven, 33; Japanese earthenware
smoker, 32; making a foil dome,
33; special techniques, 32-33;
true smoking, 31
Smoke-cooked recipes, 24, 49, 55,
57, 61, 64, 67, 74, 80, 83, 84,
86, 87, 89, 94, 95, 112, 113,
116-119, 120, 121, 125, 128,
130, 132
Soy Sauce: Chicken, Herbed, 109;
Chinese Ribs, 87; East Indian
Saté, 90; Ginger Beef Teriyaki,
54; -Ginger Marinade and Baste,
146; -Grilled Albacore Steaks,
135; Grilled Chinese Pork
Appetizers, 91; Grilled Eye of
Round Steaks, 63; Hawaiian
Bamboo-Beef Appetizers, 69;
Honolulu Steak, 53; Indonesian
Satés, 90; Japanese-Style Steak,
55; Kamo no Koma-Giri, 124;
Korean Shortrib Barbecue, 69;
-Lemon Marinade for Beef, 146;
-Mustard-Soy Marinade, 146;
Orange-, Swordfish, 132; Onigari
Yaki, 136; -Pineapple Apple
Slices, 139; Skewered Veal
Barbecue, 70; Skirt Steaks
Teriyaki, 60; Smoky Turkey with
Fruit Dressing, 120; Soy-Dipped
Hamburgers, 72; Surprised
Squab, 125; Tender Teriyaki
Steak Strips, 61; Teriyaki Turkey
Roll, 118
Spareribs, *see* Pork
Spit roasting
Accessories, 11-12, 27; balance
weight, 12; balancing meat, 25-
26; chicken, 113; Cornish game
hens, 117; fruits, 141; motor, 11;
recipes: 66, 76, 78, 80, 82, 85,
87, 92, 94, 95, 96, 105, 113, 117,
118, 121, 123, 124, 125, 141.
Rotary shish-kebab attachment,
12; special techniques, 26; spit,
12; spit forks, 12; techniques,
25-29; time chart, 28; vege-
tables, 141; Wild duck, 123
Squab, *see* Poultry
Standing rib roast, 42
Stuffing: Fruit, for turkey, 120;
Lemon Rice, for salmon, 130;
Orange-Celery for duck, 108;
Orange-Celery for duckling, 122;
Wild Rice, for buffalo steak, 107
Suckling pig, 85
Sweetbreads, 20, 30; *see also*
Variety Meats

T

T-Bone Steak, 40
Temperature chart: for grilling, 22-
23; for spit roasting, 28-29
Thawing meat, 22-23, 28-29

Thermometers: air temperature, 9,
10; grill temperature, 10; meat,
11
Tongs, 10, 12
Top sirloin roast, 42
Turkey, *see* Poultry

V

Variety Meats
Brains, Butter-Broiled, 81; *Heart:*
Peruvian Anticuchos, 80; Thick-
Sliced Beef, 80. *Kidneys:* Barbe-
cued, 81; Brochette de Rognons
d'Agneau, 102. *Liver:* Beef,
Marinated Liver Steak, 78;
Mi'Laaf Mashivi, 77; Superb, 78;
Calf, and Bacon Grill, 79; Foie de
Veau en Brochette, 77; Whole,
with Salt Pork, 78; Lamb,
Superb, 78; Whole, with Salt
Pork, 78; Veal, Superb, 78. Pigs'
Feet, 91; Sweetbreads, 30;
Tongue: Broiled, 80; Hickory-
Smoked, 80. Tripe, Strips in
Butter, 81
Veal
Kebabs, East Indian Saté, 90;
Indonesian Satés, 90; Loin, 28;
Shoulder (rolled), 28; Skewered
Barbecue, 70; steaks or chops,
22
Vegetables
Artichokes: Bottoms, 138;
Grilled Eye of Round Steaks, 63;
Hearts, 20; Mixed Vegetable
Grill, 139; Top Round Steak
with, 64; Tournedos Héloise, 48;
With Top Round Steak, 145.
Carrots, grilling idea, 138;
Cucumber, Mixed Vegetable
Grill, 139; *Eggplant:* Mixed
Vegetable Grill, 139; Roasted
Stuffed, 140; Spit Roasting, 141;
Tangy Wedges, 140. For Skewer
Cooking, 20-21; *Green Pepper:*
Grilling idea, 138; Mixed Grill,
139; Mixed Vegetable Grill, 139;
Spit roasting, 141. *Mushrooms:*
Mixed Vegetable Grill, 139;
Parboiled Vegetables en Skewer,
144. *Onions:* Parboiled Vege-
tables en Skewer, 144; spit
roasting, 141. Potatoes, spit
roasting, 141; skewer combina-
tions, 20-21; *Squash:* Acorn,
spit roasting, 141; Zucchini-
-Tomato Kebabs, 140. Tips on
Barbecuing, 137; *Tomato:* and
Zucchini Kebabs, 140; Mixed
Vegetable Grill, 139; spit roast-
ing, 141. Zucchini, Parboiled
Vegetables en Skewer, 144
Venison, *see* Game

W

Wine: and raisin sauce for duckling,
121; Brandy, Smoked Chicken
with Brandy Baste, 112;
Burgundy, Sauce for Skirt Steaks,
60; Cheddar-Sherry Sauce, 151;
Cognac, Mushrooms en
Brochette, Flambé, 141, 137;
Herb Wine Marinade, 153;
Honey-Wine Marinade for Lamb,
153; Onigari Yaki, 136; Red
Wine Marinade, 57; Red Wine
Marinade for Beef or Pork, 153
Wire brush with scraper, 12

Y

Yogurt, Chicken: Kebab Barg, 98;
Lela ka Kabab, 99; Pakistani
Kebabs, 115; Spicy, 112

Z

Zucchini, 20, 21; *see also*
Vegetables

ACKNOWLEDGMENTS

The editors would like to express their thanks to several persons who provided special advice at several stages in the preparation of this book: To Walt Rodman of the California Beef Council, and R. H. Christiansen of the American Lamb Council, who gave authoritative guidance in describing meat cuts. To Byron Allumbaugh, R. L. Heatherington, Bob Lohbeck, and Dick Root, who cooperated in providing the very best meats to picture. To Lloyd Bryan and W. A. Leak, who contributed expert know-how in the fine art of barbecue cookery.

PHOTOGRAPHERS

Cover photograph by Robert Cox. Clyde Childress, pages 14, 46 (middle, bottom); Glenn M. Christiansen, pages 13 (middle), 21, 25, 30, 34, 137; Richard Dawson, page 46 (top); Darrow M. Watt, pages 7, 8, 11, 12, 13 (left, right), 17, 18, 24, 27, 31, 32, 33, 35, 36, 37, 39, 40, 41, 42, 43, 44, 45, 47, 108, 126, 145.